THE GARDENER'S
ESSENTIAL
GERTRUDE JEKYLL

THE GARDENER'S ESSENTIAL GERTRUDE JEKYLL

Introduction by

Elizabeth Lawrence

GODINE COUNTRY CLASSICS

David R. Godine · Publisher · Boston

This is a Godine Country Classic first published in 1986 by
David R. Godine, Publisher, Inc.
Horticultural Hall
300 Massachusetts Avenue
Boston, Massachusetts 02115

Originally published in 1964 by Charles Scribner's Sons
This selection copyright © Charles Scribner's Sons

Library of Congress Cataloging in Publication Data
Jekyll, Gertrude, 1843–1932.
The gardener's essential Gertrude Jekyll.
(A Godine country classic)
Previously published: London : Breslich & Foss, 1983.
Includes index.
1. Landscape gardening. 2. Flower gardening.
3. Landscape gardening—England. 4. Flower gardening—
England. I. Title. II. Series.
SB473.J335 1986   635   85-80975
ISBN 0-87923-599-3

First printing
Printed in the United States of America

· *Contents*

❖ · The main purpose of a garden is to give its owner the best and highest kind of earthly pleasure.

It is not enough to cultivate plants well; they must also be used well. It is just the careful and thoughtful exercise of the higher qualities that makes a garden interesting, and their absence that leaves it blank, and dull, and lifeless. I am heartily in sympathy with the feeling described in these words in a friend's letter, "I think there are few things so interesting as to see in what way a person, whose perceptions you think fine and worthy of study, will give them expression in a garden."

—*Wood and Garden*

INTRODUCTION

Miss Jekyll of Munstead Wood

In an age of fine writing and fine gardening, Gertrude Jekyll excelled in both. The advice she gave to gardeners is as sound today as it was when she first offered it to her readers, and I am delighted to see it again in print.

Miss Jekyll was fifty-six when her book was published, in 1899, and she was nearing middle age when she gave up painting as a career, and turned to horticulture; but before she died, soon after her eighty-ninth birthday, she had written thirteen books, and had made plans for, or taken part in the planning of, something like three hundred and fifty gardens.

She had been a gardener all her life, and at twenty-five she made a garden at Wargrave Hill, when her family went there to live in 1868. The painter George Leslie described this garden as a wilderness of sweets, where old-fashioned flowers bloomed in profusion, and lavender hedges made marvelous growth. "Much interest in garden plants—always collecting," Miss Jekyll wrote in her journal at that time. She had already begun to experiment with new combinations of plants, introducing opium poppies and wild flowers into the flower borders—a radical step in the days of carpet bedding. "Gertrude was a pioneer spirit," her sister-in-law, Lady Jekyll, said. "Long before women had claimed their present inde-

[9]

pendence in the arts and professions, in trade, in travel, in sport, and in many difficult crafts, she had quietly and firmly established her right to self-expression."

Miss Jekyll was born in London in 1843. When she was four her parents moved to Bramley House, a country place in Surrey, where they allowed their children great freedom. She roamed the countryside, and learned to know the wildflowers intimately, not only by shape and color, but also by smell. She also knew the garden flowers by their scents, and could name the roses with her eyes shut. She always describes scents vividly. Lupines, she says, smell like a very good and delicate pepper; *Lilium pyrenaicum* like a mangy dog; some of the Schizanthus are redolent of dirty henhouses; and the scent of bracken is like "the first smell of the sea as you come near it after a long absence."

"When I pick and crush in my hand a twig of Bay," she said, "or brush against a bush of Rosemary, or tread upon a tuft of Thyme, or pass through incense-laden brakes of the Cistus, I feel that here is all that is best and purest and most refined, and nearest to poetry, in the range of faculty of the sense of smell."

Her hearing also was unusually keen. "I can nearly always tell what trees I am near by the sound of the wind in their leaves," she said, "though in the same tree it differs much from spring to autumn, as the leaves become of a harder and drier texture. The Birches have a small, quick, high-pitched sound; so near that of the falling of rain that I am often deceived into thinking it really is rain, when it is only their own leaves hitting each other with a small rain-like patter. The voice of Oak leaves is also rather high-pitched, though lower than that of the Birch. Chestnut leaves in a mild breeze sound much more deliberate; a sort of slow slither." The noise of all the Poplars, she adds, is disturbing, but the murmur of Scotch Firs is delightfully soothing.

She thought her unusually keen hearing was by way of compensation for her poor eyesight. Her natural focus was two inches, but she trained herself to close observation, and often saw things that those with perfect vision overlooked. As she drove about in her dog-cart she never missed the smallest flower along the roadside, and when she found something

[10]

INTRODUCTION

new she observed it minutely. In *Children and Gardens,* she says to her young readers: "If you will take any flower you please and look it carefully over and turn it about, and smell it and feel it and try to find out all its little secrets, not of flower only but of bud leaf and stem as well, you will discover many wonderful things."

In this fashion she examines the wood-sorrel, "the tenderest and loveliest of wood plants. The white flower in the mass has a slight lilac tinge; when I look close I see that this comes from a fine veining of reddish-purple colour on the white ground. White seems a vaguely-indefinite word when applied to the colouring of flowers; in the case of this tender little blossom the white is not very white, but about as white as the lightest part of a pearl. The downy stalk is flesh-coloured and half-transparent, and the delicately-formed calyx is painted with faint tints of dull green edged with transparent greenish buff, and is based and tipped with a reddish-purple that recalls the veining of the petals. Each of these has a touch of clear yellow on its inner base that sets off the bunch of tiny whitish stamens."

Miss Jekyll's art, like all that is good, grew out of her environment. She was fortunate in that she was able to develop her own style in a part of the country that she had known and loved since childhood. She knew the heath and woodland and the sandy hills, and the yellow-grey sandstone of the quarries; she knew the flowers of the fields and hedgerows, and the plants in cottage gardens. She understood country ways, and the craftsmen and their materials. Following the example of William Robinson in his revolt against carpet gardening, she searched gardens and nurseries for old-fashioned hardy plants to replace the bedding-out plants of the glass house.

She was also fortunate in having to work with her an architect equally devoted to the traditions of the district. Edwin Lutyens (later Sir Edwin) was nineteen when they first met, and was at work on his first commission. Miss Jekyll was forty-six, and well established as a gardener and a designer of gardens. Together they drove about the countryside studying ancient farm houses and cottages.

The knowledge they acquired was put to use in building Miss Jekyll's house at Munstead Wood.* When it was finished it looked as if it had been there for two hundred years, she said, and "seemed to have taken to itself the soul of a more ancient dwelling place." Munstead Wood consisted of fifteen acres across the road from Munstead House, where Miss Jekyll lived with her mother from the time it was built, in 1878, soon after Captain Jekyll's death, until Mrs. Jekyll died in 1895. The garden at Munstead Wood was laid out some time before the house was built, a portion at a time, with no special plan. Later Miss Jekyll fitted the parts together as best she could, and related the whole to the paved court, with its tank and stone steps, that Sir Edwin designed for the garden side of the house.

Each section of the garden was devoted to a season, or to some particular kind or type of plant. A place where two woodland paths came together was planted for winter, with heaths and hellebores, *Pieris floribunda,* and the large, round, wine-tinted leaves of Megasea. There was a spring garden for early bulbs and flowers that bloom from late March to late May; the Hidden Garden for the interval between spring and summer; the June garden around the little cottage called the Hut; the main border for summer; and for October the Michaelmas daisies had a garden to themselves. There was also a nut walk; a rock garden for alpines; a wide, green wood walk; and a network of smaller paths that threaded the woods and led from one delightful planting to another. All were grouped about two wide lawns, and special attention was given to the parts where lawn and woods met.

The chief feature of Munstead Wood was the celebrated south border,

*I wrote to Francis Jekyll, Miss Jekyll's nephew and biographer, to ask what has become of Munstead Wood. Mr. Jekyll answered from Munstead Hut, in May 1964. He says the property was sold fifteen years ago, and divided into four parts, and the garden as Miss Jekyll created it has ceased to exist. I am glad he is living in the Hut (where Miss Jekyll lived when the house was being built) and I hope there are some "tabbies" there still. "Dear little Hut!" Miss Jekyll wrote, "How sorry I was to leave it. . . . How I loved the small and simple ways of living, the happy absence of all complications. . . . How deliciously simple it all was, how small and few the bills—a pound a week for the house keeping."

eighteen feet wide and a hundred and eighty feet long,* with a high stone wall for background. The color scheme was the same at each end; blue, white, pale yellow and grey, then purple, white, pink, and grey foliage; the color then changed from both ends through yellow and orange to brilliant red. J. C. N. Forrestier describes it in *Bagatelle et Ses Jardins:* "I remember having seen in July a charming border, where the flowers were arranged in tones of chestnut and nasturtium; snapdragons, Indian pinks, zinnias, gaillardias, nasturtiums; *Helenium cupreatum,* coreopsis, dahlias, hollyhocks,—at the end of the border a quantity of *Eryngium amethystinum,* brushing with powder blue the stalks of the hollyhocks. Above all of these pale colors, a slender arch of a climbing rose of luminous color, called Ophire. Miss Jekyll, the skilful artist of Munstead Wood—perhaps to please a Frenchman—called it her 'Pompadour effect.'"

Miss Jekyll liked to use warm colors, reds and yellows, in "graduating harmonies culminating into gorgeousness," and cool colors in contrasts. "Texture plays so important a part in the appearance of colour-surface," she says, "that one can hardly think in colour without also thinking of texture. A piece of black satin and a piece of black velvet may be woven of the same batch of material, but when the satin is finished and the velvet cut, the appearance is often so dissimilar that they may look quite different in color." Her familiarity with braids and brocades, lace and damask, increased her delight in the texture and pattern of leaves: the back of the leaf of *Alchemilla alpina,* she said, is silvery-green satin of the highest quality. "The satin lining, as is plain to see, comes up and over the front edge of the leaf with a brightness that looks like polished silver against the dull green surface." She had also a great feeling for form, both for the individual beauty of such things as acanthus and yucca, and for placing each plant or group so that it would become a part of a harmonious whole. "In gardening," she wrote Mrs. Boyle, "I try to paint living pictures with living flowers, paying attention to throwing them into groups both for form and colour. . . . I wish I could show you some of my garden pictures that seem fairly successful: the Primrose Garden in its season a

*In another place she describes it as 14' wide and 200' long.

river of gold and silver flowering through a copse of silver-stemmed young birch trees for a hundred yards or more. Another of this year's pictures that pleased me, was a large isolated group of foxgloves with bracken about their base, backed by a dusky wood of Scotch firs."

The primroses were the celebrated Munstead Strain, developed by crossing the variety Golden Plover with a very pale, almost white polyanthus found in a cottage garden. The flowers are all white and yellow, but vary greatly in detail. As she herself says, Miss Jekyll never spared herself in the way of actual labor, and one of her chores was dividing the primroses. Every year, when they were taken up, she sat for two days on a low stool cutting them apart, while one boy brought freshly dug plants, and another took the divisions to be carefully replanted in dug-over and freshly manured soil. It was very pleasant to sit there, in a clearing half shaded by oak, chestnut and hazel, and on one of those days she wrote, "The still air, with only the very gentlest south-westerly breath in it, brings up the mighty boom of the great ship guns from the old seaport, thirty miles away, and the pheasants answer to the sound as they do to thunder. The early summer air is of a perfect temperature, the soft coo of the wood doves comes down from the near wood, the nightingale sings almost overhead. . . . but oh, the midges!"

Among other plants she developed and put on the market, were Lent hellebores, columbines, double pink poppies, and white foxgloves.

Miss Jekyll felt that plants should be the chief ornaments of a garden, and that such features as were added should be useful as well as beautiful: seats and sundials, pots and tubs for plants, dipping wells, summer houses and pergolas. She particularly liked the pergola, for displaying roses and climbing plants, and often makes use of a photograph of the charming one in her sister's garden in Venice, with rows of white lilies blooming on either side of the path. She made frequent visits to her sister in her younger days, and once, crossing the Piazza, she met Ruskin.

Miss Jekyll considered stone the most desirable material for garden features, particularly if it could be had nearby. The garden walls at Munstead Wood were built of Bargate stone from the local quarries, and so was the two-storey Thunder House for watching storms as they gathered beyond the fields and the chalk hills. She made excellent use of the same stone in dry walls and steps of the series of terraces at Millmead. Next to her own garden, I think Millmead must be the most perfect example of her style, for in planning it she had only herself to please. She bought a strip of land, seventy-five by four hundred feet, on a steep hillside, and built the house and laid out the garden before she began to look about for a tenant. Sir Edwin Lutyens designed the house, and together with the garden it was an example of "satisfactory indoor and outdoor planning." Miss Jekyll made the most of the site, allowing the garden to overlook the pretty meadow and the millstream at the foot of the slope, framing the view of the village church and the distant hills, giving a fine old pear tree a little enclosure of its own, and taking advantage of natural springs to make a tank and a stone dipping well. Flowers in careless profusion filled the borders and tumbled over the walls, and even seeded themselves in the stone steps. Miss Jekyll thought these unplanned effects the best of all, and she never liked the garden to be too neat. "I hold the heresy," she said, "of not minding a little moss on the paths, and of rather preferring a few scattered cluster rose petals on its brown-green velvet." But there was nothing careless in her planning. "In the way it is done," she said, "lies the whole difference between commonplace gardening and gardening that very rightly claims to rank as a fine art." She was an artist first, and a gardener second; her training in painting gave her an understanding of design, and a mastery of form and color.

All of the well-known gardeners of the day were welcomed to Munstead Wood. One was the Honorable Mrs. Boyle (E.V.B.) of Huntercombe Manor, with whom Miss Jekyll corresponded, and another was Mrs. C. W. Earle who wrote, in *Pot-Pouri from a Surrey Garden* (1896), "There has been in this year's 'Guardian' a succession of monthly articles on a Surrey Garden, written by Miss Jekyll of Munstead Wood, Godalming. I give her address, as she now sells her surplus plants, all more or less suited to light soils, to the management of which she has for many years past given special attention . . . All the plants and flowers about which Miss Jekyll writes she actually grows on the top of her Surrey hill. Her garden is a most instructive one, and encouraging too." I rather suspect that under the guise of giving her free advertisement, Mrs. Earle was putting Miss Jekyll in her place as being "in trade."

Miss Ellen Willmott, whose garden at Warley Place, Essex, was as celebrated as Munstead Wood, was of course a frequent visitor, and in 1909 the Countess von Arnim, the "Elizabeth" of the German garden was there. I can think of no two gardeners less likely to be charmed with one another than Elizabeth and Miss Jekyll. I should like to know what each one of them wrote in her journal that night.

Mr. Bowles went to Munstead, though I cannot remember any mention of it in his books, and the Reverend C. Wolley Dod, and Canon Ellacombe. In 1880 Dean Hole paid a visit, bringing William Robinson with him. Miss Jekyll had met Mr. Robinson five years before, when she called at his office. She became a regular contributor to his magazine, 'The Garden,' and for a short while was on its staff. Mr. Robinson often visited Munstead Wood, and "more than once," Francis Jekyll, her nephew, says in his *Memoir*,* "lent his experienced hand in the laying out of the garden."

All of these were welcomed, but as her fame spread, through her books and her honors (the George Robert White Medal of Honor from the Massachusetts Horticultural Society; the Victoria Medal of Honor, and the Veitchian Gold Cup), she was beset by stangers who wanted to visit Munstead Wood, and meet its mistress. By the time she had written her second book, she was begging her readers to stay away. "It is always pleasant to hear from or to see old friends," she wrote in the preface to *Home and Garden,* "and indeed all who work hard in their own gardens, yet, as a would-be quiet worker, who is by no means overstrong, I venture to plead with my kind and numerous, though frequently unknown friends, that I may be allowed a somewhat larger measure of peace and privacy." Later she wrote to a friend, "If I could only know who were the genuine applicants, I would still make exceptions. You can have no idea what I have suffered from Americans, Germans and journalists."

One of these Americans was Edith Wharton, who, with "a hundred

Gertrude Jekyll A Memoir by Francis Jekyll.

questions to ask, a thousand things to learn," went to Great Warley* in a party of fashionable people, none of whom was interested in horticulture. "I put one timid question to Miss Jekyll," she says in her autobiography, "who answered curtly, and turned her back on me to point out a hybrid iris to an eminent statesman who knew neither what a hybrid nor an iris was; and for the rest of the visit she gave me no chance of exchanging a word with her."

As many of Miss Jekyll's friends were writers, she often appears in their books. George Leslie, in *Our River,* describes her as a lady of singular and remarkable accomplishments: "Clever and witty in conversation, active and energetic in mind and body, and possessed of artistic talents of no common order. . . . there is hardly any handicraft the mysteries of which she has not mastered—carving, modelling, housepainting, carpentry, smith's work, repoussé work, gilding, wood-inlaying, embroidery, gardening, and all manner of herb and flower knowledge and culture, everything being carried on with perfect method and completeness."

In Miss Jekyll's house there was a gallery, sixty feet long and ten feet wide, with glassed-in cupboards in which she kept the pretty things "such as are almost unconsciously gathered together by a person of accumulative proclivity." Here, she says in *Home and Garden,* "are memories of many lands and of many persons: of countries I shall never see again, for my travelling days are over; of kindly little gifts from friends who are no longer among the living. Some of the small objects are of absolutely no intrinsic value but of a loveliness that is beyond all price, such as beautiful shells and feathers. Then there are tiny ancient tear-bottles, both brilliant and dainty in iridescent colouring of their decaying surface-flakes; a little silver Buddha; delicate pieces of Venetian glass; bronze coins green with age; old Church embroideries of gold and colours upon white silk now faded and discoloured; ostrich eggs of ivory white and emu eggs of dim dusty green; little objects innumerable—eight foot by four of them as a carpenter would say—a life's history in a hieroglyphic writing that is

*Surely this is a mistake. She must be thinking of Miss Willmott's place?

legible to one person only, but that to all comers presents a somewhat pretty show."

In *Reperusals and Recollections*, Logan Pearsall Smith relates how, on a visit to Munstead House, not long before Miss Jekyll died, he was told that she would like to see him. He crossed the road, and taking from its hiding place the key to the door in the garden wall, he let himself in to Munstead Wood; following shady paths until he came to an open lawn, he saw the house before him. No one was about. The silence cast a spell. It was like a scene in a fairy tale: "the locked gate and secret key, the walk through the wood to the beautiful old house which its venerable inhabitant had built for herself so long ago, and over which brooded the silence and solitude of her extreme old age." Standing there alone he remembered a time when he had walked through the garden with Miss Jekyll herself, and had asked her if she really enjoyed it all. It is difficult, he had said, "to possess one's own possessions;" the artist is apt to see only the imperfections in the thing he has created. Miss Jekyll had agreed. "But," she said, "now and then when I am thinking of something else I come round the corner suddenly on the house and garden; I catch it unawares. It seems to me all right; and then I enjoy it—I enjoy it very much I can tell you."

Although she travelled widely in her youth, at nineteen going to Rhodes, Constantinople, and Athens with the Charles Newtons, and later spending a winter in Algiers, and often visited her sister in Venice, and spent many summers with the Blumenthals at their chalet above Montreux, Miss Jekyll paid her last visit to London in 1904, and stayed at home more and more as she grew older. She was only fifty-seven when she began to beg her readers to leave her in peace, but she wrote eight years later (in *Children and Gardens*) that she could still, when no one was looking, climb over a five-barred gate or jump a ditch. "I think it is because I have been more or less a gardener all my life," she said, "that I still feel like a child in many ways, although from the number of years I have lived I ought to know that I am quite an old woman." At seventy-two she was laying out paths on a knoll of Hydon Heath, and directing four Boy Scouts in clearing out the undergrowth. In 1932, she wrote Miss Wilmott that

INTRODUCTION

it was very hard not to be able to do "all the little things about the garden
that want doing directly you notice them," and to have to be hauled about
in a wheel chair instead of having "leisurely solitary prowls of close
intimacy with growing things." Even so, she made plans that year for a
garden for Mr. Round of Cottage Wood, and had some writing under way
when she died, on the eighth of December, 1933, just after her eighty-
ninth birthday.

Too much has been made of Miss Jekyll's lack of personal beauty—she
has even been called ugly. Logan Pearsall Smith speaks of her "plain but
splendid face," and all of her life artists wanted to sketch and paint her.
On the voyage to Turkey, Mary Newton made a charming sketch of her
in her cabin, a sweet and serious young girl, intent upon her watercolor
pad. When she was twenty-one J. J. Carter sketched her on horseback,
a graceful, spirited, slender figure in a becoming riding habit. Susan
Mackenzie made a drawing of her as an imposing young woman, rather
statuesque in her elaborate black gown. And at seventy-seven, William
Nicholson with great difficulty persuaded her to sit for him. "I feel grateful
to Providence," he wrote Lady Jekyll, "for the chance she gave me of
recording so lovable a character. I am so glad if you think I have put a
little of her serene charm into my painting."

No wonder she was serene. All of her happy life was lived in the
security of a large, loving, and prosperous family, who had perfect faith
in God, themselves and the British Empire.

Elizabeth Lawrence

THE SELECTIONS HAVE BEEN TAKEN FROM

- *Wood and Garden*

- *Home and Garden*

- *Lilies for English Gardens*

- *Wall and Water Gardens*

- *Roses for English Gardens*

- *Flower Decoration in the House*

- *Colour in the Flower Garden*

- *Gardens for Small Country Houses*

- *Annuals and Biennials*

- *Garden Ornament*

· The original spelling, except for a few obvious typographical errors, has been maintained throughout. The plant names, which are inconsistent as to italics and initial capitals, have been left as they appeared in each book.

A GARDENING CREDO

SOURCES

🌱 · *Wood and Garden*

✳ · *Home and Garden*

✿ · *Wall and Water Gardens*

🌱   INTRODUCTORY

I lay no claim either to literary ability, or to botanical knowledge, or even to knowing the best practical methods of cultivation; but I have lived among outdoor flowers for many years, and have not spared myself in the way of actual labour, and have come to be on closely intimate and friendly terms with a great many growing things, and have acquired certain instincts which, though not clearly defined, are of the nature of useful knowledge.

But the lesson I have thoroughly learnt, and wish to pass on to others, is to know the enduring happiness that the love of a garden gives. I rejoice when I see any one, and especially children, inquiring about flowers, and wanting gardens of their own, and carefully working in them. For love of gardening is a seed that once sown never dies, but always grows and grows to an enduring and ever-increasing source of happiness.

I am strongly for treating garden and wooded ground in a pictorial way, mainly with large effects, and in the second place with lesser beau-

tiful incidents, and for so arranging plants and trees and grassy spaces
that they look happy and at home, and make no parade of conscious
effort. I try for beauty and harmony everywhere, and especially for harmony of colour. A garden so treated gives the delightful feeling of repose,
and refreshment, and purest enjoyment of beauty, that seems to my understanding to be the best fulfilment of its purpose; while to the diligent
worker its happiness is like the offering of a constant hymn of praise. For
I hold that the best purpose of a garden is to give delight and to give
refreshment of mind, to soothe, to refine, and to lift up the heart in a
spirit of praise and thankfulness. It is certain that those who practise
gardening in the best ways find it to be so.

I have learned much, and am always learning, from other people's
gardens, and the lesson I have learned most thoroughly is, never to say "I
know"—there is so infinitely much to learn, and the conditions of different gardens vary so greatly, even when soil and situation appear to be
alike and they are in the same district.

I have learnt much from the little cottage gardens that help to make
our English waysides the prettiest in the temperate world. One can
hardly go into the smallest cottage garden without learning or observing
something new. It may be some two plants growing beautifully together
by some happy chance, or a pretty mixed tangle of creepers, or something that one always thought must have a south wall doing better on an
east one. But eye and brain must be alert to receive the impression and
studious to store it, to add to the hoard of experience. And it is important
to train oneself to have a good flower-eye; to be able to see at a glance
what flowers are good and which are unworthy, and why, and to keep an
open mind about it; not to be swayed by the petty tyrannies of the
"florist" or show judge; for, though some part of his judgment may be
sound, he is himself a slave to rules, and must go by points which are
defined arbitrarily and rigidly, and have reference mainly to the show-
table, leaving out of account, as if unworthy of consideration, such mat-

ters as gardens and garden beauty, and human delight, and sunshine, and varying lights of morning and evening and noonday. But many, both nursery-men and private people, devote themselves to growing and improving the best classes of hardy flowers, and we can hardly offer them too much grateful praise, or do them too much honour. For what would our gardens be without the Roses, Pæonies, and Gladiolus of France, and the Tulips and Hyacinths of Holland, to say nothing of the hosts of good things raised by our home growers, and of the enterprise of the great firms whose agents are always searching the world for garden treasures?

Let no one be discouraged by the thought of how much there is to learn. Looking back upon nearly thirty years of gardening (the earlier part of it in groping ignorance with scant means of help), I can remember no part of it that was not full of pleasure and encouragement. For the first steps are steps into a delightful Unknown, the first successes are victories all the happier for being scarcely expected, and with the growing knowledge comes the widening outlook, and the comforting sense of an ever-increasing gain of critical appreciation. Each new step becomes a little surer, and each new grasp a little firmer, till, little by little, comes the power of intelligent combination, the nearest thing we can know to the mighty force of creation.

And a garden is a grand teacher. It teaches patience and careful watchfulness; it teaches industry and thrift; above all, it teaches entire trust. "Paul planteth and Apollos watereth, but God giveth the increase." The good gardener knows with absolute certainty that if he does his part, if he gives the labour, the love, and every aid that his knowledge of his craft, experience of the conditions of his place, and exercise of his personal wit can work together to suggest, that so surely as he does this diligently and faithfully, so surely will God give the increase. Then with the honestly-earned success comes the consciousness of encouragement to renewed effort, and, as it were, an echo of the gracious words, "Well done, good and faithful servant."

[25]

ON GARDENING

❦ THINGS WORTH DOING

The heading of this chapter might embrace the conclusions of all the deepest philosophies, but none the less has relation to the simplest thoughts and acts of every-day life. Is it worth having? Is it worth doing? These questions form a useful mental sieve, through which to pass many matters in order to separate the husk from the grain. And nowhere have we occasion to use it with more vigour than in matters pertaining to the garden.

When I had less knowledge of garden flowers and shrubs than I have been able to gather through many later years, I got together all the plants I was able to collect; not with a view to having them as a collection, but in order to become acquainted with them, the better to see which I could use on my own ground or recommend to others whose gardens were of different natures. And in this way I have discarded numbers of plants, some because I thought them altogether unworthy, some because the colour of the flower displeased me, others because they threatened to become troublesome weeds, and others again because, though beautiful and desirable, they were very unhappy and home-sick in my dry soil, and it was quite evident that they were no plants for me. Several of these were natives of the Alps, that missed the cool shade of the towering rocks, and the constant trickle of moisture to the root, and the overhead bath of mountain mist. It is only in the case of a thing so indispensable as the White Lily that I go on trying against nearly certain failure, and hoping almost against hope, and am rewarded perhaps only one year in seven by a clump doing fairly well, in spite of having carefully tried all the nostrums kindly given me by my many friends of highest horticultural ability. Still the White Lily is one of the good things worth doing, and after all, as a last resource, one can pot it in loam and lime and so compel it to live and flower.

A GARDENING CREDO

And I found that one thing well worth doing was to get together as many kinds as I could of any one plant in general cultivation, and grow them together, and compare them at their blooming season and see which was really the best and most beautiful; for in equal or even greater proportion with the growth of critical appreciation, there comes an intolerance of rubbish, and by the constant exercise of the critical faculty the power of judging becomes unconscious, and, as it were, another natural sense. And though I am far from venturing to think that the conclusions of my judgment are infallible, yet I believe that they are soundly based and of good general utility, and therefore fairly trustworthy for the guidance of others.

I think it is a fair test of the genuineness of the profession of the many people who now declare that they love plants and gardens, to see if they are willing to take any trouble of this kind for themselves. For though there are now whole shelves-full of the helpful books that had no existence in my younger days, yet there are many things that can only be ascertained by careful trying in individual gardens.

Now that there is so much to choose from, we should not let any mental slothfulness stand in the way of thinking and watching and comparing, so as to arrive at a just appreciation of the merits and uses of all our garden plants.

It is not possible to use to any good effect all the plants that are to be had. In my own case I should wish to grow many more than just those I have, but if I do not find a place where my critical garden conscience approves of having any one plant I would rather be without it. It is better to me to deny myself the pleasure of having it, than to endure the mild sense of guilt of having placed it where it neither does itself justice nor accords with its neighbours, and where it reproaches me every time I pass it.

I feel sure that it is in a great measure just because this is so little understood, that gardens are so often unsatisfactory and uninteresting. If owners could see, each in their own garden, what is the thing most worth doing, and take some pains to work out that one idea or group of ideas, gardens would not be so generally dull and commonplace.

Often in choosing plants and shrubs people begin the wrong way. They know certain things they would like to have, and they look through catalogues and order these, and others that they think, from the description, they would also like, and then plant them without any previous consideration of how or why.

Often when I have had to do with other people's gardens they have said: "I have bought a quantity of shrubs and plants; show me where to place them;" to which I can only answer: "That is not the way in which I can help you; show me your spaces and I will tell you what plants to get for them."

Many places that would be beautiful if almost let alone are spoiled by doing away with some simple natural feature in order to put in its place some hackneyed form of gardening. Such places should be treated with the most deliberate and careful consideration. Hardly a year passes that I do not see in my own neighbourhood examples of this kind that seem to me extremely ill-judged. Houses great and small are being built on tracts of natural heath-land. A perfect undergrowth of wild Heaths is there already. If it is old and overgrown, it can be easily renewed by clearing it off and lightly digging the ground over, when the Heaths will quickly spring up again. Often there are already thriving young Scotch Firs and Birches.

There are many people who almost unthinkingly will say, "But I like a variety." Do they really think and feel that variety is actually desirable as an end in itself, and is of more value than a series of thoughtfully composed garden pictures? There are no doubt many who, from want of a certain class of refinement of education or natural gift of teachable aptitude, are unable to understand or appreciate, at anything like its full value, a good garden picture, and to these no doubt a quantity of individual plants give a greater degree of pleasure than such as they could derive from the contemplation of any beautiful arrangement of a lesser number. When I see this in ordinary gardens, I try to put myself into the same mental attitude, and so far succeed, in that I can perceive that it represents one of the earlier stages in the love of a garden, and that one must not quarrel with it, because a garden is for its owner's pleasure, and whatever the degree or form of that pleasure, if only it be sincere, it is right and reasonable, and adds to human happiness in one of the purest and best of ways. And often I find I have to put upon myself this kind of drag, because when one has passed through the more elementary stages which deal with isolated details, and has come to a point when one feels some slight power of what perhaps may be called generalship; when the means and material that go to the making of a garden seem to be within one's grasp and awaiting one's command, then comes the danger of being inclined to lay down the law, and of advocating the ultimate effects that one feels oneself to be most desirable in an intolerant spirit of cock-sure pontification. So I try, when I am in a garden of the ordinary kind where the owner likes variety, to see it a little from the same point of view; and in the arboretum, where one of each of a hundred different kinds of Conifers stand in their fine young growth, to see and admire the individuals only, and to stifle my own longing to see a hundred of one sort at a time, and to keep down the shop-window feeling, and the idea of a worthless library made up of odd single volumes where there should be complete sets, and the comparison of an inconsequent jumble of words with a clearly-written sentence, and other ready similitudes that come crowding through the brain of the garden-artist (if I may give myself a title so honourable), who desires not only to see the beautiful plants and trees, but to see them used in the best and largest and most worthy of ways.

There is no spot of ground, however arid, bare, or ugly, that cannot be tamed into such a state as may give an impression of beauty and delight. It cannot always be done easily; many things worth doing are not done easily; but there is no place under natural conditions that cannot be graced with an adornment of suitable vegetation.

ON GARDENING

More than once I have had pleasure in taking in hand some spot of ground where it was said "nothing would grow." On two occasions it was a heap of about fifty loads of sand wheeled out of the basement of a building; in one case placed under some Scotch Firs, in another under Oaks and Chestnuts. Both are now as well covered with thriving plants and shrubs as any other parts of the garden they are in, clothed in the one case with Aucubas, hardy Ferns, Periwinkles, and Honesty, and in the other with Aucubas, Ferns, and the two grand Mulleins, *Verbascum olympicum* and *V. phlomoides*. It should be remembered that the Aucuba is one of the few shrubs that enjoys shade.

Throughout my life I have found one of the things most worth doing was to cultivate the habit of close observation. Like all else, the more it is exercised the easier it becomes, till it is so much a part of oneself that one may observe almost critically and hardly be aware of it. A habit so acquired stands one in good stead in all garden matters, so that in an exhibition of flowers or in a botanic garden one can judge of the merits of a plant hitherto unknown to one, and at once see in what way it is good, and why, and how it differs from those of the same class that one may have at home.

And I know from my own case that the will and the power to observe does not depend on the possession of keen sight. For I have sight that is both painful and inadequate; short sight of the severest kind, and always progressive (my natural focus is two inches); but the little I have I try to make the most of, and often find that I have observed things that have escaped strong and long-sighted people.

As if by way of compensation I have very keen hearing, and when I hear a little rustling rush in the grass and heath, or in the dead leaves under the trees, I can tell whether it is snake or lizard, mouse or bird. Many birds I am aware of only by the sound of their flight. I can nearly always tell what trees I am near by the sound of the wind in their leaves, though in the same tree it differs much from spring to autumn, as the leaves become of a harder and drier texture. The Birches have a small, quick, high-pitched sound; so near that of falling rain that I am often deceived into thinking it really is rain, when it is only their own leaves hitting each other with a small rain-like patter. The voice of Oak leaves is also rather high-pitched, though lower than that of Birch. Chestnut leaves in a mild breeze sound much more deliberate; a sort of slow slither. Nearly all trees in gentle wind have a pleasant sound, but I confess to a distinct dislike to the noise of all the Poplars; feeling it to be painfully fussy, unrestful, and disturbing. On the other hand, how soothing and delightful is the murmur of Scotch Firs both near and far. And what pleasant muffled music is that of a wind-waved field of corn, and especially of ripe barley. The giant Grasses, Reeds, and Bamboo sound curiously dry. The great Reed, *Arundo Donax*, makes more noise in a moderate breeze than when the wind blows a gale, for then the long ribbon-like leaves are blown straight out and play much less against each other; the Arabs say, "It whispers in the breeze and is silent in the storm." But of all the plants I know, the one whose foliage has the strangest sound is the Virginian Allspice (*Calycanthus floridus*), whose leaves are of so dry and harsh a quality that they seem to grate and clash as they come together.

As for the matter of colour, what may be observed is simply without end. Those who have had no training in the way to see colour nearly always deceive themselves into thinking that they see it as they know it is locally, whereas the trained eye sees colour in due relation and as it truly *appears to be*. I remember driving with a friend of more than ordinary intelligence, who stoutly maintained that he saw the distant wooded hill quite as green as the near hedge. He knew it was green and could not see it otherwise, till I stopped at a place where a part of the face, but none of the sky-bounded edge of the wooded distance, showed through a tiny opening among the near green branches, when, to his immense surprise, he saw it was blue. A good way of showing the same thing is to tear a roundish hole in any large bright-green leaf, such as a Burdock, and to hold it at half-arm's length so that a part of a distant landscape is seen through the hole, and the eye sees also the whole surface of the leaf. As long as the sight takes in both, it will see the true relative colour of the distance. I constantly do this myself, first looking at the distance without the leaf-frame in order to see how nearly I can guess the truth of the far colour. Even in the width of one ploughed field, especially in autumn when the air is full of vapour, in the farther part of the field the newly-turned earth is bluish-purple, whereas it is a rich brown at one's feet.

On some of those cold, cloudless days of March, when the sky is of a darker and more intensely blue colour than one may see at any other time of the year, and geese are grazing on the wide strips of green common, so frequent in my neighbourhood, I have often noticed how surprisingly blue is the north side of a white goose. If at three o'clock in the afternoon of such a day one stands facing north-west and also facing the goose, its side next one's right hand is bright blue and its other side is bright yellow, deepening to orange as the sun "westers" and sinks, and shows through a greater depth of moisture-laden atmosphere.

The way colour is applied in brilliant flowers is the subject of a never-ending and always delightful investigation. All painters know how difficult it is to get a brilliant colouring of clear, unmuddled scarlet. It can only be done, especially in water-colour, by running the scarlet over a preparation of clear strong yellow. This is exactly how nature gets over the same difficulty in flowers of that colour.

It always seems to me that one of the things most worth doing about a garden is to try to make every part of it beautiful; not the pleasure garden only, but some of the rougher accessories also, so that no place is unsightly. For the faggot-stack can be covered with Gourds or Vegetable Marrows, or quick growing rambling things like the wild Bindweed (*Convolvulus*), or the garden variety with still larger white bloom; and the sides of the coke-enclosure, built of posts and upright oak slabbing, can have hardy Chrysanthemums below and a happy tangle of wild Clematis above; and sheds that would be otherwise unbeautiful can be adorned with rampant Vine and Jasmine and the free-growing Clematises and Virginia Creeper. For my own part, I wish I had more of such places in order to have a wider scope for such plantings; while in other gardens I groan in spirit to see the many opportunities wasted, and unsightliness reigning supreme where there might be pictures of delightful beauty. And to get into the habit of considering and composing such arrangements, and to worry out the way of doing them, is by no means one of the least of the pleasures of a garden.

CULTIVATION

My garden, though it is full of limitations, and in all ways falls short of any worthy ideal, enables me here and there to point out something that is worth doing, and to lay stress on the fact that the things worth doing are worth taking trouble about. But it is a curious thing that many people, even among those who profess to know something about gardening, when I show them something fairly successful—the crowning reward of much care and labour—refuse to believe that any pains have been taken about it. They will ascribe it to chance, to the goodness of my soil, and even more commonly to some supposed occult influence of my own—to anything rather than to the plain fact that I love it well enough to give it plenty of care and labour. They assume a tone of complimentary banter, kindly meant no doubt, but to me rather distasteful, to this effect: "Oh yes, of course it will grow for you; anything will grow for you; you have only to look at a thing and it will grow." I have to pump up a laboured smile and accept the remark with what grace I can, as a necessary civility to the stranger that is within my gates, but it seems to me evident that those who say these things do not understand the love of a garden.

I could not help rejoicing when such a visitor came to me one October. I had been saying how necessary good and deep cultivation was, especially in so very poor and shallow a soil as mine. Passing up through the copse where there were some tall stems of *Lilium giganteum* bearing the great upturned pods of seed, my visitor stopped and said, "I don't believe a word about your poor soil—look at the growth of that Lily. Nothing could make that great stem ten feet high in a poor soil, and there it is, just stuck into the wood!" I said nothing, knowing that presently I could show a better answer than I could frame in words. A little farther up in the copse we came upon an excavation about twelve feet across and four deep, and by its side a formidable mound of sand, when my friend said, "Why are you making all this mess in your pretty wood? are you quarrying stone, or is it for the cellar of a building? and what on earth are you going to do with that great heap of sand? why, there must be a dozen loads of it." That was my moment of secret triumph, but I hope I bore it meekly as I answered, "I only wanted to plant a few more of those big Lilies, and you see in my soil they would not have a chance unless the ground was thoroughly prepared; look at the edge of the scarp and see how the solid yellow sand comes to within four inches of the top; so I have a big wide hole dug; and look, there is the donkey-cart coming with the first load of Dahlia-tops and soft plants that have been for the summer in the south border. There will be several of those little cartloads, each holding three barrowfuls. As it comes into the hole, the men will chop it with the spade and tread it down close, mixing in a little sand. This will make a nice cool, moist bottom of slowly-rotting vegetable matter. Some more of the same kind of waste will come from the kitchen garden—cabbage-stumps, bean-haulm, soft weeds that have been hoed up, and all the greenest stuff from the rubbish-heap. Every layer will be chopped and pounded, and trampled down so that there should be as little sinking as possible afterwards. By this time the hole will be filled to within a foot of the top; and now we must get together some better stuff—road-scrapings and trimmings mixed with some older rubbish-heap mould, and for the top of all, some of our precious loam, and the soil of an old hotbed and some well-decayed manure, all well mixed, and then we are ready for the Lilies. They are planted only just underground, and then the whole bed has a surfacing of dead leaves, which helps to keep down weeds, and also looks right with the surrounding wild ground. The remains of the heap of sand we must deal with how we can; but there are hollows here and there in the roadway and paths, and a place that can be levelled up in the rubbish-yard, and some kitchen-garden paths that will bear raising, and so by degrees it is disposed of."

❧ NOVELTY AND VARIETY

When I look back over thirty years of gardening, I see what extraordinary progress there has been, not only in the introduction of good plants new to general cultivation, but also in the home production of improved kinds of old favourites. In annual plants alone there has been a remarkable advance. And here again, though many really beautiful things are being brought forward, there seems always to be an undue value assigned to a fresh development, on the score of its novelty.

Now it seems to me, that among the thousands of beautiful things already at hand for garden use, there is no merit whatever in novelty or variety unless the thing new or different is distinctly more beautiful, or in some such way better than an older thing of the same class.

And there seems to be a general wish among seed growers just now to dwarf all annual plants. Now, when a plant is naturally of a diffuse habit, the fixing of a dwarfer variety may be a distinct gain to horticulture—it may just make a good garden plant out of one that was formerly of indifferent quality; but there seems to me to be a kind of stupidity in inferring from this that all annuals are the better for dwarfing. I take it that the bedding system has had a good deal to do with it. It no doubt enables ignorant gardeners to use a larger variety of plants as senseless colour-masses, but it is obvious that many, if not most, of the plants are individually made much uglier by the process. Take, for example, one of the dwarfest Ageratums: what a silly little dumpy, formless, pincushion of a thing it is! And then the dwarfest of the China Asters. Here is a plant (whose chief weakness already lies in a certain over-stiffness) made stiffer and more shapeless still by dwarfing and by cramming with too many petals. The Comet Asters of later years are a much-improved type of flower, with a looser shape and a certain degree of approach to grace and beauty. When this kind came out it was a noteworthy novelty, not because it was a novelty, but because it was a better and more beautiful thing. Also among the same Asters the introduction of a better class of red colouring, first of the blood-red and then of the so-called scarlet shades, was a good variety, because it was the distinct bettering of the colour of a popular race of garden-flowers, whose red and pink colourings had hitherto been of a bad and rank quality.

It is quite true that here and there the dwarf kind is a distinctly useful thing, as in the dwarf Nasturtiums. In this grand plant one is glad to have dwarf ones as well as the old trailing kinds. I even confess to a certain liking for the podgy little dwarf Snapdragons; they are ungraceful little dumpy things, but they happen to have come in some tender colourings of pale yellow and pale pink, that give them a kind of absurd prettiness, and a certain garden-value. I also look at them as a little floral joke that is harmless and not displeasing, but they cannot for a moment compare in beauty with the free-growing Snapdragon of the older type. This I always think one of the best and most interesting and admirable of garden-plants. Its beauty is lost if it is crowded up among other things in a border; it should be grown in a dry wall or steep rocky bank, where its handsome bushy growth and finely-poised spikes of bloom can be well seen.

One of the annuals that I think is entirely spoilt by dwarfing is Love-in-a-Mist, a plant I hold in high admiration. Many years ago I came upon some of it in a small garden, of a type that I thought extremely desirable, with a double flower of just the right degree of fulness, and of an unusually fine colour. I was fortunate enough to get some seed, and have never grown any other, nor have I ever seen elsewhere any that I think can compare with it.

A GARDENING CREDO

The Zinnia is another fine annual that has been much spoilt by its would-be improvers. When a Zinnia has a hard, stiff, tall flower, with a great many rows of petals piled up one on top of another, and when its habit is dwarfed to a mean degree of squatness, it looks to me both ugly and absurd, whereas a reasonably double one, well branched, and two feet high, is a handsome plant.

I also think that Stocks and Wallflowers are much handsomer when rather tall and branching. Dwarf Stocks, moreover, are invariably spattered with soil in heavy autumn rain.

An example of the improver not knowing where to stop in the matter of colouring, always strikes me in the Gaillardias, and more especially in the perennial kind, that is increased by division as well as by seed. The flower is naturally of a strong orange-yellow colour, with a narrow ring of red round the centre. The improver has sought to increase the width of the red ring. Up to a certain point it makes a livelier and brighter-looking flower; but he has gone too far, and extended the red till it has become a red flower with a narrow yellow edge. The red also is of a rather dull and heavy nature, so that instead of a handsome yellow flower with a broad central ring, here is an ugly red one with a yellow border. There is no positive harm done, as the plant has been propagated at every stage of development, and one may choose what one will; but to see them together is an instructive lesson.

No annual plant has of late years been so much improved as the Sweet Pea, and one reason why its charming beauty and scent are so enjoyable is, that they grow tall, and can be seen on a level with the eye. There can be no excuse whatever for dwarfing this, as has lately been done. There are already plenty of good flowering plants under a foot high, and the little dwarf white monstrosity, now being followed by coloured ones of the same habit, seems to me worthy of nothing but condemnation. It would be as right and sensible to dwarf a Hollyhock into a podgy mass a foot high, or a Pentstemon, or a Foxglove. Happily these have as yet escaped dwarfing, though I regret to see that a deformity that not unfrequently appears

[37]

among garden Foxgloves, looking like a bell-shaped flower topping a stunted spike, appears to have been "fixed," and is being offered as a "novelty." Here is one of the clearest examples of a new development which is a distinct debasement of a naturally beautiful form, but which is nevertheless being pushed forward in trade: it has no merit whatever in itself, and is only likely to sell because it is new and curious.

And all this parade of distortion and deformity comes about from the grower losing sight of beauty as the first consideration, or from his not having the knowledge that would enable him to determine what are the points of character in various plants most deserving of development, and in not knowing when or where to stop. Abnormal size, whether greatly above or much below the average, appeals to the vulgar and uneducated eye, and will always command its attention and wonderment. But then the production of the immense size that provokes astonishment, and the mis-applied ingenuity that produces unusual dwarfing, are neither of them very high aims.

And much as I feel grateful to those who improve garden flowers, I venture to repeat my strong conviction that their efforts in selection and other methods should be so directed as to keep in view the attainment of beauty in the first place, and as a point of honour; not to mere increase of size of bloom or compactness of habit—many plants have been spoilt by excess of both; not for variety or novelty as ends in themselves, but only to welcome them, and offer them, if they are distinctly of garden value in the best sense. For if plants are grown or advertised or otherwise pushed on any other account than that of their possessing some worthy form of beauty, they become of the same nature as any other article in trade that is got up for sale for the sole benefit of the seller, that is unduly lauded by advertisement, and that makes its first appeal to the vulgar eye by an exaggerated and showy pictorial representation; that will serve no useful purpose, and for which there is no true or healthy demand.

No doubt much of it comes about from the unwholesome pressure of trade competition, which in a way obliges all to follow where some lead. I

A GARDENING CREDO

trust that my many good friends in the trade will understand that my remarks are not made in any personal sense whatever. I know that some of them feel much as I do on some of these points, but that in many ways they are helpless, being all bound in a kind of bondage to the general system. And there is one great evil that calls loudly for redress, but that will endure until some of the mightiest of them have the energy and courage to band themselves together and to declare that it shall no longer exist among them.

❧ THE WORSHIP OF FALSE GODS

Several times I have spoken in a disparaging manner of the show-table; and I have not done so lightly, but with all the care and thought and power of observation that my limited capacity· is worth; and, broadly, I have come to this: that shows, such as those at the fortnightly meetings of the Royal Horticultural Society, and their more important one in the early summer, whose object is to bring together beautiful flowers of all kinds, to a place where they may be seen, are of the utmost value; and that any shows anywhere for a like purpose, and especially where there are no money prizes, are also sure to be helpful. And the test question I put to myself at any show is this, Does this really help the best interests of horticulture? And as far as I can see that it does this, I think the show right and helpful; and whenever it does not, I think it harmful and misleading.

The love of gardening has so greatly grown and spread within the last few years, that the need of really good and beautiful garden flowers is already far in advance of the demand for the so-called "florist" flowers, by which I mean those that find favour in the exclusive shows of Societies for the growing and exhibition of such flowers as Tulips, Carnations, Dahlias, and Chrysanthemums. In support of this I should like to know what proportion of demand there is, in Dahlias, for instance, between the show kinds, whose aim and object is the show-table, and the decorative kinds, that are indisputably better for garden use. Looking at the catalogue of a leading Dahlia nursery, I find that the decorative kinds fill ten pages, while the show kinds, including Pompones, fill only three. Is not this some indication of what is wanted in gardens?

I am of opinion that the show-table is unworthily used when its object is to be an end in itself, and that it should be only a means to a better end, and that when it exhibits what has become merely a "fancy," it loses sight of its honourable position as a trustworthy exponent of horti-culture, and has degenerated to a baser use. When, as in Chrysanthemum shows, the flowers on the board are of *no use anywhere but on that board*, and for the purpose of gaining a money prize, I hold that the show-table has a debased aim, and a debasing influence. Beauty, in all the best sense, is put aside in favour of set rules and measurements, and the production of a thing that is of no use or value; and individuals of a race of plants capable of producing the highest and most delightful forms of beauty, and of brightening our homes, and even gardens, during the dim days of early winter, are teased and tortured and fatted and bloated into ugly and useless monstrosities for no purpose but to gain money. And when private gardeners go to these shows and see how the prizes are awarded, and how all the glory is accorded to the first-prize bloated monster, can we wonder that the effect on their minds is confusing, if not absolutely harmful?

Shows of Carnations and Pansies, where the older rules prevail, are equally misleading, where the single flowers are arranged in a flat circle of paper. As with the Chrysanthemum, every sort of trickery is allowed in arranging the petals of the Carnation blooms: petals are pulled out or stuck in, and they are twisted about, and groomed and combed, and manipulated with special tools—"dressed," as the show-word has it—dressed so elaborately that the dressing only stops short of applying actual paint and perfumery. Already in the case of Carnations a better influence is being felt, and at the London shows there are now classes for border Carnations set up in long-stalked bunches just as they grow. It is only like this that their value as outdoor plants can be tested; for many of the show sorts have miserably weak stalks, and a very poor, lanky habit of growth.

Then the poor Pansies have single blooms laid flat on white papers, and are only approved if they will lie quite flat and show an outline of a perfect circle. All that is most beautiful in a Pansy, the wing-like curves, the waved or slightly fluted radiations, the scarcely perceptible undulation of surface that displays to perfection the admirable delicacy of velvety texture; all the little tender tricks and ways that make the Pansy one of the best-loved of garden flowers; all this is overlooked, and not only passively overlooked, but overtly contemned. The show-pansy judge appears to have no eye, or brain, or heart, but to have in their place a pair of compasses with which to describe a circle! All idea of garden delight seems to be excluded, as this kind of judging appeals to no recognition of beauty for beauty's sake, but to hard systems of measurement and rigid arrangement and computation that one would think more applicable to astronomy or geometry than to any matter relating to horticulture.

I do most strongly urge that beauty of the highest class should be the aim, and not anything of the nature of fashion or "fancy," and that every effort should be made towards the raising rather than the lowering of the standard of taste.

The Societies which exist throughout the country are well organised; many have existed for a great number of years; they are the local sources of horticultural education, to which large circles of people naturally look for guidance; and though they produce—especially at the Rose shows—quantities of beautiful things, it cannot but be perceived by all who have had the benefit of some refinement of education, that in very many cases they either deliberately teach, or at any rate allow to be seen with their sanction, what cannot fail to be debasing to public taste.

I will take just two examples to show how obvious methods of leading taste are not only overlooked, but even perverted; for it is not only in the individual blooms that much of the show-teaching is unworthy, but also in the training of the plants; so that a plant that by nature has some beauty of form, is not encouraged or even allowed to develop that beauty, but is trained into some shape that is not only foreign to its own nature, but is absolutely ugly and ungraceful, and entirely stupid. The natural habit of the Chrysanthemum is to grow in the form of several upright stems. They spring up sheaf-wise, straight upright for a time, and only bending a little outward above, to give room for the branching heads of bloom. The stems are rather stiff, because they are half woody at the base. In the case of pot-plants it would seem right only so far to stake or train them as to give the necessary support by a few sticks set a little outward at the top, so that each stem may lean a little over, after the manner of a Bamboo, when their clustered heads of flower would be given enough room, and be seen to the greatest advantage.

But at shows, the triumph of the training art seems to be to drag the poor thing round and round over an internal scaffolding of sticks, with an infinite number of ties and cross-braces, so that it makes a sort of shapeless ball, and to arrange the flowers so that they are equally spotted all over it, by tying back some almost to snapping-point, and by dragging forward others to the verge of dislocation. I have never seen anything so ugly in the way of potted plants as a certain kind of Chrysanthemum that has in-curved flowers of a heavy sort of dull leaden-looking red-purple colour trained in this manner. Such a sight gives me a feeling of shame, not unmixed with wrathful indignation. I ask myself, What is it for? and I get no answer. I ask a practical gardener what it is for, and he says, "Oh, it is one of the ways they are trained for shows." I ask him, Does he think it pretty, or is it any use? and he says, "Well, they think it makes a nice variety;" and when I press him further, and say I consider it a very nasty variety, and does he think nasty varieties are better than none, the question is beyond him, and he smiles vaguely and edges away, evidently thinking my conversation perplexing, and my company undesirable. I look again at the unhappy plant, and see its poor leaves fat with an un-wholesome obesity, and seeming to say, We were really a good bit mil-dewed, but have been doctored up for the show by being crammed and stuffed with artificial aliment!

A GARDENING CREDO

My second example is that of *Azalea indica*. What is prettier in a room than one of these in its little tree form, a true tree, with tiny trunk and wide-spreading branches, and its absurdly large and lovely flowers? Surely it is the most perfect room ornament that we can have in tree shape in a moderate-sized pot; and where else can one see a tree loaded with lovely bloom whose individual flowers have a diameter equal to five times that of the trunk?

But the show decrees that all this is wrong, and that the tiny, brittle branches must be trained stiffly round till the shape of the plant shows as a sort of cylinder. Again I ask myself, What is this for? What does it teach? Can it be really to teach with deliberate intention that instead of displaying its natural and graceful tree form it should aim at a more desirable kind of beauty, such as that of the chimneypot or drainpipe, and that this is so important that it is right and laudable to devote to it much time and delicate workmanship?

I cannot but think, as well as hope, that the strong influences for good that are now being brought to bear on all departments of gardening may reach this class of show, for there are already more hopeful signs in the admission of classes for groups arranged for decoration.

The prize-show system no doubt creates its own evils, because the judges, and those who frame the schedules, have been in most cases men who have a knowledge of flowers, but who are not people of cultivated taste, and in deciding what points are to constitute the merits of a flower they have to take such qualities as are within the clearest understanding of people of average intelligence and average education—such, for instance, as size that can be measured, symmetry that can be easily estimated, thickness of petal that can be felt, and such qualities of colour as appeal most strongly to the uneducated eye; so that a flower may possess features or qualities that endow it with the highest beauty, but that exclude it, because the hard and narrow limits of the show-laws provide no means of dealing with it. It is, therefore, thrown out, not because they have any fault to find with it, but because it does not concern them; and the ordinary gardener, to whose practice it might be of the highest value, accepting the verdict of the show-judge as an infallible guide, also treats it with contempt and neglect.

Now, all this would not so much matter if it did not delude those whose taste is not sufficiently educated to enable them to form an opinion of their own in accordance with the best and truest standards of beauty; for I venture to repeat that what we have to look for for the benefit of our gardens, and for our own bettering and increase of happiness in those gardens, are things that are beautiful, rather than things that are round, or straight, or thick, still less than for those that are new, or curious, or astonishing. For all these false gods are among us, and many are they who are willing to worship.

🍃 BEGINNING AND LEARNING

Many people who love flowers and wish to do some practical gardening are at their wit's end to know what to do and how to begin. Like a person who is on skates for the first time, they feel that, what with the bright steel runners, and the slippery surface, and the sense of helplessness, there are more ways of tumbling about than of progressing safely in any one direction. And in gardening the beginner must feel this kind of perplexity and helplessness, and indeed there is a great deal to learn, only it is pleasant instead of perilous, and the many tumbles by the way only teach and do not hurt. The first few steps are perhaps the most difficult, and it is only when we know something of the subject and an eager beginner comes with questions that one sees how very many are the things that want knowing. And the more ignorant the questioner, the more difficult it is to answer helpfully. When one knows, one cannot help presupposing some sort of knowledge on the part of the querist, and where this is absent the answer we can give is of no use. The ignorance, when fairly complete, is of such a nature that the questioner does not know what to ask, and the answer, even if it can be given, falls upon barren ground. I think in such cases it is better to try and teach one simple thing at a time, and not to attempt to answer a number of useless questions. It is disheartenng when one has tried to give a careful answer to have it received with an Oh! of boredom or disappointment, as much as to say, You can't expect me to take all that trouble; and there is the still more unsatisfactory sort of applicant, who plies a string of questions and will not wait for the answers! The real way is to try and learn a little from everybody and from every place. There is no royal road. It is no use asking me or any one else how to dig—I mean sitting indoors and asking it. Better go and watch a man digging, and then take a spade and try to do it, and go on trying till it comes, and you gain the knack that is to be learnt with all tools, of doubling the power and halving the effort; and meanwhile you will be learning other things, about your own arms and legs and back, and perhaps a little robin will come and give you moral support, and at the same time keep a sharp look-out for any worms you may happen to turn up; and you will find out that there are all sorts of ways of learning, not only from people and books, but from sheer trying.

The grand way to learn, in gardening as in all things else, is to wish to learn, and to be determined to find out—not to think that any one person can wave a wand and give the power and knowledge. And there will be plenty of mistakes, and there must be, just as children must pass through the usual childish complaints. And some people make the mistake of trying to begin at the end, and of using recklessly what may want the utmost caution, such, for instance, as strong chemical manures.

Some ladies asked me why their plant had died. They had got it from the very best place, and they were sure they had done their very best for it, and—there it was, dead. I asked what it was, and how they had treated it. It was some ordinary border plant, whose identity I now forget; they had made a nice hole with their new trowel, and for its sole benefit they had bought a tin of Concentrated Fertiliser. This they had emptied into the hole, put in the plant, and covered it up and given it lots

of water, and—it had died! And yet these were the best and kindest of
women, who would never have dreamed of feeding a new-born infant
on beefsteaks and raw brandy. But they learned their lesson well, and
at once saw the sense when I pointed out that a plant with naked roots
just taken out of the ground or a pot, removed from one feeding-place
and not yet at home in another, or still more after a journey, with the
roots only wrapped in a little damp moss and paper, had its feeding
power suspended for a time, and was in the position of a helpless invalid.
All that could be done for it then was a little bland nutriment of weak
slops and careful nursing; if the planting took place in the summer it
would want shading and only very gentle watering, until firm root-hold
was secured and root-appetite became active, and that in rich and well-
prepared garden ground such as theirs strong artificial manure was in any
case superfluous.

When the earlier ignorances are overcome it becomes much easier to
help and advise, because there is more common ground to stand on. In
my own case, from quite a small child, I had always seen gardening going
on, though not of a very interesting kind. Nothing much was thought of
but bedding plants, and there was a rather large space on each side of the
house for these, one on gravel and one on turf. But I had my own little
garden in a nook beyond the shrubbery, with a seat shaded by a *Boursault elegans* Rose, which I thought then, and still think, one of the
loveliest of its kind. But my first knowledge of garden plants came
through wild ones. Some one gave me that excellent book, the Rev. C. A.
Johns' "Flowers of the Field." For many years I had no one to advise me
(I was still quite small) how to use the book, or how to get to know
(though it stared me in the face) how the plants were in large related
families, and I had not the sense to do it for myself, nor to learn the
introductory botanical part, which would have saved much trouble afterwards; but when I brought home my flowers I would take them one by
one and just turn over the pages till I came to the picture that looked
something like. But in this way I got a knowledge of individuals, and

[46]

afterwards the idea of broad classification and relationship of genera to species may have come all the easier. I always think of that book as the most precious gift I ever received. I distinctly trace to its teaching my first firm steps in the path of plant knowledge, and the feeling of assured comfort I had afterwards in recognising the kinds when I came to collect garden plants; for at that time I had no other garden book, no means of access to botanic gardens or private collections, and no helpful adviser. One copy of "Johns" I wore right out; I have now two, of which one is in its second binding, and is always near me for reference. I need hardly say that this was long before the days of the "English Flower-Garden," or its helpful predecessor, "Alpine Plants."

By this time I was steadily collecting hardy garden plants wherever I could find them, mostly from cottage gardens. Many of them were still unknown to me by name, but as the collection increased I began to compare and discriminate, and of various kinds of one plant to throw out the worse and retain the better, and to train myself to see what made a good garden plant, and about then began to grow the large yellow and white bunch Primroses, whose history is in another chapter. And then I learnt that there were such places (though then but few) as nurseries, where such plants as I had been collecting in the cottage gardens, and even better, were grown. And I went to Osborne's at Fulham (now all built over), and there saw the original tree of the fine Ilex known as the Fulham Oak, and several spring-flowering bulbs I had never seen before, and what I felt sure were numbers of desirable summer-flowering plants, but not then in bloom. Soon after this I began to learn something about Daffodils, and enjoyed much kind help from Mr. Barr, visiting his nursery (then at Tooting) several times, and sometimes combining a visit to Parker's nursery just over the way, a perfect paradise of good hardy plants. I shall never forget my first sight here of the Cape Pondweed (*Aponogeton distachyon*) in full flower and great vigour in the dipping tanks, and overflowing from them into the ditches.

Also I was delighted to see the use as labels of old wheel-spokes. I could not help feeling that if one had been a spoke of a cab-wheel, and had passed all one's working life in being whirled and clattered over London pavements, defiled with street mud, how pleasant a way to end one's days was this; to have one's felloe end pointed and dipped in nice wholesome rot-resisting gas-tar and thrust into the quiet cool earth, and one's nave end smoothed and painted and inscribed with some such soothing legend as *Vinca minor* or *Dianthus fragrans!*

I think it is desirable, when a certain degree of knowledge of plants and facility of dealing with them has been acquired, to get hold of a clear idea of what one most wishes to do. The scope of the subject is so wide, and there are so many ways to choose from, that having one general idea helps one to concentrate thought and effort that would otherwise be wasted by being diluted and dribbled through too many probable channels of waste.

Ever since it came to me to feel some little grasp of knowledge of means and methods, I have found that my greatest pleasure, both in garden and woodland, has been in the enjoyment of beauty of a pictorial kind. Whether the picture be large as of a whole landscape, or of lesser extent as in some fine single group or effect, or within the space of only a few inches as may be seen in some happily-disposed planting of Alpines, the intention is always the same; or whether it is the grouping of trees in the wood by the removal of those whose lines are not wanted in the picture, or in the laying out of broad grassy ways in woody places, or by ever so slight a turn or change of direction in a wood path, or in the alteration of some arrangement of related groups for form or for massing of light and shade, or for any of the many local conditions that guide one towards forming a decision, the intention is still always the same—to try and make a beautiful garden-picture. And little as I can as yet boast of being able to show anything like the number of these I could wish, yet during the flower-year there is generally something that at least in part answers to the effort.

A GARDENING CREDO

I do not presume to urge the acceptance of my own particular form of pleasure in a garden on those to whom, from different temperament or manner of education, it would be unwelcome; I only speak of what I feel, and to a certain degree understand; but I had the advantage in earlier life of some amount of training in appreciation of the fine arts, and this, working upon an inborn feeling of reverent devotion to things of the highest beauty in the works of God, has helped me to an understanding of their divinely-inspired interpretations by the noblest minds of men, into those other forms that we know as works of fine art.

And so it comes about that those of us who feel and understand in this way do not exactly attempt to imitate Nature in our gardens, but try to become well acquainted with her moods and ways, and then discriminate in our borrowing, and so interpret her methods as best we may to the making of our garden-pictures.

I have always had great delight in the study of colour, as the word is understood by artists, which again is not a positive matter, but one of relation and proportion. And when one hears the common chatter about "artistic colours," one receives an unpleasant impression about the education and good taste of the speaker; and one is reminded of an old saying which treats of the unwisdom of rushing in "where angels fear to tread," and of regret that a good word should be degraded by misuse. It may be safely said that no colour can be called artistic in itself; for, in the first place, it is bad English, and in the second, it is nonsense. Even if the first objection were waived, and the second condoned, it could only be used in a secondary sense, as signifying something that is useful and suitable and right in its place. In this limited sense the scarlet of the soldier's coat, and of the pillar-box and mail-cart, and the bright colours of flags, or of the port and starboard lights of ships, might be said to be just so far "artistic" (again if grammar would allow), as they are right and good in their places. But then those who use the word in the usual ignorant-random way have not even this simple conception of its meaning. Those who know nothing about colour in the more refined sense (and like a knowledge of everything else it wants learning) get no farther than to enjoy it only when most crude and garish—when, as George Herbert says, it "bids the rash gazer wipe his eye," or when there is some violent opposition of complementary colour—forgetting, or not knowing, that though in detail the objects brought together may make each other appear brighter, yet in the mass, and especially when mixed up, the one actually neutralises the other. And they have no idea of using the colour of flowers as precious jewels in a setting of quiet environment, or of suiting the colour of flowering groups to that of the neighbouring foliage, thereby enhancing the value of both, or of massing related or harmonious colourings so as to lead up to the most powerful and brilliant effects; and yet all these are just the ways of employing colour to the best advantage.

But the most frequent fault, whether in composition or in colour, is the attempt to crowd too much into the picture; the simpler effect obtained by means of temperate and wise restraint is always the more telling.

❀ STUDY

Nothing is a better lesson in the knowledge of plants than to sit down in front of them, and handle them and look them over just as carefully as possible; and in no way can such study be more pleasantly or conveniently carried on than by taking a light seat to the rock-wall and giving plenty of time to each kind of little plant, examining it closely and asking oneself, and it, why this and why that. Especially if the first glance shows two tufts, one with a better appearance than the other; not to stir from the place until one has found out why and how it is done, and all about it. Of course a friend who has already gone through it all can help on the lesson more quickly, but I doubt whether it is not best to do it all for oneself.

A GARDENING CREDO

❧ WEEDING

Weeding is a delightful occupation, especially after summer rain, when the roots come up clear and clean. One gets to know how many and various are the ways of weeds—as many almost as the moods of human creatures. How easy and pleasant to pull up are the soft annuals like Chickweed and Groundsel, and how one looks with respect at deep-rooted things like Docks, that make one go and fetch a spade.

❖ TOOLS

There is a lovable quality about the actual tools. One feels so kindly to the thing that enables the hand to obey the brain. Moreover, one feels a good deal of respect for it; without it brain and hand would be helpless. When the knife that has been in one's hand or one's pocket for years has its blade so much worn by constant sharpening that it can no longer be used, with what true regret does one put it aside, and how long it is before one can really make friends with the new one! I do not think any workman really likes a new tool. There is always some feeling about it as of something strange and unfamiliar and uncongenial, somewhat of the feeling that David had about Saul's armour. What an awkward thing a new spade is, how long and heavy and rough of handle! And then how amiable it becomes when it is half worn, when the square corners that made the thrust so hard are ground away, when the whole blade has grown shorter, when the handle has gained that polish, the best polish of all, that comes of long hand-friction. No carpenter likes a new plane; no house-painter likes a new brush. It is the same with tools as with clothes;

[51]

the familiar ease can only come of use and better acquaintance. I suppose no horse likes a new collar; I am quite sure I do not like new boots!

❀ WORK

If it were possible to simplify life to the utmost, how little one really wants! And is it a blessing or a disadvantage to be so made that one *must* take keen interest in many matters; that, seeing something that one's hand may do, one cannot resist doing or attempting it, even though time be already overcrowded, and strength much reduced, and sight steadily failing? Are the people happier who are content to drift comfortably down the stream of life, to take things easily, not to *want* to take pains or give themselves trouble about what is not exactly necessary? I know not which, as worldly wisdom, is the wiser; I only know that to my own mind and conscience pure idleness seems to me to be akin to folly, or even worse, and that in some form or other I must obey the Divine command: "Work while ye have the light."

DESIGN
AND ORNAMENT

🌱   THE BEDDING FASHION AND ITS INFLUENCE

It is curious to look back at the old days of bedding-out, when that and that only meant gardening to most people, and to remember how the fashion, beginning in the larger gardens, made its way like a great inundating wave, submerging the lesser ones, and almost drowning out the beauties of the many little flowery cottage plots of our English waysides. And one wonders how it all came about, and why the bedding system, admirable for its own purpose, should have thus outstepped its bounds, and have been allowed to run riot among gardens great and small throughout the land. But so it was, and for many years the fashion, for it was scarcely anything better, reigned supreme.

It was well for all real lovers of flowers when some quarter of a century ago a strong champion of the good old flowers arose, and fought strenuously to stay the devastating tide, and to restore the healthy liking for the good old garden flowers. Many soon followed, and now one may say that all England has flocked to the standard. Bedding as an all-prevailing fashion is now dead; the old garden-flowers are again honoured and loved, and every encouragement is freely offered to those who will improve old kinds and bring forward others.

And now that bedding as a fashion no longer exists, one can look at it more quietly and fairly, and see what its uses really are, for in its own place and way it is undoubtedly useful and desirable. Many great country-houses are only inhabited in winter, then perhaps for a week or two at Easter, and in the late summer. There is probably a house-party at Easter, and a succession of visitors in the late summer. A brilliant garden, visible from the house, dressed for spring and dressed for early autumn, is exactly what is wanted—not necessarily from any special love of flowers, but as a kind of bright and well-kept furnishing of the immediate environment of the house. The gardener delights in it; it is all routine work; so many hundreds or thousands of scarlet Geranium, of yellow Calceolaria, of blue Lobelia, of golden Feverfew, or of other coloured material. It wants no imagination; the comprehension of it is within the range of the most limited understanding; indeed its prevalence for some twenty years or more must have had a deteriorating influence on the whole class of private gardeners, presenting to them an ideal so easy of attainment and so cheap of mental effort.

But bedding, though it is gardening of the least poetical or imaginative kind, can be done badly or beautifully. In the *parterre* of the formal garden it is absolutely in place, and brilliantly-beautiful pictures can be made by a wise choice of colouring. I once saw, and can never forget, a bedded garden that was a perfectly satisfying example of colour-harmony; but then it was planned by the master, a man of the most refined taste, and not by the gardener. It was a *parterre* that formed part of the garden in one of the fine old places in the Midland counties. I have no distinct recollection of the design, except that there was some principle of fan-shaped radiation, of which each extreme angle formed one centre. The whole garden was treated in one harmonious colouring of full yellow, orange, and orange-brown; half-hardy annuals, such as French and African Marigolds, Zinnias, and Nasturtiums, being freely used. It was the most noble treatment of one limited range of colouring I have ever seen in a garden; brilliant without being garish, and sumptuously gorgeous without the reproach of gaudiness—a precious lesson in temperance and restraint in the use of the one colour, and an admirable exposition of its powerful effect in the hands of a true artist.

I think that in many smaller gardens a certain amount of bedding may be actually desirable; for where the owner of a garden has a special liking for certain classes or mixtures of plants, or wishes to grow them thoroughly well and enjoy them individually to the full, he will naturally grow them in separate beds, or may intentionally combine the beds, if he will, into some form of good garden effect. But the great fault of the bedding system when at its height was, that it swept over the country as a tyrannical fashion, that demanded, and for the time being succeeded in effecting, the exclusion of better and more thoughtful kinds of gardening; for I believe I am right in saying that it spread like an epidemic disease, and raged far and wide for nearly a quarter of a century.

Its worst form of all was the "ribbon border," generally a line of scarlet Geranium at the back, then a line of Calceolaria, then a line of blue Lobelia, and lastly, a line of the inevitable Golden Feather Feverfew, or what our gardener used to call Featherfew. Could anything be more tedious or more stupid? And the ribbon border was at its worst when its lines were not straight, but waved about in weak and silly sinuations.

And when bedding as a fashion was dead, when this false god had been toppled off his pedestal, and his worshippers had been converted to better beliefs, in turning and rending him they often went too far, and did injustice to the innocent by professing a dislike to many a good plant, and renouncing its use. It was not the fault of the Geranium or of the Calceolaria that they had been grievously misused and made to usurp too large a share of our garden spaces. Not once but many a time my visitors have expressed unbounded surprise when they saw these plants in my garden, saying, "I should have thought that you would have despised Geraniums." On the contrary, I love Geraniums. There are no plants to come near them for pot, or box, or stone basket, or for massing in any sheltered place in hottest sunshine; and I love their strangely pleasant smell, and their beautiful modern colouring of soft scarlet and salmon-scarlet and salmon-pink, some of these grouping beautifully together. I have a space in connection with some formal stonework of steps, and tank, and paved walks, close to the house, on purpose for the summer placing of large pots of Geranium, with sometimes a few Cannas and Lilies. For a quarter of the year it is one of the best things in the garden, and delightful in colour. Then no plant does so well or looks so suitable in some earthen pots and boxes from Southern Italy that I always think the best that were ever made, their shape and well-designed ornament traditional from the Middle Ages, and probably from an even more remote antiquity.

There are, of course, among bedding Geraniums many of a bad, raw quality of colour, particularly among cold, hard pinks, but there are so many to choose from that these can easily be avoided.

I remember some years ago, when the bedding fashion was going out, reading some rather heated discussions in the gardening papers about methods of planting out and arranging various tender but indispensable plants. Some one who had been writing about the errors of the bedding system wrote about planting some of these in isolated masses. He was pounced upon by another, who asked, "What is this but bedding?" The second writer was so far justified, in that it cannot be denied that any planting in beds is bedding. But then there is bedding and bedding—a right and a wrong way of applying the treatment. Another matter that roused the combative spirit of the captious critic was the filling up of bare spaces in mixed borders with Geraniums, Calceolarias, and other such plants. Again he said, "What is this but bedding? These are bedding plants." When I read this it seemed to me that his argument was, These plants may be very good plants in themselves, but because they have for some years been used wrongly, therefore they must not now be used rightly! In the case of my own visitors, when they have expressed surprise at my having "those horrid old bedding plants" in my garden, it seemed quite a new view when I pointed out that bedding plants were only passive agents in their own misuse, and that a Geranium was a Geranium long before it was a bedding plant! But the discussion raised in my mind a wish to come to some conclusion about the difference between bedding in the better and worse sense, in relation to the cases quoted, and it appeared to me to be merely in the choice between right and wrong placing—placing monotonously or stupidly, so as merely to fill the space, or placing with a feeling for "drawing" or proportion. For I had very soon found out that, if I had a number of things to plant anywhere, whether only to fill up a border or as a detached group, if I placed the things myself, carefully exercising what power of discrimination I might have acquired, it looked fairly right, but that if I left it to one of my garden people (a thing I rarely do) it looked all nohow, or like bedding in the worst sense of the word.

Wild gardening is a delightful, and in good hands a most desirable, pursuit, but no kind of gardening is so difficult to do well, or is so full of pitfalls and of paths of peril. Because it has in some measure become fashionable, and because it is understood to mean the planting of exotics in wild places, unthinking people rush to the conclusion that they can put any garden plants into any wild places, and that that is wild gardening. I have seen woody places that were already perfect with their own simple charm just muddled and spoilt by a reckless planting of garden refuse, and heathy hillsides already sufficiently and beautifully clothed with native vegetation made to look lamentably silly by the planting of a nurseryman's mixed lot of exotic Conifers.

In my own case, I have always devoted the most careful consideration to any bit of wild gardening I thought of doing, never allowing myself to decide upon it till I felt thoroughly assured that the place seemed to ask for the planting in comtemplation, and that it would be distinctly a gain in pictorial value; so there are stretches of Daffodils in one part of the copse, while another is carpeted with Lily of the Valley. A cool bank is covered with Gaultheria, and just where I thought they would look well as little jewels of beauty, are spreading patches of Trillium and the great yellow Dog-tooth Violet. Besides these there are only some groups of the Giant Lily. Many other exotic plants could have been made to grow in the wooded ground, but they did not seem to be wanted; I thought where the copse looked well and complete in itself it was better left alone.

But where the wood joins the garden some bold groups of flowering plants are allowed, as of Mullein in one part and Foxglove in another; for when standing in the free part of the garden, it is pleasant to project the sight far into the wood, and to let the garden influences penetrate here and there, the better to join the one to the other.

FLOWER GROUPS

I always think it desirable to group together flowers that bloom at the same time. It is impossible, and even undesirable, to have a garden in blossom all over, and groups of flower-beauty are all the more enjoyable for being more or less isolated by stretches of intervening greenery.

SOME GARDEN PICTURES

When the eye is trained to perceive pictorial effect, it is frequently struck by something—some combination of grouping, lighting and colour —that is seen to have that complete aspect of unity and beauty that to the artist's eye forms a picture. Such are the impressions that the artist-gardener endeavours to produce in every portion of the garden. Many of these good intentions fail, some come fairly well, a few reward him by a success that was beyond anticipation. When this is the case it is probably due to some cause that had been overlooked but that had chanced to complete his intention, such as the position of the sun in relation to some wished-for colour-picture. Then there are some days during the summer when the quality of light seems to tend to an extraordinary beauty of effect. I have never been able to find out how the light on these occasions differs from that of ordinary fine summer days, but, when these days come, I know them and am filled with gladness.

In the case of my own garden, as far as deliberate intention goes, what is aimed at is something quite simple and devoid of complication; generally one thing or a very limited number of flowering things at a time, but that one, or those few things, carefully placed so as to avoid fuss, and to please the eye and give ease to the mind. In many cases the aim has been to show some delightful colour-combination without regard to the other considerations that go to the making of a more ambitious picture. It may be a group in a shrub border, or a combination of border and climbing plants, or some carefully designed company of plants in the rock garden. I have a little rose that I call the Fairy Rose. It came to me from a cottage garden, and I have never seen it elsewhere. It grows about a foot high and has blush-pink flowers with the colour deepening to the centre. In character the flower is somewhere between the lovely Blush Boursault at its best and the little De Meaux. It is an inch and a half across and of beautiful form, especially in the half-opened bud. Wishing to enjoy its beauty to the utmost, and to bring it comfortably within sight, I gave it a shelf in raised rock-work and brought near and under it a clear pale lilac Viola and a good drift of *Achillea umbellata*. It was worth doing. Another combination that gives me much pleasure is that of the pink Pompon Rose Mignonette with Catmint and whitish foliage, such as Stachys or *Artemisia stelleriana*. I may have mentioned this before, but it is so pretty that it deserves repetition.

In a shrubbery border the fine *Spiræa Aruncus* is beautiful with an interplanting of *Thalictrum purpureum*. At the end of a long flower-clump there is a yew hedge coming forward at right angles to the length of the border. Behind the hedge is a stone wall with an arch, through which the path in front of the border passes. Over the stone arch and rambling partly over the yews are the vigorous many-flowered growths of *Clematis Flammula*. In the end of the border are pale sulphur-coloured Hollyhocks. Both in form and colour this was a delightful picture; the foam-like masses of the Clematis resting on the dusky richness of the yew; the straight shafts of the Hollyhock giving clear colour and agreeing with the upright lines of the sides of the archway, which showed dimly in the shade. These are only a few incidents out of numbers that occur or are intentionally arranged.

There is a place near my house where a path leads down through a nut-walk to the further garden. It is crossed by a shorter path that ends at a Birch tree with a tall silvered trunk. It seemed desirable to accentuate the point where the paths cross; I therefore put down four square plat-forms of stone "pitching" as a place for the standing of four Hydrangeas in tubs. Just before the tree is a solid wooden seat and a shallow wide step done with the same stone pitching. Tree and seat are surrounded on three sides by a rectangular planting of yews. The tender greys of the rugged lower bark of the Birch and the silvering of its upper stem tell finely against the dark velvet-like richness of the Yew and the leaf-mass of other trees beyond; the pink flowers and fresh green foliage of the Hydrangeas are also brilliant against the dusky green. It is just one simple picture that makes one glad for three months of the later summer and early autumn. The longer cross-path, which on the right leads in a few yards to steps up to the paved court on the north side of the house, on the left passes down the nut-walk. The Birch tree and seat are immediately to the right. Standing a little way down the shaded nut-walk and looking back, the Hydrangeas are seen in another aspect, with the steps and house behind them in shade, and the sun shining through their pale green leaves. Sitting on the seat, the eye, passing between the pink Hydrangea flowers, sees a short straight path bounded by a wall of Tree Box to right and left, and at the far end one tub of pale blue Hydrangea in shade, backed by a repetition of the screen of Yews such as enclose the Birch tree.

The beautiful White Lily cannot be grown in the hot sandy soil of my garden. Even if its place be ever so well prepared with the loam and lime that it loves, the surrounding soil-influences seem to rob it of its needful nourishment; it makes a miserable show for one year and never appears again. The only way to grow it is in pots or tubs sunk in the soil. For some years I had wished to have an orderly planting of this lovely Lily in the lower border at the back of the Andromeda just in front of the Briars. I had no flower-pots deep enough, or wide enough at the bottom, but was able to make a contrivance with some short, broad, unglazed drain-pipes, measuring a foot long and of about the same diameter, by cementing in an artificial bottom made of pieces of roofing-tile and broken flower-pot, leaving spaces for drainage. Then three bulbs were put in each pot in a compost that I knew they would enjoy. When they were half grown the pots were sunk in holes at nearly even distances among the Andromedas, and in a few weeks my row of Lilies gave me my reward. Other Lilies (*L. longiflorum*) follow them a month later, just beyond in the wood edge among tufts of Male Fern, and a pot of Francoa is to right and left of the shallow steps.

During the last year or two some pretty incidents have occurred about these same steps; not important enough to call garden pictures, but charming and interesting and easily enjoyable because they are close to the open garden door of the sitting-room and because they teach me to look out for the desirable things that come of themselves. A seedling of the wild Clematis (*C. Vitalba*) appeared among the Briars to the left. As it was too strong a plant to let grow over them unchecked, I pulled it forward towards the steps, training one or two shoots to run along the hollow of the step and laying on them pieces of stone invisible among the foliage, to keep them from being dislodged by the skirts of visitors or the

ON GARDENING

gambols of my cats. At the same time, in a crack of the stone just below the upper step there came a seedling of the tall Chimney Campanula (*C. pyramidalis*). The second year this threw up its tall flower-stem and was well in bloom when it was wrecked by an early autumn gale, the wind wrenching out the crown and upper root-stock. But a little shred of rooted life remained and now there is again the sturdy tuft promising more flower-stems for the coming season.

Close behind the Bell-flower a spreading sheet of Wild Thyme has crept out of the turf and spread rather widely over the stone. Luckily I just saved it from the tidying process that threatened it, and as it is now well established over the stone I still have the pleasure of its bright rosy bloom when the duties of the mowing-machine rob me of the other tiny flowers—Hawkweed, Milkwort and Bedstraw—that bloom so bravely in the intervals between its ruthless but indispensable ministrations.

🌿 DRIFTS

Many years ago I came to the conclusion that in all flower borders it is better to plant in long rather than block-shaped patches. It not only has a more pictorial effect, but a thin long planting does not leave an unsightly empty space when the flowers are done and the leaves have perhaps died down. The word "drift" conveniently describes the shape I have in mind and I commonly use it in speaking of these long-shaped plantings.

🌿 EARLY BULBS

Where and how the early flowering bulbs had best be planted is a question of some difficulty. Perhaps the mixed border, where they are most usually put, is the worst place of all, for when in flower they only show as forlorn little patches of bloom rather far apart, and when their leaves die down, leaving their places looking empty, the ruthless spade or trowel stabs into them when it is desired to fill the space with some other plant. Moreover, when the border is manured and partly dug in the autumn, it is difficult to avoid digging up the bulbs just when they are in full root-growth. Probably the best plan is to devote a good space of cool bank to small bulbs and hardy ferns, planting the ferns in such groups as will leave good spaces for the bulbs; then as their leaves are going the fern fronds are developing and will cover the whole space. Another way is to have them among any groups of newly planted small shrubs, to be left there for spring blooming until the shrubs have covered their allotted space.

❧ THE FLOWER-BORDER AND PERGOLA

I have a rather large "mixed border of hardy flowers." It is not quite so hopelessly mixed as one generally sees, and the flowers are not all hardy; but as it is a thing everybody rightly expects, and as I have been for a good many years trying to puzzle out its wants and ways, I will try and describe my own and its surroundings.

There is a sandstone wall of pleasant colour at the back, nearly eleven feet high. This wall is an important feature in the garden, as it is the dividing line between the pleasure garden and the working garden; also, it shelters the pleasure garden from the sweeping blasts of wind from the north-west, to which my ground is much exposed, as it is all on a gentle slope, going downward towards the north. At the foot of the wall is a narrow border three feet six inches wide, and then a narrow alley; not a made path, but just a way to go along for tending the wall shrubs, and for getting at the back of the border. This little alley does not show from the front. Then the main border, fourteen feet wide and two hundred feet long. About three-quarters of the way along, a path cuts through the border, and passes by an arched gateway in the wall to the Pæony garden

[65]

and the working garden beyond. Just here I thought it would be well to mound up the border a little, and plant with groups of Yuccas, so that at all times of the year there should be something to make a handsome full-stop to the sections of the border, and to glorify the doorway. The two extreme ends of the border are treated in the same way with Yuccas on rather lesser mounds, only leaving space beyond them for the entrance to the little alley at the back.

There is nothing much more difficult to do in outdoor gardening than to plant a mixed border well, and to keep it in beauty throughout the summer. Every year, as I gain more experience, and, I hope, more power of critical judgment, I find myself tending towards broader and simpler effects, both of grouping and colour. I do not know whether it is by individual preference, or in obedience to some colour-law that I can instinctively feel but cannot pretend even to understand, and much less to explain, but in practice I always find more satisfaction and facility in treating the warm colours (reds and yellows) in graduated harmonies, culminating into gorgeousness, and the cool ones in contrasts; especially in the case of blue, which I like to use either in distinct but not garish contrasts, as of full blue with pale yellow, or in separate cloud-like harmonies, as of lilac and pale purple with grey foliage. I am never so much inclined to treat the blues, purples, and lilacs in associated gradations as the reds and yellows. Purples and lilacs I can put together, but not these with blues; and the pure blues always seem to demand peculiar and very careful treatment.

The western end of the flower-border begins with the low bank of Yuccas, then there are some rather large masses of important grey and glaucous foliage and pale and full pink flower. The foliage is mostly of the Globe Artichoke, and nearer the front of *Artemisia* and *Cineraria maritima*. Among this, pink Canterbury Bell, Hollyhock, Phlox, Gladiolus, and Japan Anemone, all in pink colourings, will follow one another in due succession. Then come some groups of plants bearing whitish and very pale flowers, *Polygonum compactum*, *Aconitum lycoctonum*, Double

[66]

Meadowsweet, and other Spiræas, and then the colour passes to pale yellow of Mulleins, and with them the palest blue Delphiniums. Towards the front is a wide planting of *Iris pallida dalmatica,* its handsome bluish foliage showing as outstanding and yet related masses with regard to the first large group of pale foliage. Then comes the pale-yellow *Iris flavescens,* and meanwhile the group of Delphinium deepens into those of a fuller blue colour, though none of the darkest are here. Then more pale yellow of Mullein, Thalictrum, and Paris Daisy, and so the colour passes to stronger yellows. These change into orange, and from that to brightest scarlet and crimson, coming to the fullest strength in the Oriental Poppies of the earlier year, and later in Lychnis, Gladiolus, Scarlet Dahlia, and Tritoma. The colour-scheme then passes again through orange and yellow to the paler yellows, and so again to blue and warm white, where it meets one of the clumps of Yuccas flanking the path that divides this longer part of the border from the much shorter piece beyond. This simple procession of colour arrangement has occupied a space of a hundred and sixty feet, and the border is all the better for it.

The short length of border beyond the gateway has again Yuccas and important pale foliage, and a preponderance of pink bloom, Hydrangea for the most part; but there are a few tall Mulleins, whose pale-yellow flowers group well with the ivory of the Yucca spikes and the clear pink of the tall Hollyhocks. These all show up well over the masses of grey and glaucous foliage, and against the rich darkness of dusky Yew.

Dahlias and Cannas have their places in the mixed border. When it is being dismantled in the late autumn all bare places are well dug and enriched, so that when it comes to filling-up time, at the end of May, I know that every spare bit of space is ready, and at the time of preparation I mark places for special Dahlias, according to .colour, and for groups of the tall Cannas where I want grand foliage.

There are certain classes of plants that are quite indispensable, but that leave a bare or shabby-looking place when their bloom is over. How

[67]

to cover these places is one of the problems that have to be solved. The worst offender is Oriental Poppy; it becomes unsightly soon after bloom- ing, and is quite gone by midsummer. I therefore plant *Gypsophila pa- niculata* between and behind the Poppy groups, and by July there is a delicate cloud of bloom instead of large bare patches. *Eryngium oliveri- anum* has turned brown by the beginning of July, but around the group some Dahlias have been planted, that will be gradually trained down over the space of the departed Sea-Holly, and other Dahlias are used in the same way to mask various weak places.

There is a perennial Sunflower, with tall black stems, and pale-yellow flowers quite at the top, an old garden sort, but not very good as usually grown; this I find of great value to train down, when it throws up a short flowering stem from each joint, and becomes a spreading sheet of bloom.

One would rather not have to resort to these artifices of sticking and training; but if a certain effect is wanted, all such means are lawful, provided that nothing looks stiff or strained or unsightly; and it is pleas- ant to exercise ingenuity and to invent ways to meet the needs of any case that may arise. But like everything else, in good gardening it must be done just right, and the artist-gardener finds that hardly the placing of a single plant can be deputed to any other hand than his own; for though, when it is done, it looks quite simple and easy, he must paint his own picture himself—no one can paint it for him.

I have no dogmatic views about having in the so-called hardy flower- border none but hardy flowers. All flowers are welcome that are right in colour, and that make a brave show where a brave show is wanted. It is of more importance that the border should be handsome than that all its occupants should be hardy. Therefore I prepare a certain useful lot of half-hardy annuals, and a few of what have come to be called bedding- plants. I like to vary them a little from year to year, because in no one season can I get in all the good flowers that I should like to grow; and I think it better to leave out some one year and have them the next, than to crowd any up, or to find I have plants to put out and no space to put them in. But I nearly always grow these half-hardy annuals; orange African Marigold, French Marigold, sulphur Sunflower, orange and scarlet tall Zinnia, Nasturtiums, both dwarf and trailing, *Nicotiana affinis*, Maize, and Salpiglossis. Then Stocks and China Asters. The Stocks are always the large white and flesh-coloured summer kinds, and the Asters, the White Comet, and one of the blood-red or so-called scarlet sorts.

Then I have yellow Paris Daisies, *Salvia Patens*, Heliotrope, *Calceolaria amplexicaulis*, Geraniums, scarlet and salmon-coloured and ivy-leaved kinds, the best of these being the pink Madame Crousse.

The front edges of the border are also treated in rather a large way. At the shadier end there is first a long straggling bordering patch of *Anemone sylvestris*. When it is once above ground the foliage remains good till autumn, while its soft white flower comes right with the colour of the flowers behind. Then comes a long and large patch of the larger kind of *Megasea cordifolia*, several yards in length, and running back here and there among the taller plants. I am never tired of admiring the fine solid foliage of this family of plants, remaining, as it does, in beauty both winter and summer, and taking on a splendid winter colouring of warm red bronze. It is true that the flowers of the two best-known kinds, *M. cordifolia* and *M. crassifolia*, are coarse-looking blooms of a strong and rank quality of pink colour, but the persistent beauty of the leaves more than compensates; and in the rather tenderer kind, *M. ligulata* and its varieties, the colour of the flower is delightful, of a delicate good pink, with almost scarlet stalks. There is nothing flimsy or temporary-looking about the Megaseas, but rather a sort of grave and monumental look that specially fits them for association with masonry, or for any place where a solid-looking edging or full-stop is wanted. To go back to those in the edge of the border: if the edging threatens to look too dark and hard, I plant among or just behind the plants that compose it, pink or scarlet Ivy Geranium or trailing Nasturtium, according to the colour demanded by the neighbouring group. *Heuchera Richardsoni* is another good front-edge plant; and when we come to the blue and pale-yellow group there is

[69]

a planting of *Funkia grandiflora,* whose fresh-looking pale-green leaves are delightful with the brilliant light yellow of *Calceolaria amplexicaulis,* and the farther-back planting of pale-blue Delphinium, Mullein, and sulphur Sunflower; while the same colour of foliage is repeated in the fresh green of the Indian Corn. Small spaces occur here and there along the extreme front edge, and here are planted little jewels of colour, of blue Lobelia, or dwarf Nasturtium, or anything of the colour that the place demands.

The whole thing sounds much more elaborate than it really is; the trained eye sees what is wanted, and the trained hand does it, both by an acquired instinct. It is painting a picture with living plants.

STAKING

An important matter is that of staking and supporting. The rule, as I venture to lay it down, is that sticks and stakes must never show. They must be so arranged that they give the needful support, while allowing the plant its natural freedom; but they must remain invisible. The only time when they are tolerated is for the week or two when they have been put in for Dahlias, when the plants have not yet grown up to cover them.

I hold that nothing unsightly should be seen in the garden. The shed for sticks and stakes is a lean-to at one end of the barn, showing to the garden. The roof had to be made at a very low pitch, and there was no roofing material suitable but galvanized iron. But a depth of four inches of peaty earth was put over the iron, and now it is a garden of Stonecrops and other plants that flourish in shallow soil in a hot exposure.

THE PERGOLA

I much enjoy the pergola at the end of the sunny path. It is pleasant while walking in full sunshine, and when that sunny place feels just a little too hot, to look into its cool depth, and to know that one has only to go a few steps farther to be in shade, and to enjoy that little air of wind that the moving summer clouds say is not far off, and is only unfelt just here because it is stopped by the wall. It seems wonderfully dark at first, this gallery of cool greenery, passing into it with one's eyes full of light and colour, and the open-sided summer-house at the end looks like a black cavern; but on going into it, and sitting down on one of its broad, low benches, one finds that it is a pleasant subdued light, just right to read by.

The pergola has two openings out of it on the right, and one on the left. The first way out on the right is straight into the nut-walk, which leads up to very near the house. The second goes up two or three low, broad steps made of natural sandstone flags, between groups of Ferns, into the Michaelmas Daisy garden. The opening on the left leads into a quiet space of grass the width of the flower and wall border (twenty feet), having only some peat-beds planted with Kalmia. This is backed by a Yew hedge in continuation of the main wall, and it will soon grow into a cool, quiet bit of garden, seeming to belong to the pergola. Now, standing midway in the length of the covered walk, with the eye rested and re-freshed by the leafy half-light, on turning round again towards the border it shows as a brilliant picture through the bowery framing, and the value of the simple method of using the colours is seen to full advantage.

The climbers I find best for covering the pergola are Vines, Jasmine, Aristolochia, Virginia Creeper, and Wistaria. Roses are about the worst, for they soon run up leggy, and only flower at the top out of sight.

There is much to be done in our better-class gardens in the way of pretty small structures thoroughly well-designed and built. Many a large lawn used every afternoon in summer as a family playground and place to receive visitors would have its comfort and usefulness greatly in-creased by a pretty garden-house, instead of the usual hot and ugly, crampy and uncomfortable tent. But it should be thoroughly well de-signed to suit the house and garden. A pigeon-cote would come well in the upper part, and the face or faces open to the lawn might be closed in winter with movable shutters, when it would make a useful store-place for garden seats and much else.

FORM IN PLANTING

If I have dwelt rather insistently on matters of colour, it is not that I underrate the equal importance of form and proportion, but that I think that the question of colour, as regards its more careful use, is either more commonly neglected or has had fewer exponents. As in all matters relating to design in gardening, the good placing of plants in detail is a matter of knowledge of an artistic character. The shaping of every group of plants, to have the best effect, should not only be definitely intended but should be done with an absolute conviction by the hand that feels the *drawing* that the group must have in relation to what is near, or to the whole form of the clump or border or whatever the nature of the place may be. I am only too well aware that to many this statement may convey no idea whatever, nevertheless I venture to insist upon its truth. Moreover, I am addressing this to the consideration of those who are in sympathy with my views of gardening, among whom I know there are many who, even if they have not made themselves able, by study and long practice, to show in ground-work and garden design the quality known to artists as *drawing*—by which is meant a right movement of line and form and group—can at least recognise its value—indeed its supreme importance—when it is present, and do not, in its absence, fail to feel that the thing shown is without life, spirit, or reasonable justification.

Even a proficiency in some branch of fine art does not necessarily imply ability to lay out ground. I have known, in the intimate association of half a lifetime, a landscape painter, whose interpretation of natural beauty was of the most refined and poetical quality, and who truly loved flowers and beautiful vegetation, but who was quite incapable of personally arranging a garden; although it is more usual that an artist should almost unconsciously place plants well.

It is therefore not to be expected that it is enough to buy good plants and merely to tell the gardener of average ability to plant them in groups, as is now often done with the very best intention. It is impossible for the gardener to know what is meant. In all the cases that have come under my notice, where such indefinite instruction has been given, the things have been planted in stiff blocks. Quite lately I came upon such an example in the garden of a friend who is by no means without a sense of beauty. There was a bank-like space on the outskirts of the pleasure-ground where it was wished to have a wild Heath garden. A better place could hardly be, for the soil is light and sandy and the space lies out in full sunlight. The ground had been thrown about into ridges and valleys, but without any reference to its natural form, whereas with half the labour it might have been guided into slight hollows, ridges, and promontories of good line and proportion. I found it planted as in the upper plan; the path stiffly edged with one kind of Heath on one side and another kind on the other; the back planting in rectangular blocks; near the front bushes of Veronica at exactly even distances, and between them the same number of Heaths in each interval quite stiffly planted. Some of the blocks at the back were of Violets—plants quite unsuited to the place. Yet, only leaving out the Violets, all the same plants might have been disposed so as to come quite easily and naturally as shown on the lower plan. Then a thin sowing of the finer Heath grasses, to include the pathway, where alone they would be mown, and a clever interplanting of wild Thyme and the native Wood Sage (*Teucrium Scorodonia*), common on the neighbouring heaths, would have put the whole thing together and would have given the impression, so desirable in wild planting, of the thing having so happened, rather than of its having been artificially made.

In planting or thinning trees also, the whole ultimate good of the effect will depend on this sense of form and good grouping. If these qualities are secured, the result in after years will be a poem; if they are neglected it will be nothing but a crop.

I can imagine nothing more interesting than the guiding and part-planting of large stretches of natural young woodland with some hilly ground above and water at the foot. As it is, I have to be content with my little wood of ten acres; yet I am truly glad to have even that small space to treat with reverent thankfulness and watchful care.

✳ WOOD AND SHRUBBERY EDGES

Opportunities for good gardening are so often overlooked that it may be well to draw attention to some of those that are most commonly neglected.

When woodland joins garden ground there is too often a sudden jolt; the wood ends with a hard line, sometimes with a path along it, accentuating the defect. When the wood is of Scotch Fir of some age there is a monotonous emptiness of naked trunk and bare ground. In wild moorland this is characteristic and has its own beauty; it may even pleasantly accompany the garden when there is only a view into it here and there; but when the path passes along, furlong after furlong, with no attempt to bring the wood into harmony with the garden, then the monotony becomes oppressive and the sudden jolt is unpleasantly perceived. There is the well-stocked garden and there is the hollow wood with no cohesion between the two—no sort of effort to make them join hands.

It would have been better if from the first the garden had not been brought quite so close to the wood, then the space between, anything from twenty-five to forty feet, might have been planted so as to bring them into unison. In such a case the path would go, not next the trees but along the middle of the neutral ground and would be so planted as to belong equally to garden and wood. The trees would then take their place as the bounding and sheltering feature. It is better to plan it like this at first than to gain the space by felling the outer trees, because the trees at the natural wood edge are better furnished with side branches. Such ground on the shady side of the Scotch Firs would be the best possible site for a Rhododendron walk, and for Azaleas and Kalmias, kept distinct from the Rhododendrons. Then the Scotch Fir indicates the presence of a light peaty soil; the very thing for that excellent but much-neglected undershrub *Gaultheria Shallon*. This is one of the few things that will grow actually under the Firs, not perhaps in the densest part of an old wood, but anywhere about its edges, or where any light comes in at a clearing or along a cart-way. When once established it spreads with a steady abundance of increase, creeping underground and gradually clothing more and more of the floor of the wood.

For the edges of other kinds of woodland the free Roses are always beautiful; where a Holly comes to the front, a Rose such as Dundee Rambler or the Garland will grow up it, supported by its outer branches in the most delightful way. The wild Clematis is in place here too, also the shade-loving plants already named. In deciduous woodland there is probably some undergrowth of Hazel, or of Bramble and wild Honeysuckle. White Foxgloves should be planted at the edge and a little way back, Daffodils for the time when the leaves are not yet there, and Lily of the Valley, whose charming bloom and brilliant foliage come with the young leaves of May.

Where the wood comes nearest the house with only lawn between, it is well to have a grouping of hardy Ferns and Lilies; where it is giving place to garden ground and there is a shrubby background, the smaller Polygonums, such as *P. compactum*, are in place.

The spaces more or less wide between large shrubs and turf are full of opportunities for ingenious treatment; they are just the places most often neglected, or at any rate not well enough considered. I have always taken delight in working out satisfactory ways of treating them. It seems desirable to have, next the grass, some foliage of rather distinct and important size or form. For this use the Megaseas are invaluable; the one most generally useful being the large variety of *M. cordifolia*. Funkias are also beautiful, but as their leaves come late and go with the first frosts or even earlier, whereas the Megaseas persist the whole year round, the latter are the most generally desirable. These shrub-edge spaces occur for the most part in bays, giving an inducement to invent a separate treatment for each bay.

�֍ SPECIMEN TREES I

In garden arrangement, as in all other kinds of decorative work, one has not only to acquire a knowledge of what to do, but also to gain some wisdom in perceiving what it is well to let alone. The want of such knowledge or discrimination, or whatever it may be called, is never more frequently or more conspicuously shown than in the treatment of grassy spaces in pleasure grounds, that are planted at the discretion of some one who has not the gift of knowing what kind of placing, of what trees or shrubs, is the most advisable.

Such a one naturally says, "Here is a space of turf otherwise unoccupied, let us put there a specimen tree." It may be a place in which the careful and highly cultured garden critic may say, "Here is a space of turf, let us be thankful for it, and above all things guard it from any intrusion." I call to mind two good places where there is a dignified house, and groups of grand trees, and stretches of what should be unbroken level sward. In older days it was so; the spreading branches of the great Cedars and Beeches came down to the lawn, and on summer evenings the shadow of a noble grove of ancient trees swept clear across the grassy level. The whole picture was perfect in its unity and peace, in its harmony of line and fine masses of form—full of dignity, repose, and abounding satisfaction.

Now the noble lawn-levels have been broken by a dotting about of specimen Conifers. One *Abies nordmannia*, one Thuya, one Wellingtonia, one Araucaria, one Taxodium, and so on, and so on. What once was a sanctuary of ordered peace is now a wearisome and irritating exposition of monotonous commonplace. The spiritual and poetical influences of the garden are gone. The great Cedars are still there, but from no moderately distant point can they now be seen because of the impertinent interposition of intruding "specimens."

Like many another thing done in gardens, how much better it would have been not to have done it; to have left the place unspoilt and untormented by these disastrous interlopers. If only it had just been let alone!

❀ SPECIMEN TREES II

Happily, our newer gardens are no longer peppered over with specimen conifers. Much as we honour those heads of our great nursery firms and others, whose enterprise and practical encouragement of botanical explorers has so greatly increased the number of coniferous trees that we may now choose from, the earlier mistakes in planting have in many cases been disastrous to gardens. About fifty years ago, when they were being raised and distributed, and horticultural taste was at a low ebb, a kind of fashion arose for planting conifers. It mattered not that they took no place in garden design, and that those who planted had no idea what they would be like when full grown; the object was merely to have one each of as many kinds as possible. If the intention had been simply to make a collection from the botanical point of view there would be nothing to criticise; but they were crowded into nearly every garden as exponents of the horticultural taste of the day. Now, when they are approaching maturity of growth, they have either been cut away wholesale, or their owners, of the later generation that has learnt better gardening, look ruefully at the large trees so unwisely planted. In fact, unless space is so great that experimental planting may be done on a large scale, or the foreign trees are so well known in all stages of growth that they can be used with a sure hand, it is safer to trust to our native evergreens and the few European kinds that we have long known. In their way nothing is better than the native juniper, Scotch fir and yew for our sandy uplands; yew also for chalky soils, and spruce and silver fir for cool hollows. Our noble English yew is nearly always beneficial in the garden landscape. Whether as a trimmed hedge or as a free-growing tree, its splendid richness of deepest green, and, indeed, its whole aspect, is of the utmost value.

🌷 ORNAMENTS

Where a garden scheme extends over several acres a designer can afford to be severely simple in the details of his conception. A broad grass walk which runs a hundred yards between herbaceous borders of, say, fifteen feet in width is a thing so delightful in itself that its charm is self-contained. The absence of a statue framed in clipped yews to close the vista is forgotten in the beauty of the wide sweeps of turf and blossom. Variety of growth and changeful schemes of colour provide the necessary incident. A little garden, however, if too simply treated, soon exhausts our curiosity. The more the designer lacks space, the apter should he be in making us forget his garden's limitations. Ingenious pleasantries of treatment here and there arrest the interest. By concentrating it they make the visitor oblivious of the smallness of the theatre which yields so much diversion. This is not a plea for many ornaments, still less for any one that stands out markedly from its surroundings; no more is claimed than that ornament of the right kind is even more welcome in small gardens than in big. It is admittedly difficult to get anything small enough in scale that is at the same time pleasant as sculpture in its own right.

⚙ SUNDIALS

A sundial is always welcome in pleasure ground, not only as a distinctive ornament, but as a link with the old garden of our Tudor ancestors. Although in these days, when everyone carries a watch and when clocks are many, it has all but lost its original purpose, yet it is still pleasant in summer days to read the time by the sun on an old dial. Properly speaking the dial is the horizontal plate with its gnomon only, the stone base being the part that forms the ornament in the garden landscape, but we are accustomed to call the whole thing a sundial, and the term is so convenient that it may well be generally used.

It may be assumed that the oldest of these are the original sundials of the Tudor gardens, the greater number of which were swept away when the landscape gardening of the 18th century became the fashion, and the old enclosed gardens were considered barbarous. No doubt the sundial would be the only thing that escaped destruction, and this may account for the many that now exist in gardens placed apparently hap-hazard, or at any rate without much consideration; for we find them as if lost in an expanse of grass, the baluster base coming straight out of the green without any vestige of the stone step or platform that they probably had in their original position; whereas one may be sure that in the old Tudor garden the sundial was the central object in the knotted garden or parterre, or at any rate formed some important rallying point in the garden design.

LARGE AND SMALL GARDENS

The size of a garden has very little to do with its merit. It is merely an accident relating to the circumstances of the owner. It is the size of his heart and brain and goodwill that will make his garden either delightful or dull, as the case may be, and either leave it at the usual monotonous dead-level, or raise it, in whatever degree may be, towards that of a work of fine art. If a man knows much, it is more difficult for him to deal with a small space than a larger, for he will have to make the more sacrifice; but if he is wise he will at once make up his mind about what he will let go, and how he may best treat the restricted space. Some years ago I visited a small garden attached to a villa on the outskirts of a watering-place on the south coast. In ordinary hands it would have been a perfectly commonplace thing, with the usual weary mixture, and exhibiting the usual distressing symptoms that come in the train of the ministrations of the jobbing-gardener. In size it may have been a third of an acre, and it was one of the most interesting and enjoyable gardens I have ever seen, its master and mistress giving it daily care and devotion, and enjoying to the full its glad response of grateful growth. The master had built with his own hands, on one side where more privacy was wanted, high rugged walls, with spaces for many rock-loving plants, and had made the wall die away so cleverly into the rock-garden, that the whole thing looked like a garden founded on some ancient ruined structure. And it was all done with so much taste that there was nothing jarring or strained-looking, still less anything cockneyfied, but all easy and pleasant and pretty, while the happy look of the plants at once proclaimed his sympathy with them, and his comprehensive knowledge of their wants. In the same garden was a walled enclosure where Tree Pæonies and some of the hardier of the oriental Rhododendrons were thriving, and there were pretty spaces of lawn, and flower border, and shrub clump, alike beautiful and enjoyable, all within a small space, and yet not crowded—the garden of one who was a keen flower lover, as well as a world-known botanist.

I am always thankful to have seen this garden, because it showed me, in a way that had never been so clearly brought home to me, how much may be done in a small space.

Another and much smaller garden that I remember with pleasure was in a sort of yard among houses, in a country town. The house it belonged to, a rather high one, was on its east side, and halfway along on the south; the rest was bounded by a wall about ten feet high. Opposite the house the owner had built of rough blocks of sandstone what served as a workshop, about twelve feet along the wall, and six feet wide within. A low archway of the same rough stone was the entrance, and immediately

above it a lean-to roof sloped up to the top of the wall, which just here
had been carried a little higher. The roof was of large flat sandstones,
only slightly lapping over each other, with spaces and chinks where grew
luxuriant masses of Polypody Fern. It was contrived with a cement bed,
so that it was quite weather-tight, and the room was lighted by a skylight
at one end that did not show from the garden. A small surface of lead-
flat, on a level with the top of the wall, in one of the opposite angles,
carried an old oil-jar, from which fell masses of gorgeous Tropæolum,
and the actual surface of the flat was a garden of Stonecrops. The
rounded coping of the walls, and joints in many places (for the wall
was an old one), were gay with yellow Corydalis and Snapdragons and
more Stonecrops. The little garden had a few pleasant flowering bushes,
Ribes and Laurustinus, a Bay and an Almond tree. In the coolest and shadi-
est corner were a fern-grotto and a tiny tank. The rest of the garden, only a
few yards across, was laid out with a square bed in the middle, and a
little path round, then a three-feet-wide border next the wall, all edged
with rather tall-grown Box. The middle bed had garden Roses and Carnations, and Mignonette and Stocks. All round were well-chosen plants
and shrubs, looking well and happy, though in a confined and rather
airless space. Every square foot had been made the most of with the
utmost ingenuity, but the ingenuity was always directed by good taste, so
that nothing looked crowded or out of place.

And I think of two other gardens of restricted space, both long strips of
ground walled at the sides, whose owners I am thankful to count among
my friends—one in the favoured climate of the Isle of Wight, a little
garden where I suppose there are more rare and beautiful plants brought
together within a small space than perhaps in any other garden of the
same size in England; the other in a cathedral town, now a memory only,
for the master of what was one of the most beautiful gardens I have ever
seen now lives elsewhere. The garden was long in shape, and divided
about midway by a wall. The division next the house was a quiet lawn,
with a mulberry tree and a few mounded borders near the sides that were

unobtrusive, and in no way spoilt the quiet feeling of the lawn space Then a doorway in the dividing wall led to a straight path with a double flower border. I suppose there was a vegetable garden behind the borders, but of that I have no recollection, only a vivid remembrance of that brilliantly beautiful mass of flowers. The picture was good enough as one went along, especially as at the end one came first within sound and then within sight of a rushing river, one of those swift, clear, shallow streams with stony bottom that the trout love; but it was ten times more beautiful on turning to go back, for there was the mass of flowers, and towering high above it the noble mass of the giant structure—one of the greatest and yet most graceful buildings that has ever been raised by man to the glory of God.

It is true that it is not every one that has the advantage of a garden bounded by a river and a noble church, but even these advantages might have been lost by vulgar or unsuitable treatment of the garden. But the mind of the master was so entirely in sympathy with the place, that no one that had the privilege of seeing it could feel that it was otherwise than right and beautiful.

I do not envy the owners of very large gardens. The garden should fit its master or his tastes just as his clothes do; it should be neither too large nor too small, but just comfortable. If the garden is larger than he can individually govern and plan and look after, then he is no longer its master but its slave, just as surely as the much-too-rich man is the slave and not the master of his superfluous wealth. And when I hear of the great place with a kitchen garden of twenty acres within the walls, my heart sinks as I think of the uncomfortable disproportion between the man and those immediately around him, and his vast output of edible vegetation, and I fall to wondering how much of it goes as it should go, or whether the greater part of it does not go dribbling away, leaking into unholy back-channels; and of how the looking after it must needs be subdivided; and of how many side-interests are likely to steal in, and altogether how great a burden of anxiety or matter of temptation it must give rise to. A grand truth is in the old farmer's saying, "The master's eye makes the pig fat;" but how can any one master's eye fat that vast pig of twenty acres, with all its minute and costly cultivation, its two or three crops a year off all ground given to soft vegetables, its stoves, greenhouses, orchid and orchard houses, its vineries, pineries, figgeries, and all manner of glass structures?

But happily these monstrous gardens are but few—I only know of or have seen two, and I hope never to see another.

Nothing is more satisfactory than to see the well-designed and well-organized garden of the large country house, whose master loves his garden, and has good taste and a reasonable amount of leisure.

I think that the first thing in such a place is to have large unbroken lawn spaces—all the better if they are continuous, passing round the south and west sides of the house. I am supposing a house of the best class, but not necessarily of the largest size. Immediately adjoining the house, except for the few feet needed for a border for climbing plants, is a broad walk, dry and smooth, and perfectly level from end to end. This, in the case of many houses, and nearly always with good effect, is raised two or three feet above the garden ground, and if the architecture of the house demands it, has a retaining wall surmounted by a balustrade of masonry and wrought stone. Broad and shallow stone steps lead down to the turf both at the end of the walk and in the middle of the front of the house, the wider and shallower the better, and at the foot of the wall may be a narrow border for a few climbing plants that will here and there rise above the opening of the parapet. I do not think it desirable where there are stone balusters or other distinct architectural features to let them be smothered with climbing plants, but that there should be, say, a *Pyrus japonica* or an Escallonia, and perhaps a white Jasmine, and on a larger space perhaps a cut-leaved or a Claret Vine. Some of the best effects of the kind I have seen were where the bush, being well established, rose straight out of the grass, the border being unnecessary except just at the beginning.

[83]

ON GARDENING

The large lawn space I am supposing stretches away a good distance from the house, and is bounded on the south and west by fine trees; away beyond that is all wild wood. On summer afternoons the greater part of the lawn expanse is in cool shade, while winter sunsets show through the tree stems. Towards the south-east the wood would pass into shrub plantations, and farther still into garden and wild orchard (of which I shall have something to say presently). At this end of the lawn would be the brilliant parterre of bedded plants, seen both from the shaded lawn and from the terrace, which at this end forms part of its design. Beyond the parterre would be a distinct division from the farther garden, either of Yew or Box hedge, with bays for seats, or in the case of a change of level, of another terrace wall. The next space beyond would be the main garden for hardy plants, at its southern end leading into the wild orchard. This would be the place for the free garden or the reserve garden, or for any of the many delightful ways in which hardy flowers can be used; and if it happened by good fortune to have a stream or any means of having running water, the possibilities of beautiful gardening would be endless.

Beyond this again would come the kitchen garden, and after that the stables and the home farm. If the kitchen garden had a high wall, and might be entered on this side by handsome wrought-iron gates, I would approach it from the parterre by a broad grass walk bounded by large Bay trees at equal intervals to right and left. Through these to the right would be seen the free garden of hardy flowers.

For the kitchen garden a space of two acres would serve a large country house with all that is usually grown within walls, but there should always be a good space outside for the rougher vegetables, as well as a roomy yard for compost, pits and frames, and rubbish.

And here I wish to plead on behalf of the gardener that he should have all reasonable comforts and conveniences. Nothing is more frequent, even in good places, than to find the potting and tool sheds screwed away into some awkward corner, badly lighted, much too small, and altogether

[84]

inadequate, and the pits and frames scattered about and difficult to get at. Nothing is more wasteful of time, labour, or temper. The working parts of a large garden form a complicated organisation, and if the parts of the mechanism do not fit and work well, and are not properly eased and oiled, still more, if any are missing, there must be disastrous friction and damage and loss of power. In designing garden buildings, I always strongly urge in connection with the heating system a warmed potting shed and a comfortable messroom for the men, and over this a perfectly dry loft for drying and storing such matters as shading material, nets, mats, ropes, and sacks. If this can be warmed, so much the better. There must also be a convenient and quite frost-proof place for winter storing of vegetable roots and such plants as Dahlias, Cannas, and Gladiolus; and also a well-lighted and warmed workshop for all the innumerable jobs put aside for wet weather, of which the chief will be repainting and glazing of lights, repairing implements, and grinding and setting tools. This shop should have a carpenter's bench and screw, and a smith's anvil, and a proper assortment of tools. Such arrangements, well planned and thought out, will save much time and loss of produce, besides helping to make all the people employed more comfortable and happy.

I think that a garden should never be large enough to be tiring, that if a large space has to be dealt with, a great part had better be laid out in wood. Woodland is always charming and restful and enduringly beautiful, and then there is an intermediate kind of woodland that should be made more of—woodland of the orchard type. Why is the orchard put out of the way, as it generally is, in some remote region beyond the kitchen garden and stables? I should like the lawn, or the hardy flower garden, or both, to pass directly into it on one side, and to plant a space of several acres, not necessarily in the usual way, with orchard standards twenty-five feet apart in straight rows (though in many places the straight rows might be best), but to have groups and even groves of such things as Medlars and Quinces, Siberian and Chinese Crabs, Damsons, Prunes, Service trees, and Mountain Ash, besides Apples, Pears, and

[85]

Cherries, in both standard and bush forms. Then alleys of Filbert and Cob-nut, and in the opener spaces tangles or brakes of the many beautiful bushy things allied to the Apple and Plum tribe—*Cydonia* and *Prunus triloba* and *Cratægus* of many kinds (some of them are tall bushes or small trees with beautiful fruits); and the wild Blackthorn, which, though a plum, is so nearly related to pear that pears may be grafted on it. And then brakes of Blackberries, especially of the Parsley-leaved kind, so free of growth and so generous of fruit.

Some members of the large Rose-Apple-Plum tribe grow to be large forest trees, and in my wild orchard they would go in the farther parts. The Bird-cherry (*Prunus padus*) grows into a tree of the largest size. A Mountain Ash will sometimes have a trunk two feet in diameter, and a head of a size to suit. The American kind, its near relation, but with larger leaves and still grander masses of berries, is a noble small tree; and the native white Beam should not be forgotten, and choice places should be given to Amelanchier and the lovely double Japan Apple (*Pyrus Malus floribunda*). To give due space and effect to all these good things my orchard garden would run into a good many acres, but every year it would be growing into beauty and profit. The grass should be left rough, and plentifully planted with Daffodils, and with Cowslips if the soil is strong. The grass would be mown and made into hay in June, and perhaps mown once more towards the end of September. Under the nut-trees would be Primroses and the garden kinds of wood Hyacinths and Dogtooth Violets and Lily of the Valley, and perhaps Snowdrops, or any of the smaller bulbs that most commeided themselves to the taste of the master.

Such an orchard garden, well-composed and beautifully grouped, always with that indispensable quality of good "drawing," would not only be a source of unending pleasure to those who lived in the place, but a valuable lesson to all who saw it; for it would show the value of the simple and sensible ways of using a certain class of related trees and bushes, and of using them with a deliberate intention of making the best of them, instead of the usual meaningless-nohow way of planting. This in nine cases out of ten, means either ignorance or carelessness, the planter not caring enough about the matter to take the trouble to find out what is best to be done, and being quite satisfied with a mixed lot of shrubs, as offered in nursery sales, or with the choice of the nurseryman. I do not presume to condemn all mixed planting, only stupid and ignorant mixed planting. It is not given to all people to take their pleasures alike; and I have in my mind four gardens, all of the highest interest, in which the planting is all mixed; but then the mixture is of admirable ingredients, collected and placed on account of individual merit, and a ramble round any one of these in company with its owner is a pleasure and a privilege that one cannot prize too highly. Where the garden is of such large extent that experimental planting is made with a good number of one good thing at a time, even though there was no premeditated intention of planting for beautiful effect, the fact of there being enough plants to fall into large groups, and to cover some extent of ground, produces numbers of excellent results. I remember being struck with this on several occasions when I have had the happiness of visiting Mr. G. F. Wilson's garden at Wisley, a garden which I take to be about the most instructive it is possible to see. In one part, where the foot of the hill joined the copse, there were hosts of lovely things planted on a succession of rather narrow banks. Almost unthinkingly I expressed the regret I felt that so much individual beauty should be there without an attempt to arrange it for good effect. Mr. Wilson stopped, and looking at me straight with a kindly smile, said very quietly, "That is your business, not mine." In spite of its being a garden whose first object is trial and experiment, it has left in my memory two pictures, among several lesser ones, of plant-beauty that will stay with me as long as I can remember anything, one an autumn and one a spring picture—the hedge of *Rosa rugosa* in full fruit, and a plantation of *Primula denticulata*. The Primrose was on a bit of level ground, just at the outer and inner edges of the hazel copse. The plants were both grouped and thinly sprinkled, just as nature plants

—possibly they grew directly there from seed. They were in superb and luxuriant beauty in the black peaty-looking half-boggy earth, the handsome leaves of the brilliant colour and large size that told of perfect health and vigour, and the large round heads of pure lilac flower carried on strong stalks that must have been fifteen inches high. I never saw it so happy and so beautiful. It is a plant I much admire, and I do the best I can for it on my dry hill; but the conditions of my garden do not allow of any approach to the success of the Wisley plants; still I have treasured that lesson among many others I have brought away from that good garden, and never fail to advise some such treatment when I see the likely home for it in other places.

Some of the most delightful of all gardens are the little strips in front of roadside cottages. They have a simple and tender charm that one may look for in vain in gardens of greater pretension. And the old garden flowers seem to know that there they are seen at their best; for where else can one see such Wallflowers, or Double Daisies, or White Rose bushes; such clustering masses of perennial Peas, or such well-kept flowery edgings of Pink, or Thrift, or London Pride?

Among a good many calls for advice about laying out gardens, I remember an early one that was of special interest. It was the window-box of a factory lad in one of the great northern manufacturing towns. He had advertised in a mechanical paper that he wanted a tiny garden, as full of interest as might be, in a window-box; he knew nothing—would somebody help him with advice? So advice was sent and the box prepared. If I remember rightly the size was three feet by ten inches. A little later the post brought him little plants of mossy and silvery saxifrages, and a few small bulbs. Even some stones were sent, for it was to be a rock-garden, and there were to be two hills of different heights with rocky tops, and a longish valley with a sunny and a shady side.

It was delightful to have the boy's letters, full of keen interest and eager questions, and only difficult to restrain him from killing his plants with kindness, in the way of liberal doses of artificial manure. The very smallness of the tiny garden made each of its small features the more precious. I could picture his feeling of delightful anticipation when he saw the first little bluish blade of the Snowdrop patch pierce its mossy carpet. Would it, could it really grow into a real Snowdrop, with the modest, milk-white flower and the pretty green hearts on the outside of the inner petals, and the clear green stripes within? and would it really nod him a glad good-morning when he opened his window to greet it? And those few blunt reddish horny-looking snouts just coming through the ground, would they really grow into the brilliant blue of the early Squill, that would be like a bit of midsummer sky among the grimy surroundings of the attic window, and under that grey, soot-laden northern sky? I thought with pleasure how he would watch them in spare minutes of the dinner-hour spent at home, and think of them as he went forward and back to his work, and how the remembrance of the tender beauty of the full-blown flower would make him glad, and lift up his heart while "minding his mule" in the busy restless mill.

❀ FORMAL GARDENS

Whenever I have seen the large formal gardens attached to important houses of the Palladian type that are so numerous throughout England, I have always been struck by their almost invariable lack of interest and want of any real beauty or power of giving happiness. For at the risk of becoming wearisome by a frequent reiteration of my creed in gardening, I venture to repeat that I hold the firm belief that the purpose of a garden is to give happiness and repose of mind, firstly and above all other considerations, and to give it through the representation of the best kind of pictorial beauty of flower and foliage that can be combined or invented. And I think few people will deny that this kind of happiness is much more often enjoyed in the contemplation of the homely border of hardy flowers than in many of these great gardens, where the flowers lose their attractive identity and with it their hold of the human heart, and have to take a lower rank as mere masses of colour filling so many square yards of space. Gardens of this kind are only redeemed when some master-mind, accepting the conditions of the place as they are, decides on treating it in some bold way, either in one grand scheme of colour-harmony, or as an exposition of this principle combined with the display of magnificent foliage-masses, or by some other such means as may raise it above the usual dull dead-level.

I always suppose that these great wide dull gardens, sprawling over much too large a space, are merely an outgrowth of plan-drawing. The designer sitting over his sheet of paper has it within such easy view on the small scale, and though he lays out the ground in correct proportion with the block-plan of the house, and is therefore right on paper, yet no human eye can ever see it from that point of view; and as for its use in promoting any kind of happiness, it can only be classed among others of those comfortless considerations that perplex and worry the mind with the feeling that they are too much, and yet not enough.

For the formal garden of the best type I can picture to myself endless possibilities both of beauty and delight—for though my own limited means have in a way obliged me to practise only the free and less costly ways of gardening, such as give the greatest happiness for the least expenditure, and are therefore the wisest ways for most people to walk in—yet I also have much pleasure in formal gardens of the best kinds. But it must be nothing less than the very best, and it is necessarily extremely costly, because it must entail much building beautifully designed and wrought. It must also have an unbounded supply of water, for so only could one work out all the best possibilities of such a garden.

There seems to me to be a whole mine of wealth waiting to be worked for the benefit of such gardens, for, as far as I am aware, what might now be done has never been even attempted with any degree of careful or serious study. When one thinks of the very few plants known for garden use to the ancients, and to those who built and planted the noble gardens of the Italian Renaissance, and when one compares this limited number with the vast range of beautiful shrubs and plants we now have to choose from, one cannot help seeing how much wider is the scope for keen and critical discrimination. And though some of the plants most anciently in cultivation, such as the Rose, Violet, Iris, Poppy, Jasmine, and Vine, are still among the best, yet we are no longer tied to those and a few others only. The great quantity we have now to choose from is in itself a danger, for in the best and most refined kinds of formal gardening one is more than ever bound to the practice of the most severe restraint in the choice of kinds, and to accept nothing that does not in its own place and way satisfy the critical soul with the serene contentment of an absolute conviction.

I therefore propose to give one example of a portion of a formal garden such as I hold to be one of the most pleasant and desirable kind, and such as will present somewhat of the aspect, and fill the mind with somewhat of the sentiment, of those good old gardens of Italy. And though the initial expense will be heavy—for in work of this kind the artist's design must be carried out to the smallest detail, without skimping or screwing, or those frequent and disastrous necessities of lopping or compromise that so often mar good work—yet the whole would be so solid and permanent that the cost of its after-maintenance would be small out of all proportion with that of the usual large gardens. These always seem as if purposely designed to bind upon the shoulders of their owners the ever-living burden of the most costly and wasteful kind of effort in the trim keeping of turf and Box edging and gravelled walks, with the accompanying and unavoidable vexatious noises of rumbling roar of mowing machine, clicking of shears, and clanking grind of iron roller. In the chief portions or courts of my formal garden all this fidgetty labour and worry of ugly noise would be unknown, and the only sounds of its own need or making would be the soothing and ever-delightful music of falling and running water.

All gardening in which water plays an important part implies a change

of level in the ground to be dealt with. I am taking as an example a place
where ground slopes away from the house, so that it demands some kind
of terraced treatment. First, there would be the space next to the house;
its breadth having due relation to the height of the building. From this
space a flight of easy steps (the first thing shown at the top of the plan)
would descend to the Water-Lily court, landing on a wide flagged path
that passes all round the tank. On all four sides there are also steps
leading down from the path into the water. I cannot say why it is, but
[I] have always observed that a beautiful effect is gained by steps leading
actually into water. In this case I would have the two lowest steps actually *below* the water-line. Although steps are in the first instance intended for the human foot, yet we have become so well accustomed to
the idea of them as easy means of access from one level to another that in
many cases they are also desirable as an aid to the eye, and in such a
place as I think of, the easy lines of shallow steps from the level of the
path to that of the water-surface and below it, would, I consider, be
preferable to any raised edging such as is more usually seen round built
tanks. I would give the eye the pleasant feeling of being invited to con-
template the Lilies at its utmost ease, instead of being cut off from them
by a raised barrier. On the sides of the path away from the tank is a
flower border, backed by the wall that bounds the whole area of the
court. On the three sides, to the right and left and across the tank as you
stand on the main flight of steps, the wall, midway in each space, falls
back into a half-round niche. The niche across the tank is filled with
Cannas, the taller kinds at the back for stately stature and nobility of
large leafage; the smaller ones, of lower habit and larger bloom, being
planted towards the front. Coming down the steps you see the level lines
of water-surface jewelled with the lovely floating bloom of white and pink
and tender rose colour, the steps into the tank on the near and far sides
still further insisting on the repose of the level line. The eye and mind are
thus in the best state of preparation for enjoying the bold uprightness of
growth of the Cannas. In the flower borders next the wall I would have

DESIGN AND ORNAMENT

Lilies, and plants mostly of Lily-like character, Crinums and Funkias, and of the true Lilies a limited number of kinds—the noble White Lily, *L. Harrisi, L. longiflorum, L. Browni,* and white and rosy forms of *L. speciosum.* These would grow out of the groups of the beautiful pale-foliaged *Funkia grandiflora* and of the tender green of the Lady Fern and of Harts-tongue. I would not let the walls be too much covered with creepers, for I hold that wherever delicate architecture marries with gardening, the growing things should never over-run or smother the masonry; but in the Lily court I would have some such light-running creeping things as can be easily led and trained within bounds, such as *Clematis Flammula,* blue Passion Flower, and, if climate allows, *Rhodochiton volubile, Cobæa scandens,* and *Solanum jasminoides.* These would be quite enough, and even perhaps too many.

The half-round niches to right and left are partly occupied by small basins, into which water falls, through a sculptured inlet, from a height of some feet. From these it runs under the flagged pathway into the tank. Two overflows pass underground from this to right and left of the Canna niche, from which the water is led out again into the small tanks at the angles of the paved space below the semi-circular stairway. From these it is again led away into a series of little channels and falls and then makes two rippling rills by the side of the next flights of steps and lengths of pavement. To return to the Water-Lily tank, its border spaces at the angles of the basin would have raised edges, and would be planted with dwarf flowering Cannas, mostly of one kind and colour. The enclosing walls would be about eight feet high, and as groves of beautiful trees would be in their near neighbourhood, I should wish that any foliage that could be seen from within the court should be that of Ilex.

Had I ever had occasion to design a garden in what I should consider the most reasonable interpretation of the good Italian style, I should have been sparing in the use of such walled courts, keeping them and the main stairways for the important and mid-most part of the design, as shown in the plan, whether the formal design was placed on the next level below

[93]

the house, or, as in the case I am contemplating, at a right angle to it, and coming straight down the face of the hill. In this case, wherever flights of steps occurred, there would be walls well planted above and below, stretching away to right and left, and below them long level spaces of grass. One of these long grassy spaces might well be made into a perfect picture gallery of the lovely modern developments of Water-Lily, in connection with a Water-Lily court. Straight down the middle of the turfed space might be a narrow rill of water fifteen inches wide, easy to step over, bounded by a flat kerb a foot to eighteen inches wide and level with the grass. At intervals in its length it would lead into separate small square-sided tanks only a few feet wide, but large enough to show the complete beauty of some one kind of Water-Lily at a time, so that the lovely flowers and leaves and surface of still water would be as it were enclosed in a definite frame of stone or marble.

Where at the lower or valley edge of these long grassy spaces a descent occurred to the next lower level there would be a dry wall planted with Cistus and free-growing Roses—never, *never*, sharp sloping banks of turf. I always try to avoid the spirit of intolerance in anything, but for these turf banks, so frequent in gardens, I can only feel a distinct aversion. Did such a turf bank ever give any one the slightest happiness? Did any one ever think it beautiful? The upper terrace wall above the level of the Lily court would no doubt be surmounted by a wrought-stone balustrade, but as the scheme descended towards the lowest level the architectural features would diminish, so that they would end in a flagged walk only, with steps where needful. But the treatment of this would depend on what was below. If it was all pleasure ground, or if there was a river or lake, the architectural refinements would be continued, though not obtruded; if it was a kitchen garden it would be approached by perhaps a simpler walled enclosure for Vines and Figs, the paved walk passing between two green spaces, in the centre of each of which would stand a Mulberry tree. On the upper levelled spaces right and left the formal feeling would merge into the free, for there is no reason why the two

[94]

should not be combined, and on one level at least the green expanse should be seen from end to end, the flagged path only passing across it. And all the way down there would be the living water, rippling, rushing, and falling. Open channels in which it flowed with any considerable fall would be built in little steps with falls to oblige the water to make its rippling music, and in the same way throughout the whole garden every point would be studied, so as to lose sight of no means, however trifling, or catching and guiding any local matter or attribute, quality, or circumstance that could possibly be turned to account for the increase of the beauty and interest and delightfulness of the garden.

As far as I understand the needs of such a garden as I have sketched, with a nucleus or backbone of pure formality, how grandly one could use all the best plants. How, descending the slope, at every fresh landing some new form of plant beauty would be displayed; how, coming up from below, the ascent of, say, a hundred feet, instead of being a toil, would be a progress of pleasure by the help of the smooth flagged path and the wide flights of easy steps. Every step in the garden would be nearly two feet broad and never more than five inches high, no matter how steep the incline. If ground falls so rapidly that steps of such a gradient cannot be carried straight up and down, we build out a bold landing and carry the steps in a double flight right and left, and then land again, and come down to the next level with another flight. Then we find what a good wide space is left below for a basin and a splash of water or some handsome group of plants, or both, and that the whole scheme has gained by the alteration in treatment that the form of the ground made expedient. Then there are frequent seats, so placed as best to give rest to the pilgrim and to display the garden-picture.

Where the lower flights of steps occur we are passing through woodland, with a not very wide space between the edge of the wood and the wide paved way, here unbounded by any edging. Here we have, in widespread groups, plants of rather large stature—Bamboos, and the great Knotweeds of Japan, the large Tritomas and the Giant Reeds and grasses,

Arundo, Gynerium and Eulalia, and between them the running water, now no longer confined in built channels, but running free in shallow pebbly rills. Here we have also other large-leaved plants—the immense Gunneras and the native Butter-bur, the North American Rodgersia, and the peltate Saxifrage, all happy on the lower cooler levels and gentle slopes; watered by the rill, and half shaded by the nearer trees. As the path rises it comes clear of the wood, and the garden spreads out right and left in the lower levels of its terraced spaces. One of these, perhaps the lowest, I should be disposed to plant with Bamboos on both sides of a broad green path. As the paved path mounts, the architectural features become more pronounced; the steps that were quite plain below have a slight undercutting of the lower part of the front. A little higher, and this becomes a fully moulded feature, with a distinct shadow accentuating the overhanging front edge of the step, and so by an insensible gradation we arrive at the full dress of the Lily court and terrace above.

In so slight a sketch as this one cannot attempt to describe in detail all the beautiful ways of using such good things as Roses and Clematis (among hosts of others) that such a garden suggests. But it is perhaps in gardens of formal structure that some of their many uses may best be seen; for the long straight line of the coping of a parapet may be redeemed from monotony by a leaping wave-mass of a free-growing Rose, with its spray-showers of clustered bloom, and the tender grace of the best of the small white-bloomed Clematises of spring and autumn is never seen to better advantage than when wreathing and decorating, but not hiding or overwhelming, the well-wrought stonework that bounds the terrace and crowns its wall.

THE DRY-WALLED TERRACE GARDEN

Many a garden has to be made on a hillside more or less steep. The conditions of such a site naturally suggest some form of terracing, and in connection with a house of modest size and kind, nothing is prettier or pleasanter than all the various ways of terraced treatment that may be practiced with the help of dry-walling, that is to say, rough wall-building without mortar, especially where a suitable kind of stone can be had locally.

It is well in sharply-sloping ground to keep the paths as nearly level as may be, whether they are in straight lines or whether they curve in following the natural contour of the ground. Many more beautiful garden-pictures may be made by variety in planting even quite straightly terraced spaces than at first appears possible, and the frequent flights of steps, always beautiful if easy and well proportioned, will be of the greatest value. When steps are built in this kind of rough terracing the almost invariable fault is that they are made too steep and too narrow in the tread. It is a good rule to make the steps so easy that one can run up and down them, whether of skilled workmanship or rough. There is no reason or excuse for the steep, ugly, and even dangerous steps one so often sees. Unless the paths come too close together on the upper and lower terraces, space for the more easy gradient can be cut away above, and the steps can also be carried out free below; the ground cut through above being supported by dry-walling at the sides of the steps, and where the steps stand up clear below, their sides being built up free. If for any reason this is difficult or inexpedient, a landing can be built out and the steps carried down sideways instead of up and down the face of the hill. In fact, there is no end to the pretty and interesting ways of using such walling and such groups of steps.

Where the stairway cuts through the bank and is lined on each side by the dry-walling, the whole structure becomes a garden of delightful small things. Little Ferns are planted in the joints on the shadier side as the wall goes up, and numbers of small Saxifrages and Stonecrops, Penny-wort and *Erinus*, *Corydalis* and Sandwort. Then there will be hanging sheets of *Aubrietia* and Rock Pinks, *Iberis* and *Cerastium*, and many another pretty plant that will find a happy home in the cool shelter of the

[97]

rocky joint. In some regions of the walling Wallflowers and Snapdragons and plants of Thrift can be established; as they ripen their seed it drifts into the openings of other joints, and the seedlings send their roots deep into the bank and along the cool backs of the stones, and make plants of surprising health and vigour that are longer lived than the softer-grown plants in the rich flower-borders.

I doubt if there is any way in which a good quantity of plants, and of bushes of moderate size, can be so well seen and enjoyed as in one of these roughly terraced gardens, for one sees them up and down and in all sorts of ways, and one has a chance of seeing many lovely flowers clear against the sky, and of perhaps catching some sweetly-scented tiny thing like *Dianthus fragrans* at exactly nose-height and eye-level, and so of enjoying its tender beauty and powerful fragrance in a way that had never before been found possible.

Then the beautiful details of structure and marking in such plants as the silvery Saxifrages can never be so well seen as in a wall at the level of the eye or just above or below it; and plain to see are all the pretty ways these small plants have of seating themselves on projections or nestling into hollows, or creeping over stony surface as does the Balearic Sand-wort, or standing like *Erinus* with its back pressed to the wall in an attitude of soldier-like bolt-uprightness.

In place of all this easily attained prettiness how many gardens on sloping ground are disfigured by profitless and quite indefensible steep banks of mown grass! Hardly anything can be so undesirable in a garden. Such banks are unbeautiful, troublesome to mow, and wasteful of spaces that might be full of interest. If there must be a sloping space, and if for any reason there cannot be a dry wall, it is better to plant the slope with low bushy or rambling things; with creeping Cotoneaster or Japan Honey-suckle, with Ivies or with such bushes as Savin, *Pyrus japonica*, Cistus, or Berberis; or if it is on a large scale, with the free-growing rambling Roses and double-flowered Brambles. I name these things in preference to the rather over-done Periwinkle and St. John's-wort, because Periwinkle is troublesome to weed, and soon grows into undesirably tight masses, and the Hypericum, though sometimes of good effect, is extremely monotonous in large masses by itself, and is so ground-greedy that it allows of no companionship.

There is another great advantage to be gained by the use of the terrace walls; this is the display of the many shrubs as well as plants that will hang over and throw their flowering sprays all over the face of the wall.

In arranging such gardens, I like to have only a very narrow border at the foot of each wall to accommodate such plants as the dwarf Lavender or any plant that is thankful for warmth or shelter.

In many cases, or even most, it will be best to have no border at all, but to make a slight preparation at the wall foot not apparently distinguishable from the path itself, and to have only an occasional plant or group or tuft of Fern. Seeds will fall to this point, and the trailing and sheeting plants will clothe the wall foot and path edge, and the whole thing will look much better than if it had a stiffly edged border.

❦ THE WINTER GARDEN

Going southward from the circular garden there is again the broad path, but of the local sand, which binds well; here there is an orchard of apples, pears and plums on the right, and a thick shrubbery to the left. Concealed in the middle of the shrubbery is a fifty-foot circle of grass with a bed of heaths in the center—a pleasantly secluded retreat. Five winding paths lead out of it through the shrubs and trees in different directions, giving access to various points, and also serving as unobtrusive means of escape when a tired worker desiring rest and solitude becomes aware of approaching intrusion.

From the western upper side of the circular garden a narrow path leads out, and, turning to the right, goes—whither? Another slight turn, between dry-walling to right and left, reveals a solid double arch of stone leading into an enclosed space about thirty-five feet each way. It is the winter garden—a delightful invention! Walled on all sides, the walling not high enough to exclude the low winter sun, it is absolutely sheltered. Four beds are filled with heaths, daphne, Rhododendron præcox and a few other plants. These beds, in company with the surrounding borders and the well-planted wall joints, show a full clothing of plants and a fair proportion of bloom from November to April. The brick-paved paths are always dry, and a seat in a hooded recess is a veritable sun-trap. The garden is rich in such sheltered seats, built and roofed, for, besides this one in the winter garden, and the loggia adjoining the house, there are two others at distinctive points. They are important in the garden design in addition to their practical purpose; moreover, even if in passing by they are not actually used, it is a comfort to the eye and mind both to see the well-designed structure bounding some garden picture and to know of the comfortable and refreshing refuge. There is an important summer-house on the eastern side of the lawn, with solid stone walls and a tiled roof. It is cool all day, for a slight air passes through, and the doorways, facing east and west, only admit the earliest and latest sun.

THE YEAR
IN THE GARDEN

✸   JANUARY

How endlessly beautiful is woodland in winter! To-day there is a
thin mist; just enough to make a background of tender blue mystery
three hundred yards away, and to show any defect in the grouping of
near trees. No day could be better for deciding which trees are to come
down; there is not too much at a time within sight; just one good picture-
full and no more. On a clear day the eye and mind are distracted by
seeing away into too many planes, and it is much more difficult to decide
what is desirable in the way of broad treatment of nearer objects.

The ground has a warm carpet of pale rusty fern; tree-stem and branch
and twig show tender colour-harmonies of grey bark and silver-grey lichen, only varied by the warm feathery masses of birch spray. Now the
splendid richness of the common holly is more than ever impressive, with
its solid masses of full, deep colour, and its wholesome look of perfect
health and vigour. Sombrely cheerful, if one may use such a mixture of
terms; sombre by reason of the extreme depth of tone, and yet cheerful

[103]

from the look of glad life, and from the assurance of warm shelter and protecting comfort to bird and beast and neighbouring vegetation. The picture is made complete by the slender shafts of the silver-barked birches, with their half-weeping heads of delicate, warm-coloured spray. Has any tree so graceful a way of throwing up its stems as the birch? They seem to leap and spring into the air, often leaning and curving upward from the very root, sometimes in forms that would be almost grotesque were it not for the never-failing rightness of free-swinging poise and perfect balance. The tints of the stem give a precious lesson in colour. The white of the bark is here silvery-white and there milk-white, and sometimes shows the faintest tinge of rosy flush. Where the bark has not yet peeled, the stem is clouded and banded with delicate grey, and with the silver-green of lichen. For about two feet upward from the ground, in the case of young trees of about seven to nine inches diameter, the bark is dark in colour, and lies in thick and extremely rugged upright ridges, contrasting strongly with the smooth white skin above. Where the two join, the smooth bark is parted in upright slashes, through which the dark, rough bark seems to swell up, reminding one forcibly of some of the old fifteenth-century German costumes, where a dark velvet is arranged to rise in crumpled folds through slashings in white satin. In the stems of older birches the rough bark rises much higher up the trunk and becomes clothed with delicate grey-green lichen.

❧ FEBRUARY

There is always in February some one day, at least, when one smells the yet distant, but surely coming, summer. Perhaps it is a warm, mossy scent that greets one when passing along the southern side of a hedge-bank; or it may be in some woodland opening, where the sun has coaxed out the pungent smell of the trailing ground Ivy, whose blue flowers will soon appear; but the day always comes, and with it the glad certainty that summer is nearing, and that the good things promised will never fail.

How strangely little of positive green colour is to be seen in copse and woodland. Only the moss is really green. The next greenest thing is the northern sides of the trunks of beech and oak. Walking southward they are all green, but looking back they are silver-grey. The undergrowth is of brambles and sparse fronds of withered bracken; the bracken less beaten down than usual, for the winter has been without snow; only where the soil is deeper, and the fern has grown more tall and rank, it has fallen into thick, almost felted masses, and the stalks all lying one way make the heaps look like lumps of fallen thatch. The bramble leaves—last year's leaves, which are held all the winter—are of a dark, blackish-bronze colour, or nearly red where they have seen the sun. Age seems to give them a sort of hard surface and enough of a polish to reflect the sky; the young leaves that will come next month are almost woolly at first. Grassy tufts show only bleached bents, so tightly matted that one wonders how the delicate young blades will be able to spear through. Ivy-berries, hanging in thick clusters, are still in beauty; they are so heavy that they weigh down the branches.

In summer-time one never really knows how beautiful are the forms of the deciduous trees. It is only in winter, when they are bare of leaves, that one can fully enjoy their splendid structure and design, their admirable qualities of duly apportioned strength and grace of poise, and the way the spread of the many-branched head has its equivalent in the wide-reaching ground-grasp of the root. And it is interesting to see how, in the many different kinds of tree, the same laws are always in force, and the same results occur, and yet by the employment of what varied means. For nothing in the growth of trees can be much more unlike than the habit of the oak and that of the weeping willow, though the unlikeness only comes from the different adjustment of the same sources of power and the same weights, just as in the movement of wind-blown leaves some flutter and some undulate, while others turn over and back again. Old apple-trees are specially noticeable for their beauty in winter, when their extremely graceful shape, less visible when in loveliness of spring bloom or in rich bounty of autumn fruit, is seen to fullest advantage.

❧ MARCH I

There comes a day towards the end of March when there is but little wind, and that is from the west or even south-west. The sun has gained much power, so that it is pleasant to sit out in the garden, or, better still, in some sunny nook of sheltered woodland. There is such a place among silver-trunked Birches, with here and there the splendid richness of masses of dark Holly. The rest of the background above eye-level is of the warm bud-colour of the summer-leafing trees, and, below, the fading rust of the now nearly flattened fronds of last year's bracken, and the still paler drifts of leaves from neighbouring Oaks and Chestnuts. The sunlight strikes brightly on the silver stems of the Birches, and casts their shadows clear-cut across the grassy woodland ride. The grass is barely green as yet, but has the faint winter green of herbage not yet grown and still powdered with the short remnants of the fine-leaved, last-year-mown heath grasses. Brown leaves still hang on young Beech and Oak. The trunks of the Spanish Chestnuts are elephant-grey, a notable contrast to the sudden, vivid shafts of the Birches. Some groups of the pale early Pyrenean Daffodil gleam level on the ground a little way forward.

It is the year's first complete picture of flower-effect in the woodland landscape. The place is not very far from the house, in the nearest hundred yards of the copse; where flowers seem to be more in place than further away. Looking to the left, the long ridge and south slope of the house-roof is seen through the leafless trees, though the main wall-block is hidden by the sheltering Hollies and Junipers.

Coming down towards the garden by another broad grassy way, that goes westward through the Chestnuts and then turns towards the down-hill north, there comes yet another deviation through Rhododendrons and Birches to the main lawn. But before the last turn there is a pleasant mass of colour showing in the wood-edge on the dead-leaf carpet. It is a straggling group of *Daphne Mezereon*, with some clumps of red Lent Hellebores, and, to the front, some half-connected patches of the common Dog-tooth Violet. The nearly related combination of colour is a delight to the trained colour-eye. There is nothing brilliant; it is all restrained, refined, in harmony with the veiled light that reaches the flowers through the great clumps of Hollies and tall half-overhead Chestnuts and neighbouring Beech. The colours are all a little "sad," as the old writers so aptly say of the flower-tints of secondary strength. But it is a perfect picture. One comes to it again and again as one does to any picture that is good to live with.

To devise these living pictures with simple well-known flowers seems to me the best thing to do in gardening. Whether it is the putting together of two or three kinds of plants, or even of one kind only in some happy setting, or whether it is the ordering of a much larger number of plants, as in a flower-border of middle and late summer, the intention is always the same. Whether the arrangement is simple and modest, whether it is obvious or whether it is subtle, whether it is bold and gorgeous, the aim is always to use the plants to the best of one's means and intelligence so as to form pictures of living beauty.

These early examples within the days of March are of special interest because as yet flowers are but few; the mind is less distracted by much variety than later in the year, and is more readily concentrated on the few things that may be done and observed; so that the necessary restriction is a good preparation, by easy steps, or the wider field of observation that is presented later.

Now we pass on through the dark masses of Rhododendron and the Birches that shoot up among them. How the silver stems, blotched and banded with varied browns and greys so deep in tone that they show like a luminous black, tell among the glossy Rhododendron green; and how strangely different is the way of growth of the two kinds of tree; the tall white trunks spearing up through the dense, dark, leathery leaf-masses of solid, roundish outline, with their delicate network of reddish branch and spray gently swaying far overhead!

Now we come to the lawn, which slopes a little downward to the north. On the right it has a low retaining-wall, whose top line is level; it bears up a border and pathway next the house's western face. The border and wall are all of a piece, for it is a dry wall partly planted with the same shrubby and half-shrubby things that are in the earth above. They have been comforting to look at all the winter; a pleasant grey coating of Phlomis, Lavender, Rosemary, Cistus and Santolina; and at the end and angle where the wall is highest, a mass of *Pyrus japonica*, planted both above and below, already showing its rose-red bloom. At one point at the foot of the wall is a strong tuft of *Iris stylosa* whose first blooms appeared in November. This capital plant flowers bravely all through the winter in any intervals of open weather. It likes a sunny place against a wall in poor soil. If it is planted in better ground the leaves grow very tall and it gives but little bloom.

Now we pass among some shrub-clumps, and at the end come upon a cheering sight; a tree of *Magnolia conspicua* bearing hundreds of its great white cups of fragrant bloom. Just before reaching it, and taking part with it in the garden picture, are some tall bushes of *Forsythia suspensa*, tossing out many-feet-long branches loaded with their burden of clear yellow flowers. They are ten to twelve feet high, and one looks up at much of the bloom clear-cut against the pure blue of the sky; the upper part of the Magnolia also shows against the sky. Here there is a third flower-picture; this time of warm white and finest yellow on brilliant blue, and out in open sunlight. Among the Forsythias is also a large bush of *Magnolia stellata*, whose milk-white flowers may be counted by the thousand. As the earlier *M. conspicua* goes out of bloom it comes into full bearing, keeping pace with the Forsythia, whose season runs on well into April.

It is always a little difficult to find suitable places for the early bulbs. Many of them can be enjoyed in rough and grassy places, but we also want to combine them into pretty living pictures in the garden proper.

Nothing seems to me more unsatisfactory then the usual way of having them scattered about in small patches in the edges of flower-borders, where they only show as little disconnected dabs of colour, and where they are necessarily in danger of disturbance and probably injury when their foliage has died down and their places are wanted for summer flowers.

It was a puzzle for many years to know how to treat these early bulbs, but at last a plan was devised that seems so satisfactory that I have no hesitation in advising it for general adoption.

On the further side of a path that bounds my June garden is a border about seventy feet long and ten feet wide. At every ten feet along the back is a larch post planted with a free-growing Rose. These are not only to clothe their posts but are to grow into garlands swinging on slack chains from post to post. Beyond are Bamboos, and then an old hedge-bank with Scotch Firs, Oaks, Thorns, &c. The border slopes upwards from the path, forming a bank of gentle ascent. It was first planted with hardy Ferns in bold drifts; Male Fern for the most part, because it is not only handsome but extremely persistent; the fronds remaining green into the winter; between them come the bulbs, with a general edging to the front of mossy Saxifrage.

The colour-scheme begins with the pink of *Megasea ligulata,* and with the lower-toned pinks of *Fumaria bulbosa* and the Dog-tooth Violets (*Erythronium*). At the back of these are Lent Hellebores of dull red colouring, agreeing charmingly with the colour of the bulbs. A few white Lent Hellebores are at the end; they have turned to greenish white by the time the rather late *Scilla amœna* is in bloom. Then comes a brilliant patch of pure blue with white—*Scilla sibirica* and white Hyacinths, followed by the also pure blues of *Scilla bifolia* and *Chionodoxa* and the later, more purple-blue of Grape Hyacinth. A long drift of white Crocus comes next, in beauty in the border's earliest days; and later, the blue-white of *Puschkinia;* then again pure blue and white of *Chionodoxa* and white Hyacinth.

Now the colours change to white and yellow and golden foliage, with the pretty little pale trumpet Daffodil Consul Crawford, and beyond it the stronger yellow of two other small early kinds—*N. nanus* and the charming little *N. minor*, quite distinct though so often confounded with *nanus* in gardens. With these, and in other strips and patches towards the end of the border, are plantings of the Golden Valerian, so useful for its bright yellow foliage quite early in the year. The leaves of the Orange Day-lily are also of a pale yellowish green colour when they first come up, and are used at the end of the border. These plants of golden and pale foliage are also placed in a further region beyond the plan, and show to great advantage as the eye enfilades the border and reaches the more distant places. Before the end of the bulb-border is reached there is once more a drift of harmonised faint pink colouring of *Megasea* and the little *Fumaria* (also known as *Corydalis bulbosa*) with the pale early Pyrenean Daffodil, *N. Pallidus Præcox.*

The bulb-flowers are not all in bloom exactly at the same time, but there is enough of the colour intended to give the right effect in each grouping. Standing at the end, just beyond the Dog-tooth Violets, the arrangement and progression of colour is pleasant and interesting, and in some portions vivid; the pure blues in the middle spaces being much enhanced by the yellow flowers and golden foliage that follow.

Through April and May the leaves of the bulbs are growing tall, and their seed-pods are carefully removed to prevent exhaustion. By the end of May the Ferns are throwing up their leafy crooks; by June the feathery fronds are displayed in all their tender freshness; they spread over the whole bank, and we forget that there are any bulbs between. By the time the June garden, whose western boundary it forms, has come into fullest bloom it has become a completely furnished bank of Fern-beauty.

🌺 MARCH II

In early March many and lovely are the flowering bulbs, and among them a wealth of blue, the more precious that it is the colour least frequent among flowers. The blue of *Scilla sibirica*, like all blues that have in them a suspicion of green, has a curiously penetrating quality; the blue of *Scilla bifolia* does not attack the eye so smartly. *Chionodoxa sardensis* is of a full and satisfying colour, that is enhanced by the small space of clear white throat. A bed of it shows very little variation in colour. *Chionodoxa Luciliæ*, on the other hand, varies greatly; one may pick out light and dark blue, and light and dark of almost lilac colour. The variety *C. gigantea* is a fine plant. There are some pretty kinds of *Scilla bifolia* that were raised by the Rev. J. G. Nelson of Aldborough, among them a tender flesh-colour and a good pink. *Leucojum vernum*, with its clear white flowers and polished dark-green leaves, is one of the gems of early March; and, flowering at the same time, no flower of the whole year can show a more splendid and sumptuous colour than the purple of *Iris reticulata*. Varieties have been raised, some larger, some nearer blue, and some reddish purple, but the type remains the best garden flower. *Iris stylosa*, in sheltered nooks open to the sun, when well established, gives flower from November till mid-April, the strongest rush of bloom being about the third week in March. It is a precious plant in our southern counties, delicately scented, of a tender and yet full lilac-blue. The long ribbon-like leaves make handsome tufts, and the sheltered place it needs in our climate saves the flowers from the injury they receive on their native windy Algerian hills, where they are nearly always torn into tatters.

What a charm there is about the common Dog-tooth Violet; it is pretty everywhere, in borders, in the rock-garden, in all sorts of corners. But where it looks best with me is in a grassy place strewn with dead leaves, under young oaks, where the garden joins the copse. This is a part of the pleasure-ground that has been treated with some care, and has rewarded thought and labour with some success, so that it looks less as if it had been planned than as if it might have come naturally. At one point the lawn, trending gently upward, runs by grass paths into a rock-garden, planted mainly with dwarf shrubs. Here are Andromedas, Pernettyas, Gaultherias, and Alpine Rhododendron, and with them three favourites whose crushed leaves give a grateful fragrance, Sweet Gale, *Ledum palustre,* and *Rhododendron myrtifolium.* The rock part is unobtrusive; where the ground rises rather quickly are a couple of ridges made of large, long lumps of sandstone, half buried, and so laid as to give a look of natural stratification. Hardy Ferns are grateful for the coolness of their northern flanks, and Cyclamens are happy on the ledges. Beyond and above is the copse, or thin wood of young silver Birch and Holly, in summer clothed below with bracken, but now bristling with the bluish spears of Daffodils and the buds that will soon burst into bloom. The early Pyrenean Daffodil is already out, gleaming through the low-toned copse like lamps of pale yellow light. Where the rough path enters the birch copse is a cheerfully twinkling throng of the Dwarf Daffodil (*N. nanus*), looking quite at its best on its carpet of moss and fine grass and dead leaves. The light wind gives it a graceful, dancing movement, with an active spring about the upper part of the stalk. Some of the heavier trumpets not far off answer to the same wind with only a ponderous, leaden sort of movement.

Farther along the garden joins the wood by a plantation of Rhododendrons and broad grassy paths, and farther still by a thicket of the free-growing Roses, some forming fountain-like clumps nine paces in diameter, and then again by masses of flowering shrubs, gradating by means of Sweetbriar, Water-elder, Dogwood, Medlar, and Thorn from garden to wild wood.

THE YEAR IN THE GARDEN

In the end of March, or at any time during the month when the wind is in the east or north-east, all increase and development of vegetation appears to cease. As things are, so they remain. Plants that are in flower retain their bloom, but, as it were, under protest. A kind of sullen dullness pervades all plant life. Sweet-scented shrubs do not give off their fragrance; even the woodland moss and earth and dead leaves withhold their sweet, nutty scent. The surface of the earth has an arid, infertile look; a slight haze of an ugly grey takes the colour out of objects in middle distance, and seems to rob the flowers of theirs, or to put them out of harmony with all things around. But a day comes, or, perhaps, a warmer night, when the wind, now breathing gently from the south-west, puts new life into all growing things. A marvellous change is wrought in a few hours. A little warm rain has fallen, and plants, invisible before, and doubtless still underground, spring into glad life.

※ APRIL I

It is a windy day in early April, and I take my camp-stool and wander into the wood, where one is always fairly in shelter. Beyond the fir wood is a bit of wild forest-like land. The trees are mostly Oaks, but here and there a Scotch Fir seems to have straggled away from the mass of its fellows, and looks all the handsomer for its isolation among leafless trees of quite another character. The season is backward; it still seems like the middle of March, and the ground covering of dead leaves has the bleached look that one only sees during March and the early weeks of a late April. It is difficult to believe that the floor of the wood will, a month hence, be covered with a carpet whose ground is the greenery of tender grass and fern-like wild Parsley, and whose pattern is the bloom of Primrose and wild Hyacinth. As yet the only break in the leafy carpet is made by some handsome tufts of the wild Arum, just now at their best, and by some wide-spreading sheets of Dog's Mercury, one of the earliest of the wild plants. It is not exactly beautiful, except in some cases as sheets of bright green colour, but it is welcome as a forerunner of the cheerful spring flowers. It is a poisonous plant, and one must beware of getting it into a garden, so insidious and persistently invading is its running root.

It is difficult to believe that we are well into April, the season is so backward, with frosty nights and winds that appear to blow equally cold from all quarters. To-day the wind comes from the south, though it feels more like north-east. How cold it must be in northern France! Coming back through the fir wood, the path is on the whole well sheltered, yet the wind reaches me in thin thready little chilly draughts, as if arrows of cold air were being shot from among the trees. The wind-blown firs in the mass have that pleasant sound that always reminds me of a distant sea washing upon a shingly beach.

The sun is away on my front and left, and the sharp shadows of the trees are thrown diagonally across the path, where the sunlight comes through a half-open place. Further along, for some fifty yards or more, the path is in shade, with still more distant stretches of stem-barred glints of sunny space. Here the fir-trunks tell dark against the mist-coloured background. It is not mist, for the day is quite clear, but I am on high ground, and the distance is of the tops of firs where the hillside falls steeply away to the north. Where the sun catches the edges of the nearer trunks it lights them in a sharp line, leaving the rest warmly dark; but where the trees stand in shade the trunks are of a cool grey that is almost blue, borrowing their colour, through the opening of the track behind me, from the hard blue cloudless sky. The trunks seen quite against the sunlight look a pale greenish-brown, lighter than the shadow they cast, and somewhat warmed by the sunlit dead bracken at their feet. When I move onward into the shade the blue look on the stems is gone, and I only see their true colour of warm purplish-grey, clouded with paler grey lichen. I wish I had with me some young student of painting, the varying colourings of the trees in this wood in to-day's light offer such valuable lessons in training the eye to see the colour of objects as it appears to be; the untrained eye only sees colour as it is locally. I suppose any one who has never gone through this kind of training could scarcely believe the difference it makes in the degree of enjoyment of all that is most worthy of admiration in our beautiful world. But it enables one, even in a greater degree than the other perceptions of form and proportion that the artist must acquire or cultivate, to see pictures for oneself, not merely to see objects. And the pictures so seized by the eye and brain are the best pictures of all, for they are those of the great Artist, revealed by Him direct to the seeing eye and the receiving heart.

It is not so much that people are unobservant, but that from the want of the necessary training they cannot see or receive direct from nature what is seen by the artist, and the only natural pictures that strike them are those that present some unusual strength or mass of positive colour, such as a brilliant sunset, or a group of trees in yellow glory of autumn colouring, or a field of poppies, or an orchard bearing its load of bloom. To these untrained eyes the much more numerous and delicate of Nature's pictorial moods or incidents can only be enjoyed or understood when presented in the form of a painted picture by the artist who understands Nature's speech and can act as her interpreter.

Now I come to the fringe of a plantation of Spruce Fir some thirty years old. The trees meet overhead above the narrow cart-track, and, looking in from outside in the late afternoon light it might be the mouth of a black-dark tunnel, so deep and heavy is the gruesome gloom. And indeed it is very dark, and in its depths strangely silent. It is like a place of the dead, and as if the birds and small wood beasts were forbidden to enter, for none are to be seen or heard. But about the middle of this sombre wood there is a slight clearing; a little more light comes from above, and I see by the side of the track, on the hitherto unbroken carpet of dull dead-brown, some patches and even sheets of a vivid green, and quantities of delicate white bloom. And the sight of this sudden picture of daintiest loveliness, of a value all the greater for its gloomy environment, fills the heart with lively joy and abounding thankfulness.

It is the Wood-Sorrel, tenderest and loveliest of wood plants. The white flower in the mass has a slight lilac tinge; when I look close I see that this comes from a fine veining of reddish-purple colour on the white ground. White seems a vaguely-indefinite word when applied to the colouring of flowers; in the case of this tender little blossom the white is not very white, but about as white as the lightest part of a pearl. The downy stalk is flesh-coloured and half-transparent, and the delicately-formed calyx is painted with faint tints of dull green edged with transparent greenish buff, and is based and tipped with a reddish-purple that recalls the veining of the petals. Each of these has a touch of clear yellow on its inner base that sets off the bunch of tiny whitish stamens.

The brilliant yellow-green leaf is a trefoil of three broad little hearts, each joined at its point to the upright stalk by a tiny stalklet just long enough to keep the leaf-divisions well apart. In the young foliage the leaflets are pressed down to the stalk and folded together. The mature ones also fold and sleep at night. Each little heart does not fold upon itself, but each half is closely pressed against the half of its neighbour, so that the whole looks like a blunt, three-winged arrow-head or bolt-head.

I sit at the edge of the hillside path, and look down the old lane. A steep sandy bank rises to the left. Above it is a wood of Oak and Hazel, enriched with groups of mighty Hollies. To the right, also steeply rising, is rather open woodland. In the hollow is a thick mass of dead leaves, and below them a rich leaf-mould, for the old lane holds not only the leaves that fall into it, but the many more that are blown in from all sides. Twenty yards ahead and nearly in the bottom is a large Beech, showing by its evident age that for a hundred and fifty years, and who knows how long before, the road has been out of use. Still nearer and a little to the side is a great Holly. Its smooth pale grey stem fifteen inches thick rises unbranched for twelve feet; then the lower branches sweep boldly down and the outer boughs meet the steep banks. The great Beech-tree arches overhead, and the old hollow way goes steeply down till its further progress is hidden by a bend and by the projection of the right-hand bank. Dog's Mercury here grows thickly, and the sunlight from beyond makes it show as a mass of brilliant green colour.

As I sit quite quiet I hear in the wood high up on my left some small animal hunting among the dead leaves. By the smallness of the sound it should be a field-mouse; the movement is not heavy enough for a weasel, still less for a stoat; it is the sound of an animal of less than three ounces weight. Now I move on to a place where some underwood has lately been cut, and then to where the ground is naturally open; a half-acre of wild turf on the sunny hillside, of the fine grasses native to the sandy soil, with occasional tufts of the pretty Wood-Sage that will blossom in the full summer. The little Cinquefoil, with a flower like a small wild Strawberry, is in bloom, and Dog-Violets and Stitchwort, and here and there is a fine clump of Burdock, whose grandly-formed leaves with their boldly-waved edges I always think worthy of a place in a garden.

Just above this open space is a low hedgerow of Hazels, with still rising wooded ground above. What a pretty and pleasant place that wise rabbit has chosen for his "bury," as the country folk call it; at the foot of the low sandy bank, and where it is kept quite dry by the roots of the old Hazels. Just above is a carpet of wild Hyacinth backed by Hollies, and a little garden of the same comes right up to his front-door, where a tuft or two is partly buried by some of his more recent works of excavation. Here also are more Burdocks. Their leaves have almost the grandeur of those of the Gourd tribe, but without their luscious weakness, and the vigour of the Rhubarb without its coarseness. I never cease to admire their grand wave of edge and the strength of line in the "drawing" from root to leaf-point. It is a plant that for leaf effect in the early year should be in every garden; it would hold its place as worthily as Veratrum or Artichoke. Later in the year there are other plants of bold leaf-beauty, but in April and May they are so few that none should be overlooked.

🌼 APRIL II

In early April there is quite a wealth of flower among plants that belong half to wood and half to garden. *Epimedium pinnatum*, with its delicate, orchid-like spike of pale-yellow bloom, flowers with its last

ON GARDENING

year's leaves, but as soon as it is fully out the young leaves rush up, as if hastening to accompany the flowers. *Dentaria pinnata*, a woodland plant of Switzerland and Austria, is one of the handsomest of the white-flowered *cruciferæ*, with well-filled heads of twelve to fifteen flowers, and palmate leaves of freshest green. Hard by, and the best possible plant to group with it, is the lovely Virginian Cowslip (*Mertensia virginica*), the very embodiment of the freshness of early spring. The sheaf of young leafage comes almost black out of the ground, but as the leaves develop, their dull, lurid colouring changes to a full, pale green of a curious texture, quite smooth, and yet absolutely unreflecting. The dark colouring of the young leaves now only remains as a faint tracery of veining on the backs of the leaves and stalks, and at last dies quite away as the bloom expands. The flower is of a rare and beautiful quality of colour, hard to describe—a rainbow-flower of purple, indigo, full and pale blue, and daintiest lilac, full of infinite variety and indescribable charm. The flowers are in terminal clusters, richly filled; lesser clusters springing from the axils of the last few leaves and joining with the topmost one to form a gracefully drooping head. The lurid colouring of the young leaves is recalled in the flower-stem and calix, and enhances the colour effect of the whole. The flower of the common Dog-tooth Violet is over, but the leaves have grown larger and handsomer. They look as if, originally of a purplish-red colour, some liquid had been dropped on them, making confluent pools of pale green, lightest at the centre of the drop. The noblest plant of the same family (*Erythronium giganteum*) is now in flower—a striking and beautiful wood plant, with turn-cap shaped flowers of palest straw-colour, almost white, and large leaves, whose markings are not drop-like as in the more familiar kind, but are arranged in a regular sequence of bold splashings, reminding one of a *Maranta*. The flowers, single or in pairs, rise on stems a foot or fifteen inches high; the throat is beautifully marked with flames of rich bay on a yellow ground, and the handsome group of golden-anthered stamens and silvery pistil make up a flower of singular beauty and refinement. That valuable Indian Primrose,

[118]

P. denticulata, is another fine plant for the cool edge or shady hollows of woodland in rather good, deep soil.

But the glory of the copse just now consists in the great stretches of Daffodils. Through the wood run shallow, parallel hollows, the lowest part of each depression some nine paces apart. Local tradition says they are the remains of old pack-horse roads; they occur frequently in the forest-like heathery uplands of our poor-soiled, sandy land, running, for the most part, three or four together, almost evenly side by side. The old people account for this by saying that when one track became too much worn another was taken by its side. Where these pass through the birch copse the Daffodils have been planted in the shallow hollows of the old ways, in spaces of some three yards broad by thirty or forty yards long— one kind at a time. Two of such tracks, planted with *Narcissus princeps* and *N. Horsfieldi,* are now waving rivers of bloom, in many lights and accidents of cloud and sunshine full of pictorial effect. The planting of Daffodils in this part of the copse is much better than in any other portions where there were no guiding trackways, and where they were planted in haphazard sprinklings.

There are balmy days in mid-April, when the whole garden is fragrant with Sweetbriar. It is not "fast of its smell," as Bacon says of the damask rose, but gives it so lavishly that one cannot pass near a plant without being aware of its gracious presence. Passing upward through the copse, the warm air draws a fragrance almost as sweet, but infinitely more subtle, from the fresh green of the young birches; it is like a distant whiff of Lily of the Valley. Higher still the young leafage of the larches gives a delightful perfume of the same kind. It seems as if it were the office of these mountain trees, already nearest the high heaven, to offer an incense of praise for their new life.

The snowy Mespilus (*Amelanchier*) shows like puffs of smoke among the firs and birches, full of its milk-white, cherry-like bloom—a true woodland shrub or small tree. It loves to grow in a thicket of other trees, and to fling its graceful sprays about through their branches. It is a doubtful native, but naturalised and plentiful in the neighbouring woods. As seen in gardens, it is usually a neat little tree of shapely form, but it is more beautiful when growing at its own will in the high woods.

Marshy hollows in the valleys are brilliant with Marsh Marigold (*Caltha palustris*); damp meadows have them in plenty, but they are largest and handsomest in the alder-swamps of our valley bottoms, where their great luscious clumps rise out of pools of black mud and water.

🥀 MAY

While May is still young, Cowslips are in beauty on the chalk lands a few miles distant, but yet within pleasant reach. They are finest of all in orchards, where the grass grows tall and strong under the half-shade of the old apple-trees, some of the later kinds being still loaded with bloom. The blooming of the Cowslip is the signal for a search for the Morell, one of the very best of the edible fungi. It grows in open woods or where the undergrowth has not yet grown high, and frequently in old parks and pastures near or under elms. It is quite unlike any other fungus; shaped like a tall egg, with the pointed end upwards, on a short, hollow stalk, and looking something like a sponge. It has a delicate and excellent flavour, and is perfectly wholesome.

The pretty little Woodruff is in flower; what scent is so delicate as that of its leaves? They are almost sweeter when dried, each little whorl by itself, with the stalk cut closely away above and below. It is a pleasant surprise to come upon these fragrant little stars between the leaves of a book. The whole plant revives memories of rambles in Bavarian woodlands, and of Maitrank, that best of the "cup" tribe of pleasant drinks, whose flavour is borrowed from its flowering tips.

In the first week in May oak-timber is being felled. The wood is handsomer, from showing the grain better, when it is felled in the winter, but it is delayed till now because of the value of the bark for tanning, and just now the fast-rising sap makes the bark strip easily. A heavy fall is taking place in the fringes of a large wood of old Scotch fir. Where the oaks grow there is a blue carpet of wild Hyacinth; the pathway is a slightly hollowed lane, so that the whole sheet of flower right and left is nearly on a level with the eye, and looks like solid pools of blue. The oaks not yet felled are putting forth their leaves of golden bronze. The song of the nightingale and the ring of the woodman's axe gain a rich musical quality from the great fir wood. Why a wood of Scotch fir has this wonderful property of a kind of musical reverberation I do not know; but so it is. Any sound that occurs within it is, on a lesser scale, like a sound in a cathedral. The tree itself when struck gives a musical note. Strike an oak or an elm on the trunk with a stick, and the sound is mute; strike a Scotch fir, and it is a note of music.

BETWEEN SPRING AND SUMMER

When the Spring flowers are done, and before the full June days come with the great Flag Irises and the perennial Lupines, there is a kind of mid-season. If it can be given a space of ground it will be well bestowed. I have a place that I call the Hidden Garden, because it is in a corner that might so easily be overlooked if one did not know where to find it. No important path leads into it, though two pass within ten yards of it on either side. It is in a sort of clearing among Ilex and Holly, and the three small ways into it are devious and scarcely noticeable from the outside.

The main path goes down some shallow, rough stone steps with a sunny bank to the left and a rocky mound to the right. The mound is crowned with small shrubs, Alpine Rhododendrons and Andromeda. Both this and the left-hand bank have a few courses of rough dry-walling next the path on its lowest level. A little cross-path curves into the main one from the right.

The path leaves the garden again by a repetition of the rough stone steps. The mossy growth of *Arenaria balearica* clings closely to the stones on their cooler faces, and the frond-like growths of Solomon's Seal hang out on either side as a fitting prelude to the dim mysteries of the wide green wood-path beyond.

It is a garden for the last days of May and the first fortnight of June.

Passing through the Yew tunnel, the little place bursts on the sight with good effect. What is most striking is the beauty of the blue-lilac *Phlox divaricata* and that of two clumps of Tree Peony—the rosy Baronne d'Alès and the pale salmon-pink Comtesse de Tuder. The little garden, with its quiet environment of dark foliage, forbids the use of strong colouring, or perhaps one should say that it suggested a restriction of the scheme of colouring to the tenderer tones. There seemed to be no place here for the gorgeous Oriental Poppies, although they too are finest in partial shade, or for any strong yellows, their character needing wider spaces and clearer sunlight.

The Hollies and Ilexes all round are growing fast, and before many years are over the little garden will become too shady for the well-being of the flowers that now occupy it. It will then change its character and become a Fern garden.

All gardening involves constant change. It is even more so in woodland. A young bit of wood such as mine is for ever changing. Happily, each new development reveals new beauty of aspect or new possibility of good treatment, such as, rightly apprehended and then guided, tends to a better state than before.

Meanwhile the little tree-embowered garden has a quiet charm of its own. It seems to delight in its character of a Hidden Garden, and in the pleasant surprise that its sudden discovery provokes. For between it and its owner there is always a pretty little play of pretending that there is no garden there, and of being much surprised and delighted at finding, not only that there is one, but quite a pretty one.

One of my desires that can never be fulfilled is to have a rocky hill-side in full sun, so steep as to be almost precipitous, with walls of bare rock only broken by ledges that can be planted. I would have great groups of Yucca standing up against the sky and others in the rock-face, and some bushes of this great *Euphorbia* and only a few other plants, all of rather large grey effect; *Phlomis*, Lavender, Rosemary and Cistus, with *Othonna* hanging down in long sheets over the bare face of the warm rock. It would be a rock-garden on an immense scale, planted as Nature plants, with not many different things at a time. The restriction to a few kinds of plants would give the impression of spontaneous growth; of that large, free, natural effect that is so rarely achieved in artificial planting. Besides natural hillsides, there must be old quarries within or near the pleasure-grounds of many places in our islands where such a scheme of planting could worthily be carried out.

᪻ JUNE I

What is one to say about June—the time of perfect young summer, the fulfilment of the promise of the earlier months, and with as yet no sign to remind one that its fresh young beauty will ever fade? For my own part I wander up into the wood and say, "June is here—June is here; thank God for lovely June!" The soft cooing of the wood-dove, the glad song of many birds, the flitting of butterflies, the hum of all the little winged people among the branches, the sweet earth-scents—all seem to say the same, with an endless reiteration, never wearying because so gladsome. It is the offering of the Hymn of Praise! The lizards run in and out of the heathy tufts in the hot sunshine, and as the long day darkens the night-jar trolls out his strange song, so welcome because it is the prelude to the perfect summer night; here and there a glow-worm shows its little lamp. June is here—June is here; thank God for lovely June!

᪻ JUNE II

"Thou sentest a gracious rain upon thine inheritance; and refreshedst it when it was weary."

The whole garden is singing this hymn of praise and thankfulness. It is the middle of June; no rain had fallen for nearly a month, and our dry soil had become a hot dust above, a hard cake below. A burning wind from the east that had prevailed for some time, had brought quantities of noisome blight, and had left all vegetation, already parched with drought, a helpless prey to the devouring pest. Bushes of garden Roses had their buds swarming with green-fly, and all green things, their leaves first coated and their pores clogged with viscous stickiness, and then covered with adhering wind-blown dust, were in a pitiable state of dirt and suffocation. But last evening there was a gathering of grey cloud, and this ground of grey was traversed by those fast-travelling wisps of fleecy blackness that are the surest promise of near rain the sky can show. By bedtime rain was falling steadily, and in the night it came down on the roof in a small thunder of steady downpour. It was pleasant to wake from time to time and hear the welcome sound, and to know that the clogged leaves were being washed clean, and that their pores were once more drawing in the breath of life, and that the thirsty roots were drinking their fill. And now, in the morning, how good it is to see the brilliant light of the blessed summer day, always brightest just after rain, and to see how every tree and plant is full of new life and abounding gladness; and to feel one's own thankfulness of heart, and that it is good to live, and all the more good to live in a garden.

JULY

After the wealth of bloom of June, there appear to be but few flowers in the garden; there seems to be a time of comparative emptiness between the earlier flowers and those of autumn. It is true that in the early days of July we have Delphiniums, the grandest blues of the flower year. They are in two main groups in the flower border, one of them nearly all of the palest kind—not a solid clump, but with a thicker nucleus, thinning away for several yards right and left. Only white and pale-yellow flowers are grouped with this, and pale, fresh-looking foliage of maize and Funkia. The other group is at some distance, at the extreme western end. This is of the full and deeper blues, following a clump of Yuccas, and grouped about with things of important silvery foliage, such as Globe Artichoke and Silver Thistle (*Eryngium*).

In the end of July we have some of the hottest of the summer days, only beginning to cool between six and seven in the evening. One or two evenings I go to the upper part of the wood to cut some fern-pegs for pegging Carnation layers, armed with fag-hook and knife and rubber, and a low rush-bottomed stool to sit on. The rubber is the stone for sharpening the knife—a long stone of coarse sandstone grit, such as is used for scythes. Whenever I am at work with a knife there is sure to be a rubber not far off, for a blunt knife I cannot endure, so there is a stone in each department of the garden sheds, and a whole series in the workshop, and one or two to spare to take on outside jobs. The Bracken has to be cut with a light hand, as the side-shoots that will make the hook of the peg are easily broken just at the important joint. The fronds are of all sizes, from two to eight feet long; but the best for pegs are the moderate-sized, that have not been weakened by growing too close together. Where they are crowded the main stalk is thick, but the side ones are thin and weak; whereas, where they get light and air the side branches are carried on stouter ribs, and make stronger and better-balanced pegs. The cut fern is lightly laid in a long ridge with the ends all one way, and the operator sits at the stalk end of the ridge, a nice cool shady place having been chosen. Four cuts with the knife make a peg, and each frond makes three pegs in about fifteen seconds. With the fronds laid straight and handy it goes almost rhythmically, then each group of three pegs is thrown into the basket, where they clash on to the others with a hard ringing sound. In about four days the pegs dry to a surprising hardness; they are better than wooden ones, and easier and quicker to make.

People who are not used to handling Bracken should be careful how they cut a frond with a knife; they are almost sure to get a nasty little cut on the second joint of the first finger of the right hand—not from the knife, but from the cut edge of the fern. The stalk has a silicious coating, that leaves a sharp edge like a thin flake of glass when cut diagonally with a sharp knife; they should also beware how they pick or pull off a mature frond, for even if the part of the stalk laid hold of is bruised and twisted, some of the glassy structure holds together and is likely to wound the hand.

🦋 AUGUST I

August is the month of China Asters. I find many people are shy of these capital plants, perhaps because the mixtures, such as are commonly grown, contain rather harsh and discordant colours; also perhaps because a good many of the kinds, having been purposely dwarfed in order to fit them for pot-culture and bedding, are too stiff to look pretty in general gardening. Such kinds will always have their uses, but what is wanted now in the best gardening is more freedom of habit. I have a little space that I give entirely to China Asters. I have often had the pleasure of showing it to some person who professed a dislike to them, and with great satisfaction have heard them say, with true admiration: "Oh! but I had no idea that China Asters could be so beautiful."

It is only a question of selection, for the kinds are now so many and the colourings so various that there are China Asters to suit all tastes and uses. My own liking is for those of the pure violet-purple and lavender colours, with whites; and to plants with these clear, clean tints my Aster garden is restricted. In other places I grow some of the tenderer pinks, a good blood-red, and a clear pale yellow; but these are kept quite away from the purples. The kinds chosen are within the Giant Comet, Ostrich Plume and Victoria classes—all plants with long-stalked bloom and a rather free habit of growth. For some years I was much hindered from getting the colours I wanted from the inaccurate way in which they are described in seed-lists. Finally I paid a visit to the trial-grounds of one of our premier seed-houses, and saw all the kinds and the colourings and made my own notes. I cannot but think that a correct description of the colours, instead of a fanciful one, would help both customer and seed-merchant. As it is, the customer, in order to get the desired flowers, has to *learn a code*. I have often observed, in comparing French and English seed-lists, that the French do their best to describe colours accurately, but that the English use some wording which does not describe the colour, but appears to be intended as a complimentary euphemism. Thus, if I want a Giant Comet of that beautiful pale silvery lavender, perhaps the loveliest colour of which a China Aster is capable, I have to ask for "azure blue." If I want a full lilac, I must order "blue"; if a full purple it is "dark blue." If I want a strong, rich violet-purple, I must beware of asking for purple, for I shall get a terrible magenta such as one year spoilt the whole colour-scheme of my Aster garden. It is not as if the right colour-words were wanting, for the language is rich in them—violet, lavender, lilac, mauve, purple;—these, with slight additions, will serve to describe the whole of the colourings falsely called blue. The word blue should not be used at all in connexion with these flowers. There are no blue China Asters.

🌿　AUGUST II

Here and there in the copse, among the thick masses of green Bracken, is a frond or two turning yellow. This always happens in the first or second week of August, though it is no indication of the approaching yellowing of the whole. But it is taken as a signal that the Fern is in full maturity, and a certain quantity is now cut to dry for protection and other winter uses. Dry Bracken lightly shaken over frames is a better protection than mats, and is almost as easily moved on and off.

The Ling is now in full flower, and is more beautiful in the landscape than any of the garden Heaths; the relation of colouring, of greyish foliage and low-toned pink bloom with the dusky spaces of purplish-grey shadow, are a precious lesson to the colour-student.

The fern-walk is at its best. It passes from the garden upwards to near the middle of the copse. The path, a wood-path of moss and grass and short-cut heath, is a little lower than the general level of the wood. The mossy bank, some nine feet wide, and originally cleared for the purpose, is planted with large groups of hardy Ferns, with a preponderance (due to preference) of Dilated Shield Fern and Lady Fern. Once or twice in the length of the bank are hollows, sinking at their lowest part to below the path-level, for *Osmunda* and *Blechnum*. When rain is heavy enough to run down the path it finds its way into these hollow places.

By the middle of August the garden assumes a character distinctly autumnal. Much of its beauty now depends on the many non-hardy plants, such as Gladiolus, Canna, and Dahlia, on Tritomas of doubtful hardiness, and on half-hardy annuals—Zinnia, Helichrysum, Sunflower, and French and African Marigold.

🏵 SEPTEMBER I

Now is the moment to get to work on the rock-garden; there is no time of year so precious for this work as September. Small things planted now, while the ground is still warm, grow at the root at once, and get both anchor-hold and feeding-hold of the ground before frost comes. Those that are planted later do not take hold, and every frost heaves them up, sometimes right out of the ground. Meanwhile those that have got a firm root-hold are growing steadily all the winter, underground if not above; and when the first spring warmth comes they can draw upon the reserve of strength they have been hoarding up, and make good growth at once.

Except in the case of a rockery only a year old, there is sure to be some part that wants to be worked afresh, and I find it convenient to do about a third of the space every year. Many of the indispensable Alpines and rock-plants of lowly growth increase at a great rate, some spreading over much more than their due space, the very reason of this quick-spreading habit being that they are travelling to fresh pasture; many of them prove it clearly by dying away in the middle of the patch, and only showing vigorous vitality at the edges.

﹡ SEPTEMBER II

The fierce gales and heavy rains of the last days of September wrought sad havoc among the flowers. Dahlias were virtually wrecked. Though each plant had been tied to three stakes, their masses of heavy growth could not resist the wrenching and twisting action of the wind, and except in a few cases where they were well sheltered, their heads lie on the ground, the stems broken down at the last tie. If anything about a garden could be disheartening, it would be its aspect after such a storm of wind. Wall shrubs, only lately made safe, as we thought, have great gaps torn out of them, though tied with tarred string to strong iron staples, staples and all being wrenched out. Everything looks battered, and whipped, and ashamed; branches of trees and shrubs lie about far from their sources of origin; green leaves and little twigs are washed up into thick drifts; apples and quinces, that should have hung till mid-October, lie bruised and muddy under the trees. Newly-planted roses and hollies have a funnel-shaped hole worked in the ground at their base, showing the power of the wind to twist their heads, and giving warning of a corresponding disturbance of the tender roots. There is nothing to be done but to look round carefully and search out all disasters and repair them as well as may be, and to sweep up the wreckage and rubbish, and try to forget the rough weather, and enjoy the calm beauty of the better days that follow, and hope that it may be long before such another angry

storm is sent. And indeed a few quiet days of sunshine and mild temperature work wonders. In a week one would hardly know that the garden
had been so cruelly torn about. Fresh flowers take the place of bruised
ones, and wholesome young growths prove the enduring vitality of vegetable life. Still we cannot help feeling, towards the end of September,
that the flower year is nearly at an end, though the end is a gorgeous one,
with its strong yellow masses of the later perennial Sunflowers and Marigolds, Goldenrod, and a few belated Gladioli; the brilliant foliage of
Virginian Creepers, the leaf-painting of *Vitis Coignetiæ*, and the strong
crimson of the Claret Vine.

The nights are growing chilly, with even a little frost, and the work for
the coming season of dividing and transplanting hardy plants has already begun. Plans are being made for any improvements or alterations
that involve ground work. Already we have been at work on some broad
grass rides through the copse that were roughly levelled and laid with
grass last winter. The turf has been raised and hollows filled in, grass
seed sown in bare patches, and the whole beaten and rolled to a good
surface, and the job put out of hand in good time before the leaves
begin to fall.

OCTOBER

The bracken in the copse stands dry and dead, but when leaves are
fluttering down and the chilly days of mid-October are upon us, its warm,
rusty colouring is certainly cheering; the green of the freshly grown
mossy carpet below looks vividly bright by contrast. Some bushes of
Spindle-tree (*Euonymus europæus*) are loaded with their rosy seed-pods;
some are already burst, and show the orange-scarlet seeds—an audacity
of colouring that looks all the brighter for the even, lustreless green of
the leaves and of the green-barked twigs and stems.

The hardy Azaleas are now blazing masses of crimson, almost scarlet leaf; the old *A. pontica*, with its large foliage, is as bright as any. With them are grouped some of the North American Vacciniums and Andromedas, with leaves almost as bright. The ground between the groups of shrubs is knee-deep in heath. The rusty-coloured withered bloom of the wild heath on its purplish-grey masses and the surrounding banks of dead fern make a groundwork and background of excellent colour-harmony.

Towards the end of October outdoor flowers in anything like quantity cannot be expected, and yet there are patches of bloom here and there in nearly every corner of the garden. The pretty Mediterranean Periwinkle (*Vinca acutiflora*) is in full bloom. As with many another southern plant that in its own home likes a cool and shady place, it prefers a sunny one in our latitude. The flowers are of a pale and delicate grey-blue colour, nearly as large as those of the common *Vinca major*, but they are borne more generously as to numbers on radical shoots that form thick, healthy-looking tufts of polished green foliage. It is not very common in gardens, but distinctly desirable.

In the bulb-beds the bright-yellow *Sternbergia lutea* is in flower. At first sight it looks something like a Crocus of unusually firm and solid substance; but it is an Amaryllis, and its pure and even yellow colouring is quite unlike that of any of the Crocuses. The numerous upright leaves are thick, deep green, and glossy. It flowers rather shyly in our poor soil, even in well-made beds, doing much better in chalky ground.

❦ NOVEMBER

As soon as may be in November the big hardy flower-border has to be thoroughly looked over. The first thing is to take away all "soft stuff." This includes all dead annuals and biennials and any tender things that have been put in for the summer, also Paris Daisies, Zinnias, French and African Marigolds, Helichrysums, Mulleins, and a few Geraniums. Then

Dahlias are cut down. The waste stuff is laid in big heaps on the edge of the lawn just across the footpath, to be loaded into the donkey-cart and shot into some large holes that have been dug in the wood.

Now, in the third week of November, the most pressing work is the collecting of leaves for mulching and leaf-mould. The oaks have been late in shedding their leaves, and we have been waiting till they are down. Oak-leaves are the best, then hazel, elm, and Spanish chestnut. Birch and beech are not so good; beech-leaves especially take much too long to decay. This is, no doubt, the reason why nothing grows willingly under beeches. Horse and cart and three hands go out into the lanes for two or three days, and the loads that come home go three feet deep into the bottom of a range of pits. The leaves are trodden down close and covered with a layer of mould, in which winter salad stuff is immediately planted. The mass of leaves will soon begin to heat, and will give a pleasant bottom-heat throughout the winter. Other loads of leaves go into an open pen about ten feet square and five feet deep. Two such pens, made of stout oak post and rail and upright slabs, stand side by side in the garden yard. The one newly filled has just been emptied of its two-year-old leaf-mould, which has gone as a nourishing and protecting mulch over beds of Daffodils and choice bulbs and Alströmerias, some being put aside in reserve for potting and various uses. The other pen remains full of the leaves of last year, slowly rotting into wholesome plant-food.

With works of wood-cutting and stump-grubbing near at hand, we look over the tools and see that all are in readiness for winter work. Axes and hand-bills are ground, fag-hooks sharpened, picks and mattocks sent to the smithy to be drawn out, the big cross-cut saw fresh sharpened and set, and the hand-saws and frame-saws got ready. The rings of the bittle are tightened and wedged up, so that its heavy head may not split when the mighty blows, flung into the tool with a man's full strength, fall on the heads of the great iron wedges.

The leaves are all down by the last week of November, and woodland assumes its winter aspect; perhaps one ought rather to say, some one of its infinite variety of aspects, for those who live in such country know how many are the winter moods of forest land, and how endless are its variations of atmospheric effect and pictorial beauty—variations much greater and more numerous than are possible in summer.

With the wind in the south-west and soft rain about, the twigs of the birches look almost crimson, while the dead bracken at their foot, half-draggled and sodden with wet, is of a strong, dark rust colour. Now one sees the full value of the good evergreens, and, rambling through wood-land, more especially of the Holly, whether in bush or tree form, with its masses of strong green colour, dark and yet never gloomy. Whether it is the high polish of the leaves, or the lively look of their wavy edges, with the short prickles set alternately up and down, or the brave way the tree has of shooting up among other thick growth, or its massive sturdiness on a bare hillside, one cannot say, but a Holly in early winter, even without berries, is always a cheering sight. John Evelyn is eloquent in his praise of this grand evergreen, and lays special emphasis on this quality of cheerfulness.

❧   DECEMBER

A spell of frosty days at the end of December puts a stop to all plant-ing and ground work. Now we go into the copse and cut the trees that have been provisionally marked, judged, and condemned, with the object of leaving the remainder standing in graceful groups. The men wonder why I cut some of the trees that are best and straightest and have good tops, and leave those with leaning stems. Anything of seven inches or less diameter is felled with the axe, but thicker trees with the cross-cut saw. For these our most active fellow climbs up the tree with a rope, and makes it fast to the trunk a good way up, then two of them, kneeling, work the saw. When it has cut a third of the way through, the rope is pulled on the side opposite the cut to keep it open and let the saw work free. When still larger trees are sawn down this is done by driving in a wedge behind the saw, when the width of the saw-blade is rather more than buried in the tree. When the trunk is nearly sawn through, it wants care and judgment to see that the saw does not get pinched by the weight of the tree; the clumsy workman who fails to clear his saw gets laughed at, and probably damages his tool. Good straight trunks of oak and chestnut are put aside for special uses; the rest of the larger stuff is cut into cordwood lengths of four feet. The heaviest of these are split up into four pieces to make them easier to load and carry away, and eventually to saw up into firewood.

The best of the birch tops are cut into pea-sticks, a clever, slanting cut with the hand-bill leaving them pointed and ready for use. Throughout the copse are "stools" of Spanish chestnut cut about once in five years. From this we get good straight stakes for Dahlias and Hollyhocks, also bean-poles; while the rather straight-branched boughs are cut into branching sticks for Michaelmas Daisies, and special lengths are got ready for various kinds of plants—Chrysanthemums, Lilies, Pæonies, and so on. To provide all this in winter, when other work is slack or impossible, is an important matter in the economy of a garden, for all gardeners know how distressing and harassing it is to find themselves without the right sort of sticks or stakes in summer, and what a troublesome job it then is to have to look them up and cut them, of indifferent quality, out of dry faggots. By the plan of preparing all in winter no precious time is lost, and a tidy withe-bound bundle of the right sort is always at hand.

FLOWERS,
SHRUBS, TREES

🌼   IRIS STYLOSA

I never tire of admiring and praising *Iris Stylosa*, which has proved itself such a good plant for English gardens; at any rate, for those in our southern counties. Lovely in form and colour, sweetly-scented and with admirable foliage, it has in addition to these merits the unusual one of a blooming season of six months' duration. The first flowers come with the earliest days of November, and its season ends with a rush of bloom in the first half of April. Then is the time to take up old tufts and part them, and plant afresh; the old roots will have dried up into brown wires, and the new will be pushing. It thrives in rather poor soil, and seems to bloom all the better for having its root-run invaded by some stronger plant. When I first planted a quantity I had brought from its native place, I made the mistake of putting it in a well-prepared border. At first I was

[137]

ON GARDENING

delighted to see how well it flourished, but as it gave me only thick
masses of leaves a yard long, and no flowers, it was clear that it wanted to
be less well fed. After changing it to poor soil, at the foot of a sunny wall
close to a strong clump of Alströmeria, I was rewarded with a good crop
of flowers; and the more the Alströmeria grew into it on one side and
Plumbago Larpentæ on the other, the more freely the brave little Iris
flowered. The flower has no true stem; what serves as a stem, sometimes a
foot long, is the elongated tube, so that the seed-pod has to be looked for
deep down at the base of the tufts of leaves, and almost under ground.
The specific name, *stylosa,* is so clearly descriptive, that one regrets that
the longer, and certainly uglier, *unguicularis* should be preferred by
botanists.

What a delight it was to see it for the first time in its home in the hilly
wastes, a mile or two inland from the town of Algiers! Another lovely
blue Iris was there too, *I. alata* or *scorpioides,* growing under exactly
the same conditions; but this is a plant unwilling to be acclimatised in
England. What a paradise it was for flower-rambles, among the giant
Fennels and the tiny orange Marigolds, and the immense bulbs of *Scilla
maritima* standing almost out of the ground, and the many lovely Bee-
orchises and the fairy-like *Narcissus scrotinus,* and the groves of Prickly
Pear wreathed and festooned with the graceful tufts of bell-shaped flower
and polished leaves of *Clematis cirrhosa!*

🏵 THE PRIMROSE GARDEN

It must be some five-and-twenty years ago that I began to work at
what I may now call my own strain of Primroses, improving it a little
every year by careful selection of the best for seed. The parents of the
strain were a named kind, called Golden Plover, and a white one, without
name, that I found in a cottage garden. I had also a dozen plants about
eight or nine years ago from a strong strain of Mr. Anthony Waterer's

that was running on nearly the same lines; but a year later, when I had flowered them side by side, I liked my own one rather the best, and Mr. Waterer, seeing them soon after, approved of them so much that he took some to work with his own. I hold Mr. Waterer's strain in great admiration, and, though I tried for a good many years, never could come near him in red colourings. But as my own taste favoured the delicately-shaded flowers, and the ones most liked in the nursery seemed to be those with strongly contrasting eye, it is likely that the two strains may be working still farther apart.

They are, broadly speaking, white and yellow varieties of the strong bunch-flowered or Polyanthus kind, but they vary in detail so much, in form, colour, habit, arrangement, and size of eye and shape of edge, that one year thinking it might be useful to classify them I tried to do so, but gave it up after writing out the characters of sixty classes! Their possible variation seems endless. Every year among the seedlings there appear a number of charming flowers with some new development of size, or colour of flower, or beauty of foliage, and yet all within the narrow bounds of—white and yellow Primroses.

Their time of flowering is much later than that of the true or single-stalked Primrose. They come into bloom early in April, though a certain number of poorly-developed flowers generally come much earlier, and they are at their best in the last two weeks of April and the first days of May. When the bloom wanes, and is nearly overtopped by the leaves, the time has come that I find best for dividing and replanting. The plants then seem willing to divide, some almost falling apart in one's hands, and the new roots may be seen just beginning to form at the base of the crown. The plants are at the same time relieved of the crowded mass of flower-stem, and, therefore, of the exhausting effort of forming seed, a severe drain on their strength. A certain number will not have made more than one strong crown, and a few single-crown plants have not flowered; these, of course, do not divide. During the flowering time I keep a good look-out for those that I judge to be the most beautiful and desirable, and mark them for seed. These are also taken up, but are kept apart, the flower stems reduced to one or two of the most promising, and they are then planted in a separate place—some cool nursery corner. I find that the lifting and replanting in no way checks the growth or well-being of the seed-pods.

I remember some years ago a warm discussion in the gardening papers about the right time to sow the seed. Some gardeners of high standing were strongly for sowing it as soon as ripe, while others equally trustworthy advised holding it over till March. I have tried both ways, and have satisfied myself that it is a matter for experiment and decision in individual gardens. As nearly as I can make out, it is well in heavy soils to sow when ripe, and in light ones to wait till March. In some heavy soils Primroses stand well for two years without division; whereas in light ones, such as mine, they take up the food within reach in a much shorter time, so that by the second year the plant has become a crowded mass of weak crowns that only throw up poor flowers, and are by then so much exhausted that they are not worth dividing afterwards. In my own case, having tried both ways, I find the March sown ones much the best.

The seed is sown in boxes in cold frames, and pricked out again into boxes when large enough to handle. The seedlings are planted out in June, when they seem to go on without any check whatever, and are just right for blooming next spring.

The Primrose garden is in a place by itself—a clearing half shaded by Oak, Chestnut, and Hazel. I always think of the Hazel as a kind nurse to Primroses; in the copses they generally grow together, and the finest Primrose plants are often nestled close in to the base of the nut-stool. Three paths run through the Primrose garden, mere narrow tracks between the beds, converging at both ends, something like the lines of longitude on a globe, the ground widening in the middle where there are two good-sized Oaks, and coming to a blunt point at each end, the only other planting near it being two other long-shaped strips of Lily of the Valley.

FLOWERS, SHRUBS, TREES

Every year, before replanting, the Primrose ground is dug over and well manured. All day for two days I sit on a low stool dividing the plants; a certain degree of facility and expertness has come of long practice. The "rubber" for frequent knife-sharpening is in a pail of water by my side; the lusciously fragrant heap of refuse leaf and flower-stem and old stocky root rises in front of me, changing its shape from a heap to a ridge, as when it comes to a certain height and bulk I back and back away from it. A boy feeds me with armfuls of newly-dug-up plants, two men are digging-in the cooling cow-dung at the farther end, and another carries away the divided plants tray by tray, and carefully replants them. The still air, with only the very gentlest south-westerly breath in it, brings up the mighty boom of the great ship guns from the old seaport, thirty miles away, and the pheasants answer to the sound as they do to thunder. The early summer air is of a perfect temperature, the soft coo of the wood-dove comes down from the near wood, the nightingale sings almost overhead, but—either human happiness may never be quite complete, or else one is not philosophic enough to contemn life's lesser evils, for—oh, the midges!

❧ AURICULAS

Border Auriculas are making a brave show. Nothing in the flower year is more interesting than a bed of good seedlings of the Alpine class. I know nothing better for pure beauty of varied colouring among early flowers. Except in varieties of *Salpiglossis*, such rich gradation of colour, from pale lilac to rich purple, and from rosy pink to deepest crimson, is hardly to be found in any one family of plants. There are varieties of cloudings of smoky-grey, sometimes approaching black, invading, and at the same time enhancing, the purer colours, and numbers of shades of half-tones of red and purple, such as are comprised within the term *murrey* of heraldry, and tender blooms of one colour, sulphurs and milk-

[141]

whites—all with the admirable texture and excellent perfume that belong to the "Bear's-ears" of old English gardens. For practical purposes the florist's definition of a good Auricula is of little value; that is for the show-table, and, as Bacon says, "Nothing to the true pleasure of a garden." The qualities to look for in the bed of seedlings are not the narrowing ones of proportion of eye to tube, of exact circle in the circumference of the individual pip, and so on, but to notice whether the plant has a handsome look and stands up well, and is a delightful and beautiful thing as a whole.

🌸 ROSES

I have great delight in the best of the old garden Roses; the Provence (Cabbage Rose), sweetest of all sweets, and the Moss Rose, its crested variety; the early Damask, and its red and white striped kind; the old, nearly single, Reine Blanche. I do not know the origin of this charming Rose, but by its appearance it should be related to the Damask. A good many years ago I came upon it in a cottage garden in Sussex, and thought I had found a white Damask. The white is a creamy white, the outsides of the outer petals are stained with red, first showing clearly in the bud. The scent is delicate and delightful, with a faint suspicion of Magnolia. A few years ago this pretty old Rose found its way to one of the meetings of the Royal Horticultural Society, where it gained much praise. It was there that I recognised my old friend, and learned its name.

I am fond of the old *Rosa alba*, both single and double, and its daughter, Maiden's Blush. How seldom one sees these Roses except in cottage gardens; but what good taste it shows on the cottager's part, for what Rose is so perfectly at home upon the modest little wayside porch?

I have also learnt from cottage gardens how pretty are some of the old Roses grown as standards. I have taken the hint, and have now some big roundheaded standards, the heads a yard through, of the lovely Celeste and of Madame Plantier, that are worth looking at, though one of them is rather badly-shaped this year, for my handsome Jack (donkey) ate one side of it when he was waiting outside the studio door, while his cart-load of logs for the ingle fire was being unloaded.

❧ SOME BEAUTIFUL WAYS OF GROWING LILIES

The greater number of the Lilies look their best when seen among shrubs and green growths of handsome foliage. Their forms are so distinct as well as beautiful that they are much best in separate groups among quiet greenery—not combined with other flowers. This general rule is offered for consideration as applicable to Lilies of white, pink, lemon-yellow, or other tender colourings; not so much to those that have scarlet and orange flowers. These are admirable in combination with many other garden flowers in the mixed border and various garden spaces. The White Lily, also, which loves sunlight, is so old a garden flower, and seems so naturally to accompany the Cabbage Roses and late Dutch Honeysuckle and other old garden flowers of the early days of July, that one must allow that its place in our gardens is in combination with the other old favourites.

But if it were a question of preparing a place for the purest pleasure in the enjoyment of Lily beauty it might be best arranged in some cool, sheltered, leafy place; some shady bay in woodland close to, though removed from, the garden proper. It should be in a place that was fairly moist yet well drained, where the Lilies would rise from ground rather thickly grouped with hardy Ferns and low bushes and plants of good foliage. Mr. R. W. Wallace of Colchester says: "An ideal spot for Lilies would be an open forest glade with a small stream running through it, near the banks of which the North American peat and moisture-loving

[143]

Lilies would flourish; and higher up, away from the water, clumps of *auratum, washingtonianum, Humboldti, giganteum,* and all our finest species, would readily grow."

If Lilies were planted in such a place, one kind at a time in fair quantity, we should be better able to appreciate their beauty and their dignity than when they are crowded among numbers of other flowers in the garden borders.

The value of rather close shelter of tree and bush can scarcely be overrated, for the outlying branches of the near bushes protect young Lily growths from the late frosts that are so harmful, and the encircling trees, not near enough to rob at the root or overhang at the top, but so near as to afford passing shade and to stop all violence of wind, give just the protection that suits them best.

It is a great advantage to have the Lilies in so well sheltered a place that they need not be staked, for staking deprives the plant of one of its beautiful ways, that of swaying to the movement of the air. It would scarcely be believed by any one who had not watched them unstaked, how variously and diversely graceful are the natural movements of Lilies. If they are tied up to stakes all this is necessarily lost, as is also the naturally dignified and yet dainty poise of the whole plant.

Where the Lily groups have penetrated into true woodland, a background of wild Bracken is the best that can be. As the Lily ground approaches the garden, clumps of Solomon's Seal would be admissible, and that good woodland plant of allied character, *Smilacina racemosa,* and plenty of our best hardy Ferns, Male Fern, Lady Fern, Dilated Shield Fern, and Osmunda, and some of the fine hardy American Ferns, among them also some of the Osmundas, with Onoclea and *Adiantum pedatum.*

Where the Lilies actually join the garden ground, no plant suits them so well as the bold-leaved *Funkia grandiflora. Liliums longiflorum, Brownii, Krameri,* and *speciosum* are specially thankful for this association. The *Funkia* also enjoys partial shade, for though it flowers best in sun, yet the leaves burn in its fiercest heat. No one would ever regret a good planting of *Lilium longiflorum*, Lady Fern, and *Funkia*. *Funkia grandiflora* is the best of the family, because the leaves are of the fresh, light, yellow-green colour that is so becoming to white and tender-coloured flowers.

Sometimes, where there is a permanent group of Lilies in a place where the roots of trees would be likely to rob a special compost, it is a good plan to plant the Lilies in a sunk tub.

꙰ LILIUM GIGANTEUM

The blooming of the *Lilium giganteum* is one of the great flower events of the year. It is planted in rather large straggling groups just within the fringe of the copse. In March the bulbs, which are only just underground, thrust their sharply-pointed bottle-green tips out of the earth. These soon expand into heart-shaped leaves, looking much like Arum foliage of the largest size, and of a bright-green colour and glistening surface. The groups are so placed that they never see the morning sun. They require a slight sheltering of fir-bough, or anything suitable, till the third week of May, to protect the young leaves from the late frosts. In June the flower-stem shoots up straight and tall, like a vigorous young green-stemmed tree. If the bulb is strong and the conditions suitable, it will attain a height of over eleven feet, but among the flowering bulbs of a group there are sure to be some of various heights from differently sized bulbs; those whose stature is about ten feet are perhaps the handsomest. The upper part of the stem bears the gracefully drooping great white Lily flowers, each bloom some ten inches long, greenish when in bud, but changing to white when fully developed. Inside each petal is a purplish-red stripe. In the evening the scent seems to pour out of the great white trumpets, and is almost overpowering, but gains a delicate quality by passing through the air, and at fifty yards away is like a faint waft of incense. In the evening light, when the sun is down, the great heads of white flower have a mysterious and impressive effect when seen at some distance through the wood, and by moonlight have a strangely weird dignity. The flowers only last a few days, but when they are over the beauty of the plant is by no means gone, for the handsome leaves remain in perfection till the autumn, while the growing seed-pods, rising into an erect position, become large and rather handsome objects. The rapidity and vigour of the four months' growth from bulb to giant flowering plant is very remarkable. The stem is a hollow, fleshy tube, three inches in diameter at the base, and the large radiating roots are like those of a tree. The original bulb is, of course, gone, but when the plants that have flowered are taken up at the end of November, offsets are found clustered round the root; these are carefully detached and replanted. The great growth of these Lilies could not be expected to come to perfection in our very poor, shallow soil, for doubtless in their mountain home in the Eastern Himalayas they grow in deep beds of cool vegetable earth. Here, therefore, their beds are deeply excavated, and filled to within a foot of the top with any of the vegetable rubbish of which only too much accumulates in the late autumn. Holes twelve feet across and three feet deep are convenient graves for frozen Dahlia-tops and half-hardy Annuals; a quantity of such material chopped up and trampled down close forms a cool subsoil that will comfort the Lily bulbs for many a year. The upper foot of soil is of good compost, and when the young bulbs are planted, the whole is covered with some inches of dead leaves that join in with the natural woodland carpet.

CARNATIONS

The flower of this month [July] that has the firmest hold of the gardener's heart is the Carnation—the Clove Gilliflower of our ancestors. Why the good old name "Gilliflower" has gone out of use is impossible to say, for certainly the popularity of the flower has never waned. Indeed, in the seventeenth century it seems that it was the best-loved flower of all in England; for John Parkinson, perhaps our earliest writer on garden plants, devotes to it a whole chapter in his "Paradisus Terrestris," a distinction shared by few other flowers. He describes no less than fifty kinds, a few of which are still to be recognised, though some are lost. For instance, what has become of the *"great gray Hulo,"* which he describes as a plant of the largest and strongest habit? The "gray" in this must refer to the colour of the leaf, as he says the flower is red; but there is also a variety called the "blew Hulo," with flowers of a "purplish murrey" colouring, answering to the slate colour that we know as of not unfrequent occurrence. The branch of the family that we still cultivate as "Painted Lady" is named by him "Dainty Lady," the present name being no doubt an accidental and regrettable corruption.

🪻 DAHLIAS

Dahlias are now at their full growth. To make a choice for one's own garden, one must see the whole plant growing. As with many another kind of flower, nothing is more misleading than the evidence of the show-table, for many that there look the best, and are indeed lovely in form and colour as individual blooms, come from plants that are of no garden value. For however charming in humanity is the virtue modesty, and however becoming is the unobtrusive bearing that gives evidence of its possession, it is quite misplaced in a Dahlia. Here it becomes a vice, for the Dahlia's first duty in life is to flaunt and to swagger and to carry gorgeous blooms well above its leaves, and on no account to hang its head. Some of the delicately-coloured kinds lately raised not only hang their heads, but also hide them away among masses of their coarse foliage, and are doubly frauds, looking everything that is desirable in the show, and proving worthless in the garden. It is true that there are ways of cutting out superfluous green stuff and thereby encouraging the blooms to show up, but at a busy season, when rank leafage grows fast, one does not want to be every other day tinkering at the Dahlias.

Careful and strong staking they must always have, not forgetting one central stake to secure the main growth at first. It is best to drive this into the hole made for the plant before placing the root, to avoid the danger of sending the point of the stake through the tender tubers. Its height out of the ground should be about eighteen inches less than the expected stature of the plant. As the Dahlia grows, there should be at least three outer stakes at such distance from the middle one as may suit the bulk and habit of the plant; and it is a good plan to have wooden hoops to tie to these, so as to form a girdle round the whole plant, and for tying out the outer branches. The hoop should be only loosely fastened—best with roomy loops of osier, so that it may be easily shifted up with the growth of the plant. We make the hoops in the winter of long straight rent rods of Spanish Chestnut, bending them while green round a tub, and tying them with tarred twine or osier bands. They last several years. All this care in staking the Dahlias is labour well bestowed, for when autumn storms come the wind has such a power of wrenching and twisting, that unless the plant, now grown into a heavy mass of succulent vegetation, is braced by firm fixing at the sides, it is in danger of being broken off short just above the ground, where its stem has become almost woody, and therefore brittle.

❧ MICHAELMAS DAISIES

The early days of October bring with them the best bloom of the Michaelmas Daisies, the many beautiful garden kinds of the perennial Asters. They have, as they well deserve to have, a garden to themselves. Passing along the wide path in front of the big flower border, and through the pergola that forms its continuation, with eye and brain full of rich, warm colouring of flower and leaf, it is a delightful surprise to pass through the pergola's last right-hand opening, and to come suddenly upon the Michaelmas Daisy garden in full beauty. Its clean, fresh, pure colouring, of pale and dark lilac, strong purple, and pure white, among masses of pale-green foliage, forms a contrast almost startling after the warm colouring of nearly everything else; and the sight of a region where the flowers are fresh and newly opened, and in glad spring-like profusion, when all else is on the verge of death and decay, gives an impression of satisfying refreshment that is hardly to be equalled throughout the year. Their special garden is a wide border on each side of a path, its length bounded on one side by a tall hedge of filberts, and on the other side by clumps of yew, holly, and other shrubs. It is so well sheltered that the strongest wind has its destructive power broken, and only reaches it as a refreshing tree-filtered breeze. The Michaelmas Daisies are replanted every year as soon as their bloom is over, the ground having been newly dug and manured. The old roots, which will have increased about four-fold, are pulled or chopped to pieces, nice bits with about five crowns being chosen for replanting; these are put in groups of three to five together. Tall-growing kinds like *Novi Belgi* Robert Parker are kept rather towards the back, while those of delicate and graceful habit, such as *cordifolius elegans* and its good variety Diana are allowed to come forward. The fine dwarf *Aster Amellus* is used in rather large quantity, coming quite to the front in some places, and running in and out between the clumps of other kinds. Good-sized groups of *Pyrethrum uliginosum* are given a place among the Asters, for though of quite another family, they are Daisies, and bloom at Michael-mas, and are admirable companions to the main occupants of the bor-ders. The only other plants admitted are white Dahlias, the two differ-ently striped varieties of *Eulalia japonica*, the fresh green foliage of Indian Corn, and the brilliant light-green leafage of *Funkia grandiflora*. Great attention is paid to staking the Asters. Nothing is more deplorable than to see a neglected, overgrown plant, at the last moment, when already half blown down, tied up in a tight bunch to one stake. When we are cutting underwood in the copse in the winter, special branching spray is looked out for our Michaelmas Daisies and cut about four feet or five feet long, with one main stem and from two to five branches. Towards the end of June and beginning of July these are thrust firmly into the ground among the plants, and the young growths are tied out so as to show to the best advantage. Good kinds of Michaelmas Daisies are now so numerous that in selecting those for the special garden it is well to avoid both the ones that bloom earliest and also the very latest, so that for about three weeks the borders may show a well-filled mass of bloom.

RHODODENDRONS I

Now, in the third week of May, Rhododendrons are in full bloom on the edge of the copse. The plantation was made about nine years ago, in one of the regions where lawn and garden were to join the wood. During the previous blooming season the best nurseries were visited and careful observations made of colouring, habit, and time of blooming. The space they were to fill demanded about seventy bushes, allowing an average of eight feet from plant to plant—not seventy different kinds, but, perhaps, ten of one kind, and two or three fives, and some threes, and a few single plants, always bearing in mind the ultimate intention of pictorial aspect as a whole. In choosing the plants and in arranging and disposing the groups these ideas were kept in mind: to make pleasant ways from lawn to copse; to group only in beautiful colour harmonies; to choose varieties beautiful in themselves; to plant thoroughly well, and to avoid over-crowding. Plantations of these grand shrubs are generally spoilt or ineffective, if not absolutely jarring, for want of attention to these simple rules. The choice of kinds is now so large, and the variety of colouring so extensive, that nothing can be easier than to make beautiful combinations, if intending planters will only take the small amount of preliminary trouble that is needful.

RHODODENDRONS II

I venture to entreat those who are about to plant Rhododendrons in watery places not to plant them, as has been done so often, on a small round island. I lived for twenty years in a pretty place of some fifty acres where there were three streams and two good-sized ponds. In one of the ponds were three islands, two of them of fair size and closely wooded with Alders and large Grey Poplars and smaller underwood, but the third and smallest was the worst form of small round pudding of Rhododendrons, about thirty feet across. When ponds are being artificially made it is tempting to leave islands, and if well arranged and planted they may be beautiful, although, in nearly all cases, except where there is unlimited space, a promontory is more pictorial, and favours in a greater degree the sense of mystery as to the extent of the water and the direction of the unseen shore.

If there is or must be a small island it is far better to plant it with an Alder and a group of Silver Birch. The rounded forms of the Rhododendrons add painfully to the rounded dumpiness of the little island. It is better to group them on the shore and to plant the island with something of upright form that will give beautiful reflection in the water, or to let it be covered with non-woody vegetation.

RHODODENDRONS III

My Rhododendrons are in large clumps, with Auratum Lilies in many of the spaces between them, and hardy Ferns, Andromedas, and some of the Dwarf Rhododendrons filling up the outer spaces between them. But the Azaleas, some distance away, stand unevenly apart, among open spaces of grass and Heath, and want yearly attention because the grass and weeds so soon invade the richer preparation at their root. I often bewail the waste of these lovely shrubs when I see them planted close together in bare beds of poor soil, or, worse still, mixed up with even more starved and unhappy Rhododendrons. Though all my Azaleas are some yards apart, I sometimes wish they were still more largely spaced, although I like here and there to plant two or three of the same together, or if not the same, of such colourings as approach each other and will make a mass of closely related harmony.

AZALEAS

The last days of May see hardy Azaleas in beauty. Any of them may be planted in company, for all their colours harmonise. In this garden, where care is taken to group plants well for colour, the whites are planted at the lower and more shady end of the group; next come the pale yellows and pale pinks, and these are followed at a little distance by kinds whose flowers are of orange, copper, flame, and scarlet-crimson colourings; this strong-coloured group again softening off at the upper end by strong yellows, and dying away into the woodland by bushes of the common yellow *Azalea pontica*, and its variety with flowers of larger size and deeper colour. The plantation is long in shape, straggling over a space of about half an acre, the largest and strongest-coloured group being in an open clearing about midway in the length. The ground between them is covered with a natural growth of the wild Ling (*Calluna*) and Whortleberry, and the small, white-flowered Bed-straw, with the fine-bladed Sheep's-fescue grass, the kind most abundant in heath-land. The surrounding ground is copse, of a wild, forest-like character, of birch and small oak. A woodpath of wild heath cut short winds through the planted group, which also comprises some of the beautiful white-flowered Californian *Azalea occidentalis*, and bushes of some of the North American Vacciniums.

Azaleas should never be planted among or even within sight of Rhododendrons. Though both enjoy a moist peat soil, and have a near botanical relationship, they are incongruous in appearance, and impossible to group together for colour. This must be understood to apply to the two classes of plants of the hardy kinds, as commonly grown in gardens. There are tender kinds of the East Indian families that are quite harmonious, but those now in question are the ordinary varieties of so-called Ghent Azaleas, and the hardy hybrid Rhododendrons. In the case of small gardens, where there is only room for one bed or clump of peat plants, it would be better to have a group of either one or the other of these plants, rather than spoil the effect by the inharmonious mixture of both.

BERBERIS

What a precious thing this fine old Berberis is! What should we do in winter without its vigorous masses of grand foliage in garden and shrubbery, to say nothing of its use indoors? Frequent as it is in gardens, it is seldom used as well or thoughtfully as it deserves. There are many places where, between garden and wood, a well-considered planting of Berberis, combined with two or three other things of larger stature, such as the fruiting Barberry, and Hawthorn and Holly, would make a very enjoyable piece of shrub wild-gardening. When one reflects that *Berberis Aquifolium* is individually one of the handsomest of small shrubs, that it is at its very best in mid-winter, that every leaf is a marvel of beautiful drawing and construction, and that its ruddy winter colouring is a joy to see, enhanced as it is by the glistening brightness of the leaf-surface; and further, when one remembers that in spring the whole picture changes—that the polished leaves are green again, and the bushes are full of tufted masses of brightest yellow bloom, and fuller of bee-music than any other plant then in flower; and that even then it has another season of beauty yet to come, when in the days of middle summer it is heavily loaded with the thick-clustered masses of berries, covered with a brighter and bluer bloom than almost any other fruit can show,—when one thinks of all this brought together in one plant, it seems but right that we should spare no pains to use it well. It is the only hardy shrub I can think of that is in one or other of its varied forms of beauty throughout the year. It is never leafless or untidy; it never looks mangy like an Ilex in April, or moulting like a Holly in May, or patchy and unfinished like Yew and Box and many other evergreens when their young leafy shoots are sprouting.

CLIMBING PLANTS

When one sees climbing plants or any of the shrubs that are so often used as climbers, planted in the usual way on a house or wall, about four feet apart and with no attempt at arrangement, it gives one that feeling of regret for opportunities lost or misused that is the sentiment most often aroused in the mind of the garden critic in the great number of pleasure-grounds that are planted without thought or discernment. Not infrequently in passing along a country road, with eye alert to note the beauties that are so often presented by little wayside cottage gardens, something is seen that may well serve as a lesson in better planting. The lesson is generally one that teaches greater simplicity—the doing of one thing at a time; the avoidance of overmuch detail. One such cottage has under the parlour window an old bush of *Pyrus japonica*. It had been well spurred back and must have been a mass of gorgeous bloom in early spring. The rest of the cottage was embowered in an old Grape Vine, perhaps of all wall plants the most beautiful, and, I always think, the most harmonious with cottages or small houses of the cottage class. It would seem to be least in place on the walls of houses of classical type, though such houses are often unsuitable for any wall plants. Still there are occasions where the noble polished foliage of Magnolia comes admirably on their larger spaces, and the clear-cut refinement of Myrtle on their lesser areas of wall-surface.

It is, like all other matters of garden planning, a question of knowledge and good taste. The kind of wall or house and its neighbouring forms are taken into account and a careful choice is made of the most suitable plants. For my own part I like to give a house, whatever its size or style, some dominant note in wall-planting. In my own home, which is a house of the large cottage class, the prevailing wall-growths are Vines and Figs in the south and west, and, in a shady northward facing court between two projecting wings, *Clematis montana* on the two cooler sides, and again a Vine upon the other. At one angle on the warmer side of the house where the height to the eaves is not great, China Roses have been trained up, and Rosemary, which clothes the whole foot of the wall, is here encouraged to rise with it. The colour of the China Rose bloom and the dusky green of the Rosemary are always to me one of the most charming combinations. In remembrance of the cottage example lately quoted there is *Pyrus japonica* under the long sitting-room window. I remember another cottage that had a porch covered with the golden balls of *Kerria japonica,* and China Roses reaching up the greater part of the low walls of half timber and plastering; the pink Roses seeming to ask one which of them were the loveliest in colour; whether it was those that came against the silver-grey of the old oak or those that rested on the warm-white plaster.

Another of the tender plants that is beautiful for walls and for free rambling over other wall-growths is *Solanum jasminoides.* Its white clusters come into bloom in middle summer and persist till latest autumn. In two gardens near me it is of singular beauty; in the one case on the sunny wall of a sheltered court where it covers a considerable space, in the other against a high south retaining-wall where, from the terrace above, the flowers are seen against the misty woodland of the middle distance and the pure grey-blue of the far-away hills. Turning round on the very same spot there is the remarkable growth of the Sweet Verbena that owes its luxuriance to its roots and main shoots being under shelter. There must be unending opportunities, where there are verandahs, of having just such bowers of sweetness to brush against in passing and to waft scented air to the windows of the rooms above.

One of the many garden possessions that I ardently desire and can never have is a bit of rocky hillside; a place partly of sheer scarp and partly of tumbled and outcropping rock-mass, for the best use of these plants. There would be the place for the yellow winter Jasmine, for the Honeysuckles both bushy and rambling, for the trailing Clematises lately described, and for the native *C. Vitalba*, beautiful both in flower and fruit; for shrubs like *Forsythia suspensa* and *Desmodium penduliflorum* that like to root high and then throw down cascades of bloom, and for the wichuraiana Roses, also for Gourds and wild Vines. There should be a good quarter of a mile of it so that one might plant at perfect ease, one thing at a time or one or two in combination, in just such sized and shaped groups as would make the most delightful pictures, and in just the association that would show the best assortment.

I have seen long stretches of bare chalky banks for year after year with nothing done to dispel their bald monotony, feeling inward regret at the wasted opportunity; thinking how beautiful they might be made with a planting of two common things, *Clematis Vitalba* and Red Spur Valerian. But such examples are without end.

JUNIPER

Among the many merits of the Juniper, its tenderly mysterious beauty of colouring is by no means the least; a colouring as delicately subtle in its own way as that of cloud or mist, or haze in warm, wet woodland. It has very little of positive green; a suspicion of warm colour in the shadowy hollows, and a blue-grey bloom of the tenderest quality imaginable on the outer masses of foliage. Each tiny, blade-like leaf has a band of dead, palest, bluish-green colour on the upper surface, edged with a narrow line of dark green slightly polished; the back of the leaf is of the same full, rather dark green, with slight polish; it looks as if the green back had been brought up over the edge of the leaf to make the dark edging on the upper surface. The stems of the twigs are of a warm, almost foxy colour, becoming darker and redder in the branches. The tips of the twigs curl over or hang out on all sides towards the light, and the "set" of the individual twigs is full of variety. This arrangement of mixed colouring and texture, and infinitely various position of the spiny little leaves, allows the eye to penetrate unconsciously a little way into the mass, so that one sees as much tender shadow as actual leaf-surface, and this is probably the cause of the wonderfully delicate and, so to speak, intangible quality of colouring. Then, again, where there is a hollow place in a bush, or group, showing a cluster of half-dead stems, at first one cannot tell what the colour is, till with half-shut eyes one becomes aware of a dusky and yet luminous purple-grey.

The merits of the Juniper are not yet done with, for throughout the winter (the time of growth of moss and lichen) the rugged-barked old stems are clothed with loveliest pale-green growths of a silvery quality. Standing before it, and trying to put the colour into words, one repeats, again and again, pale-green silver—palest silvery green! Where the lichen is old and dead it is greyer; every now and then there is a touch of the orange kind, and a little of the branched staghorn pattern so common on the heathy ground. Here and there, as the trunk or branch is increasing in girth, the silvery, lichen-clad, rough outer bark has parted, and shows the smooth, dark-red inner bark; the outer covering still clinging over the opening, and looking like grey ribands slightly interlaced. Many another kind of tree-stem is beautiful in its winter dress, but it is difficult to find any so full of varied beauty and interest as that of the Juniper; it is one of the yearly feasts that never fails to delight and satisfy.

🍀 ELDER-TREE

I am very fond of the Elder-tree. It is a sociable sort of thing; it seems to like to grow near human habitations. In my own mind it is certainly the tree most closely associated with the pretty old cottage and farm architecture of my part of the country; no bush or tree, not even the apple, seems to group so well or so closely with farm buildings. When I built a long thatched shed for the many needs of the garden, in the region of pits and frames, compost, rubbish and burn-heap, I planted Elders close to the end of the building and on one side of the yard. They look just right, and are, moreover, every year loaded with their useful fruit. This is ripe quite early in September, and is made into Elder wine, to be drunk hot in winter, a comfort by no means to be despised. My trees now give enough for my own wants, and there are generally a few acceptable bushels to spare for my cottage neighbours.

🍀 WILD PLANTING

Near my home is a little wild valley, whose planting, wholly done by Nature, I have all my life regarded with the most reverent admiration.

The arable fields of an upland farm give place to hazel copses as the ground rises. Through one of these a deep narrow lane, cool and dusky in summer from its high steep banks and over-arching foliage, leads by a rather sudden turn into the lower end of the little valley. Its grassy bottom is only a few yards wide, and its sides rise steeply right and left. Looking upward through groups of wild bushes and small trees, one sees thickly-wooded ground on the higher levels. The soil is of the very poorest; ridges of pure yellow sand are at the mouths of the many rabbit-

FLOWERS, SHRUBS, TREES

burrows. The grass is of the short fine kinds of the heathy uplands. Bracken grows low, only from one to two feet high, giving evidence of the poverty of the soil, and yet it seems able to grow in perfect beauty clumps of Juniper and Thorn and Holly, and Scotch Fir on the higher ground.

On the steeply-rising banks are large groups of Juniper, some tall, some spreading, some laced and wreathed about with tangles of Honeysuckle, now in brown winter dress, and there are a few bushes of Spindle-tree, whose green stems and twigs look strangely green in winter. The Thorns stand some singly, some in close companionship, impenetrable masses or short-twigged prickly growth, with here and there a wild Rose shooting straight up through the crowded branches. One thinks how lovely it will be in early June, when the pink Rose-wreaths are tossing out of the foamy sea of white Thorn blossom. The Hollies are towering masses of health and vigour. Some of the groups of Thorn and Holly are intermingled; all show beautiful arrangements of form and colour, such as are never seen in planted places. The track in the narrow valley trends steadily upwards and bears a little to the right. High up on the left-hand side is an old wood of Scotch Fir. A few detached trees come half-way down the valley bank to meet the gnarled, moss-grown Thorns and the silver-green Junipers. As the way rises some Birches come in sight, also at home in the sandy soil. Their graceful, lissome spray moving to the wind looks active among the stiffer trees, and their white stems shine out in startling contrast to the other dusky foliage. So the narrow track leads on, showing the same kinds of tree and bush in endless variety of beautiful grouping, under the sombre half-light of the winter day. It is afternoon, and as one mounts higher a pale bar of yellow light gleams between the farther tree-stems, but all above is grey, with angry, blackish drifts of ragged wrack. Now the valley opens out to a nearly level space of rough grass, with grey tufts that will be pink bell-heather in summer, and upstanding clumps of sedge that tell of boggy places. In front and to the right are dense fir-woods. To the left is broken ground and a steep-sided hill, towards whose shoulder the track rises.

Here are still the same kinds of trees, but on the open hillside they have quite a different effect. Now I look into the ruddy heads of the Thorns, bark and fruit both of rich warm colouring, and into the upper masses of the Hollies, also reddening into wealth of berry.

Throughout the walk, pacing slowly but steadily for nearly an hour, only these few kinds of trees have been seen, Juniper, Holly, Thorn, Scotch Fir, and Birch (a few small Oaks excepted), and yet there has not been once the least feeling of monotony, nor, returning downward by the same path, could one wish anything to be altered or suppressed or differently grouped. And I have always had the same feeling about any quite wild stretch of forest land. Such a bit of wild forest as this small valley and the hilly land beyond are precious lessons in the best way of tree and shrub planting. No artificial planting can ever equal that of Nature, but one may learn from it the great lesson of the importance of moderation and reserve, of simplicity of intention, and directness of purpose, and the inestimable value of the quality called "breadth" in painting. For planting ground is painting a landscape with living things; and as I hold that good gardening takes rank within the bounds of the fine arts, so I hold that to plant well needs an artist of no mean capacity. And his difficulties are not slight ones, for his living picture must be right from all points, and in all lights.

No doubt the planting of a large space with a limited number of kinds of trees cannot be trusted to all hands, for in those of a person without taste of the more finely-trained perceptions the result would be very likely dull or even absurd. It is not the paint that makes the picture, but the brain and heart and hand of the man who uses it.

?⅛ PLANTING TREES

During the year I make careful notes of any trees or shrubs that will be wanted, either to come from the nursery or to be transplanted within my own ground, so as to plant them as early as possible. Of the two extremes it is better to plant too early than too late. I would rather plant deciduous trees before the leaves are off than wait till after Christmas, but of all planting times the best is from the middle of October till the end of November, and the same time is the best for all hardy plants of large or moderate size.

I have no patience with slovenly planting. I like to have the ground prepared some months in advance, and when the proper time comes, to do the actual planting as well as possible. The hole in the already prepared ground is taken out so that the tree shall stand exactly right for depth, though in this dry soil it is well to make the hole an inch or two deeper, in order to leave the tree standing in the centre of a shallow depression, to allow of a good watering now and then during the following summer. The hole must be made wide enough to give easy space for the most outward-reaching of the roots; they must be spread out on all sides, carefully combing them out with the fingers, so that they all lay out to the best advantage. Any roots that have been bruised, or have broken or jagged ends, are cut off with a sharp knife on the homeward side of the injury. Most gardeners when they plant, after the first spadeful or two has been thrown over the root, shake the bush with an up and down joggling movement. This is useful in the case of plants with a good lot of bushy root, such as Berberis, helping to get the grains of earth well in among the root; but in tree planting, where the roots are laid out flat, it is of course useless. In our light soil, the closer and firmer the earth is made round the newly-planted tree the better, and strong staking is most important, in order to save the newly-placed root from disturbance by dragging.

WILD FERNS

I am thankful to live in a place where many Ferns are among our wild hedge plants, and above all where there is an abundance of Bracken. For though my neighbourhood is populous, and the hedges of the most frequented ways have been stripped of their Ferns, yet I know the country so well for a good many miles round, that when I want to see any particular Fern I am nearly always able to find it, though it is true that some habitats of rather rare Ferns have been entirely destroyed. In one great swampy hollow, where, when I was a child, I remember the Royal Fern growing high above my head, not an atom now remains. It used to grow in great mounded tussocks, the crowns springing from a sort of raised table of matted black root nearly eighteen inches high. I remember leaning back against one of these and looking up and seeing how bright the sunlit rusty heads of flower looked against the late summer sky. It was then so abundant, and its home so little known, that there was no reason to hesitate about taking some pieces to plant by our ponds. I have still a strong plant, that, after several removals, has, I hope, found a final resting-place. How tough that black root-mass was! no spade, much less trowel, would divide it; after a first trial with these feebler implements we had to give it up and come back another day armed with choppers. It was no matter of regret, for the place was full of beauty. Such a wild bog-garden! Sheets of brilliant Sphagnum covering stretches of soft black bog that could not be crossed, but whose edges might be cautiously approached. Quantities of the wonderful little Sundew clutching its prey; white plumes of the silky Cotton-grass; tufts of Bog-Asphodel, neatest of small plants, with its sheaf of tiny Iris-like leaves and conspicuous spikes of deep-yellow flower; the pale and shaggy Marsh St. John's Wort, and, daintiest and loveliest of wild plants, the tiny Bog Pimpernel, its thread-like stem carrying the neat pairs of leaves through the tufts of Sphagnum, and its flowers of tenderest, loveliest pink looking up to the sun.

Of all our Ferns the one that is really important in the landscape is the Bracken; in all its many forms and aspects a thing of beauty and of highest pictorial value. Growing only a foot high on the poorest and most exposed of our sandy wastes, in sheltered woodland its average is six to seven feet, while in hedges and clumps of forest brake it rushes up among the taller growths, and shows the upper ends of its fronds at a height almost incredible. How delightful it is by the sides of our many unfenced roads; how it accommodates itself to the conditions of its position and graces every place. How perfectly it groups itself with its wild companions great and small; with the Heaths and fine Grasses of the moorlands, with the Brambles and Thorns, Hollies, Birches, Junipers, and small Oaks of the wild poor ground that has never known the plough; with the thicker woods of Fir, where in cooler ground it takes a deeper colour; while in woodland openings the blue of the heavens is reflected in the wide-spread sheets of flattened frond.

Then one thinks with satisfaction of how pleasant a shelter it is to living creatures; to the deer of park and forest, and to all the smaller feathered and furry folk of copse and moorland and roadside waste.

It is not in summer only that the Bracken is good to see, for in winter its cheerfulness of rusty warmth is distinctly comforting, as we who live on the sandy hills well know. For when we visit our neighbours in the weald or in the valleys, and see the sodden grass reeking with winter wet, and the leafless trees dripping, and the cold mists hanging to the ground we come back with glad thankfulness to our warm dry hills with their red Fern-carpet and their well-clothed Firs; to the silver-barked Birches swaying, and their crimson spray swishing, in the cheerful breeze and the clear bright light of the blessed sun.

❧ BRACKEN

Towards the end of June the bracken that covers the greater part of the ground of the copse is in full beauty. No other manner of undergrowth gives to woodland in so great a degree the true forest-like character. This most ancient plant speaks of the old, untouched land of which large stretches still remain in the south of England—land too poor to have been worth cultivating, and that has therefore for centuries endured human contempt. In the early part of the present century, William Cob-

[163]

bett, in his delightful book, "Rural Rides," speaking of the heathy head-lands and vast hollow of Hindhead, in Surrey, calls it "certainly the most villainous spot God ever made." This gives expression to his view, as farmer and political economist, of such places as were incapable of culti-vation, and of the general feeling of the time about lonely roads in waste places, as the fields for the lawless labours of smuggler and highwayman. Now such tracts of natural wild beauty, clothed with stretches of Heath and Fern and Whortleberry, with beds of Sphagnum Moss, and little natural wild gardens of curious and beautiful sub-aquatic plants in the marshy hollows and undrained wastes, are treasured as such places de-serve to be, especially when they still remain within fifty miles of a vast city. The height to which the bracken grows is a sure guide to the depth of soil. On the poorest, thinnest ground it only reaches a foot or two; but in hollow places where leaf-mould accumulates and surface soil has washed in and made a better depth, it grows from six feet to eight feet high, and when straggling up through bushes to get to the light a frond will sometimes measure as much as twelve feet. The old country people who have always lived on the same poor land say, "Where the farn grows tall anything will grow"; but that only means that there the ground is somewhat better and capable of cultivation, as its presence is a sure indication of a sandy soil. The timber-merchants are shy of buying oak trees felled from among it, the timber of trees grown on the wealden clay being so much better.

COLOUR AND SCENT

SOURCES

🌿 · *Colour in the Flower Garden*

🌹 · *Annuals and Biennials*

🌾 · *Wood and Garden*

❀ · *Home and Garden*

🌷 · *Gardens for Small Country Houses*

🌿 COLOUR IN THE FLOWER GARDEN

To plant and maintain a flower-border, *with a good scheme for colour*, is by no means the easy thing that is commonly supposed.

I believe that the only way in which it can be made successful is to devote certain borders to certain times of year; each border or garden region to be bright for from one to three months.

Nothing seems to me more unsatisfactory than the border that in spring shows a few patches of flowering bulbs in ground otherwise looking empty, or with tufts of herbaceous plants just coming through. Then the bulbs die down, and their place is wanted for something that comes later. Either the ground will then show bare patches, or the place of the bulbs will be forgotten and they will be cruelly stabbed by fork or trowel when it is wished to put something in the apparently empty space.

[167]

ON GARDENING

For many years I have been working at these problems in my own garden, and having come to certain conclusions, can venture to put them forth with some confidence. I may mention that from the nature of the ground, in its original state partly wooded and partly bare field, and from its having been brought into cultivation and some sort of shape before it was known where the house now upon it would exactly stand, the garden has less general unity of design than I should have wished. The position and general form of its various portions were accepted mainly according to their natural conditions, so that the garden ground, though but of small extent, falls into different regions, with a general, but not altogether definite, cohesion.

I am strongly of [the] opinion that the possession of a quantity of plants, however good the plants may be themselves and however ample their number, does not make a garden; it only makes a *collection*. Having got the plants, the great thing is to use them with careful selection and definite intention. Merely having them, or having them planted unassorted in garden spaces, is only like having a box of paints from the best colourman, or, to go one step further, it is like having portions of these paints set out upon a palette. This does not constitute a picture; and it seems to me that the duty we owe to our gardens and to our own bettering in our gardens is so to use the plants that they shall form beautiful pictures; and that, while delighting our eyes, they should be always training those eyes to a more exalted criticism; to a state of mind and artistic conscience that will not tolerate bad or careless combination or any sort of misuse of plants, but in which it becomes a point of honour to be always striving for the best.

It is just in the way it is done that lies the whole difference between commonplace gardening and gardening that may rightly claim to rank as a fine art. Given the same space of ground and the same material, they may either be fashioned into a dream of beauty, a place of perfect rest and refreshment of mind and body—a series of soul-satisfying pictures— a treasure of well-set jewels; or they may be so misused that everything is jarring and displeasing. To learn how to perceive the difference and how to do right is to apprehend gardening as a fine art. In practice it is to place every plant or group of plants with such thoughtful care and definite intention that they shall form a part of a harmonious whole, and that successive portions, or in some cases even single details, shall show a series of pictures. It is so to regulate the trees and undergrowth of the wood that their lines and masses come into beautiful form and harmonious proportion; it is to be always watching, noting and doing, and putting oneself meanwhile into closest acquaintance and sympathy with the growing things.

THE MAIN HARDY FLOWER BORDER

The big flower border is about two hundred feet long and fourteen feet wide. It is sheltered from the north by a solid sandstone wall about eleven feet high clothed for the most part with evergreen shrubs—Bay and Laurustinus, Choisya, Cistus and Loquat. These show as a handsome background to the flowering plants. They are in a three-foot-wide border at the foot of the wall; then there is a narrow alley, not seen from the front, but convenient for access to the wall shrubs and for working the back of the border.

As it is impossible to keep any one flower border fully dressed for the whole summer, and as it suits me that it should be at its best in the late summer, there is no attempt to have it full of flowers as early as June. Another region belongs to June; so that at that time the big border has only some incidents of good bloom, though the ground is rapidly covering with the strong patches, most of them from three to five years old, of the later blooming perennials.

The planting of the border is designed to show a distinct scheme of colour-arrangement. At the two ends there is a groundwork of grey and glaucous foliage—Stachys, Santolina, *Cineraria maritima*, Sea Kale and

[169]

Lyme Grass, with darker foliage, also of grey quality, of Yucca, *Clematis recta* and Rue. With this, at the near or western end, there are flowers of pure blue, grey-blue, white, palest yellow and palest pink; each colour partly in distinct masses and partly inter-grouped. The colouring then passes through stronger yellows to orange and red. By the time the middle space of the border is reached the colour is strong and gorgeous, but, as it is in good harmonies, it is never garish. Then the colour-strength recedes in an inverse sequence through orange and deep yellow to pale yellow, white and palest pink, with the blue-grey foliage. But at this, the eastern end, instead of the pure blues we have purples and lilacs.

Looked at from a little way forward, for a wide space of grass allows this point of view, the whole border can be seen as one picture, the cool colouring at the ends enhancing the brilliant warmth of the middle. Then, passing along the wide path next the border the value of the colour-arrangement is still more strongly felt. Each portion now becomes a picture in itself, and every one is of such a colouring that it best prepares the eye, in accordance with natural law, for what is to follow. Standing for a few moments before the end-most region of grey and blue, and saturating the eye to its utmost capacity with these colours, it passes with extraordinary avidity to the succeeding yellows. These intermingle in a pleasant harmony with the reds and scarlets, blood-reds and clarets, and then lead again to yellows. Now the eye has again become saturated, this time with the rich colouring, and has therefore, by the law of complementary colour, acquired a strong appetite for the greys and purples. These therefore assume an appearance of brilliancy that they would not have had without the preparation provided by their recently received complementary colour.

There are well-known scientific toys illustrating this law. A short word, printed in large red letters, is looked at for half a minute. The eyes are shut and an image of the same word appears, but the lettering is green. Many such experiments may be made in the open garden. The brilliant orange African Marigold has leaves of a rather dull green colour. But look steadily at the flowers for thirty seconds in sunshine and then look at the leaves. The leaves appear to be bright blue!

Even when a flower border is devoted to a special season, as mine is given to the time from mid-July to October, it cannot be kept fully furnished without resorting to various contrivances. One of these is the planting of certain things that will follow in season of bloom and that can be trained to take each other's places. Thus, each plant of *Gypsophila paniculata* when full grown covers a space a good four feet wide. On each side of it, within reasonable distance of the root, I plant Oriental Poppies. These make their leaf and flower growth in early summer when the Gypsophila is still in a young state. The Poppies will have died down by the time the Gypsophila is full grown and has covered them. After this has bloomed the seed-pods turn brown, and though a little of this colouring is not harmful in the autumn border, yet it is not wanted in such large patches. We therefore grow at its foot, or within easy reach, some of the trailing Nasturtiums and lead them up so that they cover the greater part of the brown seed-spray.

Delphiniums, which are indispensable for July, leave bare stems with quickly yellowing leafage when the flowers are over. We plant behind them the white Everlasting Pea, and again behind that Clematis Jackmanni. When the Delphiniums are over, the rapidly forming seed-pods are removed, the stems are cut down to just the right height, and the white Peas are trained over them. When the Peas go out of bloom in the middle of August, the Clematis is brought over. It takes some years for these two plants to become established; in the case of those I am describing the Pea has been four or five years planted and the Clematis seven. They cannot be hurried, indeed in my garden it is difficult to get the Clematis to grow at all. But good gardening means patience and dogged determination. There must be many failures and losses, but by always pushing on there will also be the reward of success. Those who do not know are apt to think that hardy flower gardening of the best kind is easy. It is not easy at all. It has taken me half a lifetime merely to find out

what is best worth doing, and a good slice out of another half to puzzle
out the ways of doing it.

🌹 COLOUR SCHEMES

What is meant by colour schemes is not merely the putting together
of flowers that look well side by side, but the disposition of the plants in
complete borders in such a manner that the whole effect together is
pictorial. It is done by means of progressive harmonies—harmonies
throughout being the guiding principle, contrasts the occasional exception. In the days of less enlightened gardening, about the middle of the
last century, anything that was aimed at in the way of colouring was
nearly always some violent contrast, or the putting together of crudely
coloured flowers; a pleasant harmony was scarcely thought of. Such a
combination as scarlet Geranium and blue Lobelia was then admired,
and so on with all the plants, excellent in themselves for better use, that
were then available—for garish effects were then deliberately aimed at;
now that more thoughtful ways prevail we try for something better than
garishness—we try for the nobler colour-quality of sumptuous splendour.
In acquiring this we get even more brilliancy; the eye and mind are filled
with a consciousness of delightful satisfaction of attainment instead of
their being, as it were, rudely attacked, and, in the case of the more
sensitive among us, actually shocked by a harsh crudity that has some of
the displeasing qualities of vulgarity.

Although the more reasonable and enjoyable way of putting flowers
together can be better done with the tender summer plants of stouter
habit, such as Dahlias, Cannas, Geraniums and the rest, it is well to apply
the same principle to borders of annuals. A double border so arranged
begins on the left with blue or bluish flowers with white, or both white
and a little pale yellow. There is some quality about blue that invites con-

[172]

trast as an alternative to harmony, for the scheme would be almost equally pictorial if, instead of merging the blues into yellow or pale pink, it led them to lilacs and purples; but in my own practice I prefer treating the pure blues with contrast of white or yellow. For the rest, the whole is in a harmonious sequence. Whether the blues reach the strong yellows through pink or pale yellow can be decided according to the preference or judgment of the operator, but when once the full yellows are reached, the colour progresses towards the strongest scarlets through orange and reds of lesser intensity. A double border arranged in some such way when seen from either end, or a single border that has lawn or other space in front from which it can be viewed, will in either case show the advantage of the definite colour-plan and the unity of intention. It will be a satisfying picture, with a gradual ascent to a culminating glory, instead of a jumbled incoherence of spottiness, with perhaps here and there a pretty incident, but no repose or pictorial effect.

GROUPING OF PLANTS IN POTS

The Geraniums would be very carefully assorted for colour; in one part of the scheme white and soft pink, in another the rosy scarlets, and elsewhere the salmon-reds, now so numerous and good. The last two groups might by degrees tone into the pure scarlets, of which the best I know and the most delightful in colour is Paul Crampel. The colour is pure and brilliant but not *cruel*. I can think of no other word that so well describes some scarlets of a harsh quality that gives discomfort rather than satisfaction to a sensitive colour-eye. Henry Jacoby is to me one of the cruel reds and has no place among my flowers. I have no desire to disparage a plant which is so general a favourite, but feel sure that its popularity is a good deal owing to the fact that the main gardening public is inclined rather to accept what is put before it than to take the trouble to search for something better. Although the colour of this Geranium is extremely vivid, a whole bed of it has a heavy appearance and is wanting in pictorial effect.

I have great pleasure in putting together Omphale, palest salmon-pink; Mrs. Laurence, a shade deeper; Mrs. Cannell, a salmon-scarlet approaching the quality of colour of Phlox Coquelicot, and leading these by degrees to the pure, good scarlet of Paul Crampel. A bed or clump or border planted with these, or varieties equivalent in colour, would be seen to have, in comparison with a bed of Henry Jacoby, a quite remarkable degree of life, brilliancy, beauty and interest. The colouring would be actually brighter and yet more kind and acceptable to the eye.

There are among Geraniums some of a raw magenta-pink that I regret to see in many gardens and that will certainly never be admitted into mine.

❧ COLOURS OF FLOWERS

I am always surprised at the vague, not to say reckless, fashion in which garden folk set to work to describe the colours of flowers, and at the way in which quite wrong colours are attributed to them. It is done in perfect good faith, and without the least consciousness of describing wrongly. In many cases it appears to be because the names of certain substances have been used conventionally or poetically to convey the idea of certain colours. And some of these errors are so old that they have acquired a kind of respectability, and are in a way accepted without challenge. When they are used about familiar flowers it does not occur to one to detect them, because one knows the flower and its true colour; but when the same old error is used in the description of a new flower, it is distinctly misleading. For instance, when we hear of golden buttercups, we know that it means bright-yellow buttercups; but in the case of a new flower, or one not generally known, surely it is better and more accurate to say bright yellow at once. Nothing is more frequent in plant catalogues than "bright golden yellow," when bright yellow is meant. Gold is not bright yellow. I find that a gold piece laid on a gravel path, or against a sandy bank, nearly matches it in colour; and I cannot think of any flower that matches or even approaches the true colour of gold, though something near it may be seen in the pollen-covered anthers of many flowers. A match for gold may more nearly be found among dying beech leaves, and some dark colours of straw or dry grass bents, but none of these when they match the gold are bright yellow. In literature it is quite another matter; when the poet or imaginative writer says, "a field of golden buttercups," or "a golden sunset," he is quite right, because he appeals to our artistic perception, and in such case only uses the word as an image of something that is rich and sumptuous and glowing.

The same irrelevance of comparison seems to run through all the colours. Flowers of a full, bright-blue colour are often described as of a "brilliant amethystine blue." Why amethystine? The amethyst, as we generally see it, is a stone of a washy purple colour, and though there are amethysts of a fine purple, they are not so often seen as the paler ones, and I have never seen one even faintly approaching a really blue colour. What, therefore, is the sense of likening a flower, such as a Delphinium, which is really of a splendid pure-blue colour, to the duller and totally different colour of a third-rate gem?

Another example of the same slip-slop is the term flame-coloured, and it is often preceded by the word "gorgeous." This contradictory mixture of terms is generally used to mean bright scarlet. When I look at a flame, whether of fire or candle, I see that the colour is a rather pale yellow, with a reddish tinge about its upper forks, and side wings often of a bluish white—no scarlet anywhere. The nearest approach to red is in the coals, not in the flame. In the case of the candle, the point of the wick is faintly red when compared with the flame, but about the flame there is no red whatever. A distant bonfire looks red at night, but I take it that the apparent redness is from seeing the flames through damp atmosphere, just as the harvest-moon looks red when it rises.

And the strange thing is that in all these cases the likeness to the unlike, and much less bright, colour is given with an air of conferring the highest compliment on the flower in question. It is as if, wishing to praise some flower of a beautiful blue, one called it a brilliant slate-roof blue. This sounds absurd, because it is unfamiliar, but the unsuitability of the comparison is scarcely greater than in the examples just quoted.

It seems most reasonable in describing the colour of flowers to look out for substances whose normal colour shows but little variation—such, for example, as sulphur. The colour of sulphur is nearly always the same. Citron, lemon, and canary are useful colour-names, indicating different strengths of pure pale yellow, inclining towards a tinge of the palest green. Gentian-blue is a useful word, bringing to mind the piercingly powerful hue of the Gentianella. So also is turquoise-blue, for the stone has little variety of shade, and the colour is always of the same type. Forget-me-not blue is also a good word, meaning the colour of the native water Forget-me-not. Sky-blue is a little vague, though it has come by the "crystallising" force of usage to stand for a blue rather pale than full, and not far from that of the Forget-me-not; indeed, I seem to remember written passages in which the colours of flower and firmament were used reciprocally, the one in describing the other. Cobalt is a word sometimes used, but more often misused, for only water-colour painters know just what it represents, and it is of little use, as it so rarely occurs among flowers.

Crimson is a word to beware of; it covers such a wide extent of ground, and is used so carelessly in plant-catalogues, that one cannot know whether it stands for a rich blood colour or for a malignant magenta. For the latter class of colour the term amaranth, so generally used in French plant-lists, is extremely useful, both as a definition and a warning. Salmon is an excellent colour-word, copper is also useful, the two covering a limited range of beautiful colouring of the utmost value. Blood-red is also accurately descriptive. Terra-cotta is useful but indefinite, as it may mean anything between brick-red and buff. Red-lead, if it would be accepted as a colour-word, would be useful, denoting the shades of colour between the strongest orange and the palest scarlet, frequent in the lightest of the Oriental Poppies. Amber is a misleading word, for who is to know when it means the transparent amber, whose colour approaches that of resin, or the pale, almost opaque, dull-yellow kind. And what is meant by coral-red? It is the red of the old-fashioned dull-scarlet coral, or of the pink kind more recently in favour.

The terms bronze and smoke may well be used in their place, as in describing or attempting to describe the wonderful colouring of such flowers as Spanish Iris, and the varieties of Iris of the *squalens* section. But often in describing a flower a reference to texture much helps and strengthens the colour-word. I have often described the modest little *Iris tuberosa* as a flower made of green satin and black velvet. The green portion is only slightly green, but is entirely green satin, and the black of the velvet is barely black, but is quite black-velvet-like. The texture of the flower of *ornithogalum nutans* is silver satin, neither very silvery nor very satin-like, and yet so nearly suggesting the texture of both that the words may well be used in speaking of it. Indeed, texture plays so important a part in the appearance of colour-surface, that one can hardly think of colour without also thinking of texture. A piece of black satin and a piece of black velvet may be woven of the same batch of material, but when the satin is finished and the velvet cut, the appearance is often so dissimilar that they may look quite different in colour. A working painter is never happy if you give him an oil-colour pattern to match in distemper; he must have it of the same texture, or he will not undertake to get it like.

What a wonderful range of colouring there is in black alone to a trained colour-eye! There is the dull brown-black of soot, and the velvety brown-black of the bean-flower's blotch; to my own eye, I have never found anything so entirely black in a natural product as the patch on the lower petals of *Iris iberica*. Is it not Ruskin who says of Velasquez, that

[177]

there is more colour in his black than in many another painter's whole palette? The blotch of the bean-flower appears black at first, till you look at it close in the sunlight, and then you see its rich velvety texture, so nearly like some of the brown-velvet markings on butterflies' wings. And the same kind of rich colour and texture occurs again on some of the tough flat half-round funguses, marked with shaded rings, that grow out of old posts, and that I always enjoy as lessons of lovely colour-harmony of grey and brown and black.

Much to be regretted is the disuse of the old word murrey, now only employed in heraldry. It stands for a dull red-purple, such as appears in the flower of the Virginian Allspice, and in the native Hound's-tongue, and often in seedling Auriculas. A fine strong-growing border Auricula was given to me by my valued friend the Curator of the Trinity College Botanic Garden, Dublin, to which he had given the excellently descriptive name, "Old Murrey."

Sage-green is a good colour-word, for, winter or summer, the sage-leaves change but little. Olive-green is not so clear, though it has come by use to stand for a brownish green, like the glass of a wine-bottle held up to the light, but perhaps bottle-green is the better word. And it is not clear what part or condition of the olive is meant, for the ripe fruit is nearly black, and the tree in general, and the leaf in detail, are of a cool-grey colour. Perhaps the colour-word is taken from the colour of the unripe fruit pickled in brine, as we see them on the table. Grass-green any one may understand, but I am always puzzled by apple-green. Apples are of so many different greens, to say nothing of red and yellow; and as for pea-green, I have no idea what it means.

I notice in plant-lists the most reckless and indiscriminate use of the words purple, violet, mauve, lilac, and lavender, and as they are all related, I think they should be used with the greater caution. I should say that mauve and lilac cover the same ground; the word mauve came into use within my recollection. It is French for mallow, and the flower of the wild plant may stand as the type of what the word means. Lavender stands for a colder or bluer range of pale purples, with an inclination to grey; it is a useful word, because the whole colour of the flower spike varies so little. Violet stands for the dark garden violet, and I always think of the grand colour of *Iris reticulata* as an example of a rich violet-purple. But purple equally stands for this, and for many shades redder.

Snow-white is very vague. There is nearly always so much blue about the colour of snow, from its crystalline surface and partial transparency, and the texture is so unlike that of any kind of flower, that the comparison is scarcely permissible. I take it that the use of "snow-white" is, like that of "golden-yellow," more symbolical than descriptive, meaning any white that gives an impression of purity. Nearly all white flowers are yellowish-white, and the comparatively few that are bluish-white, such, for example, as *Omphalodes linifolia*, are of a texture so different from snow that one cannot compare them at all. I should say that most white flowers are near the colour of chalk; for although the word chalky-white has been used in rather a contemptuous way, the colour is really a very beautiful warm white, but by no means an intense white. The flower that always looks to me the whitest is that of *Iberis sempervirens*. The white is dead and hard, like a piece of glazed stoneware, quite without play or variation and hence uninteresting.

GARDENS OF SPECIAL COLOURING

It is extremely interesting to work out gardens in which some special colouring predominates, and to those who, by natural endowment or careful eye-cultivation, possess or have acquired what artists understand by an eye for colour, it opens out a whole new range of garden delights.

Arrangements of this kind are sometimes attempted, for occasionally I hear of a garden for blue plants, or a white garden, but I think such ideas are but rarely worked out with the best aims. I have in mind a whole series of gardens of restricted colouring, though I have not, alas, either room or means enough to work them out for myself, and have to be satisfied with an all-too-short length of double border for a grey scheme. But, besides my small grey garden I badly want others, and especially a gold garden, a blue garden, and a green garden; though the number of these desires might easily be multiplied.

It is a curious thing that people will sometimes spoil some garden project for the sake of a word. For instance, a blue garden, for beauty's sake, may be hungering for a group of white Lilies, or for something of palest lemon-yellow, but it is not allowed to have it because it is called the blue garden, and there must be no flowers in it but blue flowers. I can see no sense in this; it seems to me like fetters foolishly self-imposed. Surely the business of the blue garden is to be beautiful as well as to be blue. My own idea is that it should be beautiful first, and then just as blue as may be consistent with its best possible beauty. Moreover, any experienced colourist knows that the blues will be more telling—more purely blue—by the juxtaposition of rightly placed complementary colour.

The Grey garden is so called because most of its plants have grey foliage, and all the carpeting and bordering plants are grey or whitish. The flowers are white, lilac, purple, and pink. It is a garden mostly for August, because August is the time when the greater number of suitable plants are in bloom, but a Grey garden could also be made for September, or even October, because of the number of Michaelmas Daisies that can be brought into use.

The Gold garden is chosen for the middle, partly because it contains the greater number of permanent shrubs and is bright and cheerful all the year round, and partly because it is the best preparation, according to natural colour-law, for the enjoyment of the compartments on either side. It is supposed that the house is a little way away to the north, with such a garden-scheme close to it as may best suit its style and calibre. Then I would have a plantation of shrubs and trees. The shade and solidity of this would rest and refresh the eye and mind, making them the more ready to enjoy the colour garden. Suddenly entering the Gold garden, even on the dullest day, will be like coming into sunshine. Through the shrub-wood there is also a path to right and left parallel to the long axis of the colour garden, with paths turning south at its two ends, joining the ends of the colour-garden paths. This has been taken into account in arranging the sequence of the compartments.

The hedges that back the borders and form the partitions are for the most part of Yew, grown and clipped to a height of seven feet. But in the case of the Gold garden, where the form is larger and more free than in the others, there is no definite hedge, but a planting of unclipped larger gold Hollies, and the beautiful Golden Plane, so cut back and regulated as to keep within the desired bounds. This absence of a stiff hedge gives more freedom of aspect and a better cohesion with the shrub-wood.

In the case of the Grey garden the hedge is of Tamarisk (*Tamarix gallica*), whose feathery grey-green is in delightful harmony with the other foliage greys. Where this joins the Gold garden the hedge is double, for it must be of gold Holly on one side and of Tamarisk on the other. At the entrances and partition where the path passes, the hedge shrubs are allowed to grow higher, and are eventually trained to form arches over the path.

In the Gold and Green gardens, the shrubs, which form the chief part of the planting, are shown as they will be after some years' growth. It is best to have them so from the first. If, in order to fill the space at once, several are planted where one only should eventually stand, the extra ones being removed later, the one left probably does not stand quite right. I strongly counsel the placing of them singly at first, and that until they have grown the space should be filled with temporary plants. Of these, in the Gold garden, the most useful will be *Œnothera lamarcki- ana*, *Verbascum olympicum*, and *V. pholomoides*, with more Spanish Broom till the gold Hollies are grown; and yellow-flowered annuals, such as the several kinds of *Chrysanthemum coronarium*, both single and double, and *Coreopsis Drummondi*; also a larger quantity of African

Marigolds, the pale primrose and the lemon-coloured. The fine tall yellow Snapdragons will also be invaluable. Flowers of a deep orange colour, such as the orange African Marigold, so excellent for their own use, are here out of place, only those of pale and middle yellow being suitable.

In such a garden it will be best to have, next the path, either a whole edging of dwarf, gold-variegated Box-bushes about eighteen inches to two feet high, or a mixed planting of these and small bushes of gold-variegated Euonymus clipped down to not much over two feet. The edge next the path would be kept trimmed to a line.

The strength of colour and degree of variation is so great that it is well worth going to a nursery to pick out all these gold-variegated plants. It is not enough to tell the gardener to get them. There should be fervour on the part of the garden's owner such as will take him on a gold-plant pilgrimage to all good nurseries within reach, or even to some rather out of reach. No good gardening comes of not taking pains. All good gardening is the reward of well-directed and strongly sustained effort.

Where, in the Gold garden, the paths meet and swing round in a circle, there may be some accentuating ornament—a sundial, a stone vase for flowers, or a tank for a yellow Water-lily. If a sundial, and there should be some incised lettering, do not have the letters gilt because it is the Gold garden; the colour and texture of gilding are quite out of place. If there is a tank, do not have goldfish; their colour is quite wrong. Never hurt the garden for the sake of the tempting word.

The word "gold" in itself is, of course, an absurdity; no growing leaf or flower has the least resemblance to the colour of gold. But the word may be used because it has passed into the language with a commonly accepted meaning.

I have always felt a certain hesitation in using the free-growing perennial Sunflowers. For one thing, the kinds with the running roots are difficult to keep in check, and their yearly transplantation among other established perennials is likely to cause disturbance and injury to their neighbours. Then, in so many neglected gardens they have been let run wild, surviving when other plants have been choked, that, half uncon-sciously, one has come to hold them cheap and unworthy of the best use. I take it that my own impression is not mine alone, for often when I have been desired to do planting-plans for flower borders, I have been asked not to put in any of these Sunflowers because "they are so common."

But nothing is "common" in the sense of base or unworthy if it is rightly used, and it seems to me that this Gold garden is just the place where these bright autumn flowers may be employed to great advantage.

The golden Planes, where the path comes in from the north, are of course deciduous, and it might be well to have gold Hollies again at the back of these, or gold Yews, to help the winter effect.

Perhaps the Grey garden is seen at its best by reaching it through the orange borders. Here the eye becomes filled and saturated with the strong red and yellow colouring. This filling with the strong, rich colour-ing has the natural effect of making the eye eagerly desirous for the complementary colour, so that, standing by the inner Yew arch and sud-denly turning to look into the Grey garden, the effect is surprisingly— quite astonishingly—luminous and refreshing. One never knew before how vividly bright Ageratum could be, or Lavender or Nepeta; even the grey-purple of Echinops appears to have more positive colour than one's expectation would assign to it. The purple of the Clematises of the Jack-manii class becomes piercingly brilliant, while the grey and glaucous foliage looks strangely cool and clear.

[A plan would show] the disposition of the plants, with grey-white edg-ing of *Cineraria maritima*, Stachys and Santolina. There are groups of Lav-ender with large-flowered Clematises placed so that they may be trained close to them and partly over them. There are the monumental forms of the taller Yuccas, *Y. gloriosa* and its variety *recurva* towards the far angles, and, nearer the front the free-blooming *Yucca filamentosa* of smaller size. The flower-colouring is of purple, pink and white. Besides the Yuccas, the other white flowers are *Lilium longiflorum* and *Lilium candidum*, the clear white Achillea The Pearl and the grey-white clouds of *Gypsophila paniculata*. The pink flowers are Sutton's Godetia Double Rose, sown in place early in May, the beautiful clear pink Hollyhock Pink Beauty, and the pale pink Double Soapwort. Clematis and white Everlasting Pea are planted so that they can be trained to cover the Gypsophila when its bloom is done and the seed-pods are turning brown. As soon as it loses its grey colouring the flowering tops are cut off, and the Pea and Clematis, already brought near, are trained over. When the Gypsophila is making its strong growth in May, the shoots are regulated and supported by some stiff branching spray that is stuck among it. A little later this is quite hidden, but it remains as a firm sub-structure when the top of the Gypsophila is cut back and the other plants are brought over.

Elymus is the blue-green Lyme Grass, a garden form of the handsome blue-leaved grass that grows on the seaward edges of many of our sea-shore sandhills. The Soapwort next to it is the double form of *Saponaria officinalis*, found wild in many places.

Of Ageratum, two kinds are used—a brightly coloured one of the dwarf kinds for places near the front, where it tells as a close mass of colour, and the tall *A. Mexicanum* for filling up further back in the border, where it shows as a diffuse purple cloud. The Nepeta is the good garden Catmint (*N. Mussini*). Its normal flowering time is June, but it is cut half back, removing the first bloom, by the middle of the month, when it at once makes new flowering shoots.

Now, after the grey plants, the Gold garden looks extremely bright and sunny. A few minutes suffice to fill the eye with the yellow influence, and then we pass to the Blue garden, where there is another delightful shock of eye-pleasure. The brilliancy and purity of colour are almost incredible. Surely no blue flowers were ever so blue before! That is the impression received. For one thing, all the blue flowers used, with the exception of Eryngium and *Clematis davidiana*, are quite pure blues; these two are grey-blues. There are no purple-blues, such as the bluest of the Campanulas and the perennial Lupines; they would not be admissible. With the blues are a few white and palest yellow flowers; the foam-white *Clematis recta*, a delightful foil to Delphinium Belladonna; white perennial Lupine with an almond-like softness of white; *Spiræa Aruncus*, another foam-coloured flower. Then milk-white Tree Lupine, in its carefully decreed place near the bluish foliage of Rue and Yucca. Then there is the tender citron of Lupine Somerset and the full canary of the tall yellow Snapdragon, the diffused pale yellow of the soft plumy Thalictrum and the strong canary of *Lilium szovitzianum*, with white Everlasting Pea and white Hollyhock at the back. White-striped Maize grows up to cover the space left empty by the Delphiniums when their bloom is over, and pots of *Plumbago capense* are dropped in to fill empty spaces. One group of this is trained over the bluish-leaved *Clematis recta*, which goes out of flower with the third week of July.

Yuccas, both of the large and small kinds, are also used in the Blue garden, and white Lilies, *candidum* and *longiflorum*. There is foliage both of glaucous and of bright green colour, besides an occasional patch of the silvery *Eryngium giganteum*. At the front edge are the two best Funkias, *F. grandiflora*, with leaves of bright yellow-green, and *F. Sieboldi*, whose leaves are glaucous. The variegated Coltsfoot is a valuable edge-plant where the yellowish white of its bold parti-colouring is in place, and I find good use for the variegated form of the handsome Grass *Glyceria* or *Poa aquatica*. Though this is a plant whose proper place is in wet ground, it will accommodate itself to the flower border, but it is well to keep it on the side away from the sun. It harmonises well in colour with the Coltsfoot; as a garden plant it is of the same class as the old Ribbon Grass, but is very much better. The great white-striped Japanese grass, *Eulalia japonica striata* is planted behind the Delphiniums at the angles, and groups well with the Maize just in front.

From the Blue garden, passing eastward, we come to the Green garden. Shrubs of bright and deep green colouring and polished leaf-surface predominate. Here are green Aucubas and Skimmias, with *Ruscus racemosus*, the beautiful Alexandrian or Victory Laurel, and more polished

ON GARDENING

foliage of *Acanthus, Funkia, Asarum, Lilium candidum* and *longiflorum,* and *Iris fœtidissima.* Then feathery masses of paler green, Male Fern and Lady Fern and *Myrrhis odorata,* the handsome fern-like Sweet Cicely of old English gardens. In the angles are again Eulalias, but these are the variety *zebrina* with the leaves barred across with yellow.

In the Green garden the flowers are fewer and nearly all white—Campanulas *latifolia* and *persicifolia,* Lilies, Tulips, Foxgloves, Snapdragons, Peonies, Hellebores—giving just a little bloom for each season to accompany the general scheme of polished and fern-like foliage. A little bloom of palest yellow shows in the front in May and June, with the flowers of Uvularia and Epimedium. But the Green garden, for proper development, should be on a much larger scale.

🔹 DELPHINIUMS AND LILIES

In "Wood and Garden," I explained rather at length the way I thought best of arranging the sequence of colour in a large border of hardy flowers, namely, in a gradual progression of colour-harmony in the case of the red and yellow flowers, whose numbers preponderate among those we have to choose from; but saying that as far as my own understanding of the colour-requirements of flowers went, it was better to treat blues with contrasts rather than with harmonies. And I had observed, when at one point, from a little distance, I could see in company the pure deep orange of the Herring-Lilies (*Lilium croceum*) with the brilliant blue of some full-blue Delphiniums, how splendid, although audacious, the mixture was, and immediately noted it, so as to take full advantage of the observation when planting-time came. In the autumn, two of the large patches of Lilies were therefore taken up and grouped in front of, and partly among, the Delphiniums; and even though neither had come to anything like full strength in the past summer (the first year after removal), yet I could see already how grandly they went together, and how well worth doing and recommending such a mixture was. The Delphiniums should be of a full deep-blue colour, not perhaps the very darkest, and not any with a purple shade.

❦ RETAINING WALLS AND THEIR PLANTING

As in arranging flower-borders, it is well to place the plants in groups of a fair quantity of one thing at a time; and, in the case of small plants, such as thrift or London Pride, to put them fairly close together. If they are spaced apart at even distances they look like buttons; but even when this has been done, either inadvertently or by an unpractised hand, it is easily remedied by adding a few plants to make the group hang together. Though it is advised that there should be no border at the foot of a planted dry wall, yet it looks well to have its junction with the grass or gravel broken here and there by some plant that enjoys such a place, as, for example, *Iris stylosa* or Plumbago larpentae in a sunny aspect, or hardy ferns and Welsh poppy and small pansies in a shady one. It is well also to make careful combinations of colour, for they not only give the prettiest pictures, but also that restful feeling of some one idea completely presented that is so desirable, so easy to accomplish, and yet so rarely seen in gardens. As an example, on a sunny wall there may be a colour-scheme of grey with purple of various shades, white and pale pink, composed of dwarf lavender, nepeta, aubrietia, cerastium, Helianthemums of the kinds that have grey leaves and white and pale pink bloom, rock pinks, stachys, the dwarf artemisias and Achillea umbrella, and in the border above, yuccas, lavender, rosemary, the larger euphorbias, China roses, phlomis and santolina with white and pink snapdragons. Phlomis and santolina both have yellow flowers, but a slight break of yellow would harm the effect but little during their time of bloom, while both are of year-long value for their good grey foliage; moreover, it is easy to remove the santolina bloom, which comes on shoots that are quite separate from

[187]

the foliage. If it were quite a high wall, larger plants could be used, especially in the upper half. Yuccas are grand coming out of rocky chinks high up, and gypsophila in great clouds, and centranthus (the red valerian) in big bushy masses.

On a shady wall there would be a preponderance of good greenery of hardy ferns, male fern and hart's-tongue, with the smaller ferns, woodsia, cheilanthes, adiantum and allosorus, with Welsh poppies, corydalis, mimulus and the smaller alpine bell-flowers, such as the lovely little Campanula pusilla, both blue and white, and the rather larger carpatica and eriocarpa. Then if the shady wall was of good size there would be columbines in quantity, white foxgloves and mulleins growing with splendid vigour and enjoying the cool root-run among the stones.

PLANTING FOR WINTER COLOUR

It would add greatly to the enjoyment of many country places if some portions were planted with evergreens expressly for winter effect. Some region on the outskirts of the garden, and between it and woodland, would be the most desirable. If well done the sense of wintry discomfort would disappear, for nearly all the growing things would be at their best, and even in summer, shrubs and plants can do no more than this. In summer, too, it would be good to see, for the green things would have such an inter-planting of free Roses, Jasmines, Clematis, Honeysuckles, Forsythia, and so on, as would make charming incidents of flower-beauty.

The place for this winter walk should be sheltered from the north and east. I have such a place in my mind's eye, where, beyond the home garden and partly wooded old shrubbery, there is a valley running up into a fir-wooded hill. The path goes up the hillside diagonally, with a very gentle gradient. In the cooler, lower portion there would be Rhododendrons and Kalmias, with lower growths of Skimmia and Gaultheria. Close to the path, on the less sunny side, would be Lent Hellebores and the delightful winter greenery of Epimedium. Then in full sun *Andromeda japonica,* and on the shelter side *Andromeda floribunda.* Both of these hard and rather brittle-wooded shrubs belong to the group properly named *Pieris,* and form dense bushes four or more feet high. At their foot would be the lower-growing Andromedas of the *Leucothoë* section, with lissome branches of a more willow-like character. These make a handsome ground-carpeting from one to two feet high, beautiful at all seasons—the leaves in winter tinted or marbled with red. Portions of the cooler side would also have fringes of Hartstongue and Polypody, both winter ferns. Then, as the path rose into more direct sunlight, there would be Cistuses—in all mild winter days giving off their strong, cordial scent—and the dwarf Rhododendrons. Behind the Cistuses would be White Broom, finely green-stemmed in winter. There would even be shrubs in flower; the thick-set yellowish bloom of Witch Hazel (*Hamamelis*) and the bright yellow of *Jasminum nudiflorum.* Then groups of Junipers, and all the ground carpeted with Heath, and so to the upper Firwood. Then, after the comforting greenery of the lower region, the lovely colour of distant winter landscape would be intensely enjoyable; for the greys and purples of the leafless woodland of middle distance have a beauty that no summer landscape can show. In clear weather the further distances have tints of an extraordinary purity, while the more frequent days of slightly distant haze have another kind of beautiful mystery.

❀ GARDENS IN FOREST CLEARINGS

The especial charm of making a flower garden in a forest clearing is that the wilful tribes of Nature can be absorbed into the new population, where they will still flaunt their wild and brilliant graces. In such gardens the outlying parts are likely never to be more brilliant than in autumn, when the gold of the furze is glittering everywhere among the darker hues of heather and the fading greens of bracken. Furze is a great ally to the garden colourist, for the large and early varieties are followed by others that are small and late. As the old and pleasant saying runs, gorse is out of bloom only when kissing's out of fashion.

The sweet scents of a garden are by no means the least of its many delights. Even January brings *Chimonanthus fragrans,* one of the sweetest and strongest scented of the year's blooms—little half-transparent yellowish bells on an otherwise naked-looking wall shrub. They have no stalks, but if they are floated in a shallow dish of water, they last well for several days, and give off a powerful fragrance in a room.

During some of the warm days that nearly always come towards the end of February, if one knows where to look in some sunny, sheltered corner of a hazel copse, there will be sure to be some Primroses, and the first scent of the year's first Primrose is no small pleasure. The garden Primroses soon follow, and, meanwhile, in all open winter weather there have been Czar Violets and *Iris stylosa,* with its delicate scent, faintly violet-like, but with a dash of tulip. *Iris reticulata* is also sweet, with a still stronger perfume of the violet character. But of all Irises I know, the sweetest to smell is a later blooming one, *I. graminea.* Its small purple flowers are almost hidden among the thick mass of grassy foliage which rises high above the bloom; but they are worth looking for, for the sake of the sweet and rather penetrating scent, which is exactly like that of a perfectly-ripened plum.

All the scented flowers of the Primrose tribe are delightful—Primrose, Polyanthus, Auricula, Cowslip. The actual sweetness is most apparent in the Cowslip; in the Auricula it has a pungency, and at the same time a kind of veiled mystery, that accords with the clouded and curiously-blended colourings of many of the flowers.

Sweetbriar is one of the strongest of the year's early scents, and closely following is the woodland incense of the Larch, both freely given off and far-wafted, as is also that of the hardy Daphnes. The first quarter of the year also brings the bloom of most of the deciduous Magnolias, all with a fragrance nearly allied to that of the large one that blooms late in summer, but not so strong and heavy.

The sweetness of a sun-baked bank of Wallflower belongs to April. Daffodils, lovely as they are, must be classed among flowers of rather rank smell, and yet it is welcome, for it means spring-time, with its own charm and its glad promise of the wealth of summer bloom that is soon to come. The scent of the Jonquil, Poeticus, and Polyanthus sections are best, Jonquil perhaps best of all, for it is without the rather coarse scent of the Trumpets and Nonsuch, and also escapes the penetrating lusciousness of *poeticus* and *Tazetta*, which in the south of Europe is exaggerated in the case of *tazetta* into something distinctly unpleasant.

What a delicate refinement there is in the scent of the wild Wood-Violet; it is never overdone. It seems to me to be quite the best of all the violet-scents, just because of its temperate quality. It gives exactly enough, and never that perhaps-just-a-trifle-too-much that may often be noticed about a bunch of frame-Violets, and that also in the south is intensified to a degree that is distinctly undesirable. For just as colour may be strengthened to a painful glare, and sound may be magnified to a torture, so even a sweet scent may pass its appointed bounds and become an overpoweringly evil smell. Even in England several of the Lilies, whose smell is delicious in open-air wafts, cannot be borne in a room. In the south of Europe a Tuberose cannot be brought indoors, and even at home I remember one warm wet August how a plant of Balm of Gilead (*Cedronella triphylla*) had its always powerful but usually agreeably-aromatic smell so much exaggerated that it smelt exactly like coal-gas! A brother in Jamaica writes of the large white Jasmine: "It does not do to bring it indoors here; the scent is too strong. One day I thought there was a dead rat under the floor (a thing which did happen once), and behold, it was a glassful of fresh white Jasmine that was the offender!"

ON GARDENING

While on this less pleasant part of the subject, I cannot help thinking of the horrible smell of the Dragon Arum; and yet how fitting an accompaniment it is to the plant, for if ever there was a plant that looked wicked and repellent, it is this; and yet, like Medusa, it has its own kind of fearful beauty. In this family the smell seems to accompany the appearance, and to diminish in unpleasantness as the flower increases in amiability; for in our native wild Arum the smell, though not exactly nice, is quite innocuous, and in the beautiful white Arum or *Calla* of our greenhouses there is as little scent as a flower can well have, especially one of such large dimensions. In Fungi the bad smell is nearly always an indication of poisonous nature, so that it would seem to be given as a warning. But it has always been a matter of wonder to me why the root of the harmless and friendly Laurustinus should have been given a particularly odious smell—a smell I would rather not attempt to describe. On moist warmish days in mid-seasons I have sometimes had a whiff of the same unpleasantness from the bushes themselves; others of the same tribe have it in a much lesser degree. There is a curious smell about the yellow roots of Berberis, not exactly nasty, and a strong odour, not really offensive, but that I personally dislike, about the root of *Chrysanthemum maximum*. On the other hand, I always enjoy digging up, dividing, and replanting the *Asarums,* both the common European and the American kinds; their roots have a pleasant and most interesting smell, a good deal like mild pepper and ginger mixed, but more strongly aromatic. The same class of smell, but much fainter, and always reminding me of very good and delicate pepper, I enjoy in the flowers of the perennial Lupines. The only other hardy flowers I can think of whose smell is distinctly offensive are *Lilium pyrenaicum,* smelling like a mangy dog, and some of the *Schizanthus,* that are redolent of dirty hen-house.

There is a class of scent that, though it can neither be called sweet nor aromatic, is decidedly pleasing and interesting. Such is that of Bracken and other Fern-fronds, Ivy-leaves, Box-bushes, Vine-blossom, Elder-flowers, and Fig-leaves. There are the sweet scents that are wholly delightful—most of the Roses, Honeysuckle, Primrose, Cowslip, Mignonette, Pink, Carnation, Heliotrope, Lily of the Valley, and a host of others; then there is a class of scent that is intensely powerful, and gives an impression almost of intemperance or voluptuousness, such as Magnolia, Tuberose, Gardenia, Stephanotis, and Jasmine; it is strange that these all have white flowers of thick leathery texture. In strongest contrast to these are the sweet, wholesome, wind-wafted scents of clover-field, of bean-field, and of new-mown hay, and the soft honey-scent of sun-baked heather, and of a buttercup meadow in April. Still more delicious is the wind-swept sweetness of a wood of Larch or of Scotch Fir, and the delicate perfume of young-leaved Birch, or the heavier scent of the flowering Lime. Out on the moorlands, besides the sweet heather-scent, is that of flowering Broom and Gorse and of the Bracken, so like the first smell of the sea as you come near it after a long absence.

How curiously scents of flowers and leaves fall into classes—often one comes upon related smells running into one another in not necessarily related plants. There is a kind of scent that I sometimes meet with about clumps of Brambles, a little like the waft of a Fir wood; it occurs again (quite naturally) in the first taste of blackberry jam, and then turns up again in Sweet Sultan. It is allied to the smell of the dying Strawberry leaves.

The smell of the Primrose occurs again in a much stronger and ranker form in the root-stock, and the same thing happens with the Violets and Pansies; in Violets the plant-smell is pleasant, though without the high perfume of the flower; but the smell of an overgrown bed of Pansy-plants is rank to offensiveness.

Perhaps the most delightful of all flower scents are those whose tender and delicate quality makes one wish for just a little more. Such a scent is that of Apple-blossom, and of some small Pansies, and of the wild Rose and the Honeysuckle. Among Roses alone the variety and degree of sweet scent seems almost infinite. To me the sweetest of all is the Provence, the old Cabbage Rose of our gardens. When something approaching this appears, as it frequently does, among the hybrid perpetuals, I always greet it as the real sweet Rose smell. One expects every Rose to be fragrant, and it is a disappointment to find that such a beautiful flower as Baroness Rothschild is wanting in the sweet scent that would be the fitting complement of its incomparable form, and to perceive in so handsome a Rose as Malmaison a heavy smell of decidedly bad quality. But such cases are not frequent.

There is much variety in the scent of the Tea-Roses, the actual tea flavour being strongest in the Dijon class. Some have a powerful scent that is very near that of a ripe Nectarine; of this the best example I know is the old rose Goubault. The half-double red Gloire de Rosamène has a delightful scent of a kind that is rare among Roses. It has a good deal of the quality of that mysterious and delicious smell given off by the dying strawberry leaves, aromatic, pungent, and delicately refined, searching and powerful, and yet subtle and elusive—the best sweet smell of all the year. One cannot have it for the seeking; it comes as it will—a scent that is sad as a forecast of the inevitable certainty of the flower-year's waning, and yet sweet with the promise of its timely new birth.

Sometimes I have met with a scent of somewhat the same mysterious and aromatic kind when passing near a bank clothed with the great St. John's Wort. As this also occurs in early autumn, I suppose it to be occasioned by the decay of some of the leaves. And there is a small yellow-flowered Potentilla that has a scent of the same character, but always freely and willingly given off—a humble-looking little plant, well worth growing for its sweetness, that much to my regret I have lost.

I observe that when a Rose exists in both single and double form the scent is increased in the double beyond the proportion that one would expect. *Rosa lucida* in the ordinary single state has only a very slight scent; in the lovely double form it is very sweet, and has acquired somewhat of the Moss-rose smell. The wild Burnet-rose (R. *spinosissima*) has very little smell; but the Scotch Briars, its garden relatives, have quite a powerful fragrance, a pale flesh-pink kind, whose flowers are very round and globe-like, being the sweetest of all.

But of all the sweet scents of bush or flower, the ones that give me the greatest pleasure are those of the aromatic class, where they seem to have a wholesome resinous or balsamic base, with a delicate perfume added. When I pick and crush in my hand a twig of Bay, or brush against a bush of Rosemary, or tread upon a tuft of Thyme, or pass through incense-laden brakes of Cistus, I feel that here is all that is best and purest and most refined, and nearest to poetry, in the range of faculty of the sense of smell.

The scents of all these sweet shrubs, many of them at home in dry and rocky places in far-away lower latitudes, recall in a way far more distinct than can be done by a mere mental effort of recollection, rambles of years ago in many a lovely southern land—in the islands of the Greek Archipelago, beautiful in form, and from a distance looking bare and arid, and yet with a scattered growth of lowly, sweet-smelling bush and herb, so that as you move among them every plant seems full of sweet sap or aromatic gum, and as you tread the perfumed carpet the whole air is scented; then of dusky groves of tall Cyprus and Myrtle, forming mysterious shadowy woodland temples that unceasingly offer up an incense of their own surpassing fragrance, and of cooler hollows in the same lands and in the nearer Orient, where the Oleander grows like the willow of the north, and where the Sweet Bay throws up great tree-like suckers of surprising strength and vigour. It is only when one has seen it grow like this that one can appreciate the full force of the old Bible simile. Then to find oneself standing (while still on earth) in a grove of giant Myrtles fifteen feet high, is like having a little chink of the door of heaven opened, as if to show a momentary glimpse of what good things may be beyond!

Among the sweet shrubs from the nearer of these southern regions, one of the best for English gardens is *Cistus laurifolius*. Its wholesome, aromatic sweetness is freely given off, even in winter. In this, as in its near

ON GARDENING

relative, *C. ladaniferus*, the scent seems to come from the gummy surface, and not from the body of the leaf. *Caryopteris Mastacanthus*, the
Mastic plant, from China, one of the few shrubs that flower in autumn,
has strongly-scented woolly leaves, something like turpentine, but more
refined. *Ledum palustre* has a delightful scent when its leaves are
bruised. The wild Bog-myrtle, so common in Scotland, has almost the
sweetness of the true Myrtle, as has also the broad-leaved North American kind, and the Sweet Fern-bush (*Comptonia asplenifolia*) from the
same country. The myrtle-leaved Rhododendron is a dwarf shrub of neat
habit, whose bruised leaves have also a myrtle-like smell, though it is less
strong than in the Gales. I wonder why the leaves of nearly all the hardy
aromatic shrubs are of a hard, dry texture; the exceptions are so few that
it seems to be a law.

If my copse were some acres larger I should like nothing better than to
make a good-sized clearing, lying out to the sun, and to plant it with
these aromatic bushes and herbs. The main planting should be of Cistus
and Rosemary and Lavender, and for the shadier edges the Myrtle-leaved
Rhododendron, and *Ledum palustre*, and the three Bog-myrtles. Then
again in the sun would be Hyssop and Catmint, and Lavender-cotton and
Southernwood, with others of the scented Artemisias, and Sage and Marjoram. All the ground would be carpeted with Thyme and Basil and
others of the dwarfer sweet-herbs. There would be no regular paths, but
it would be so planted that in most parts one would have to brush up
against the sweet bushes, and sometimes push through them, as one does
on the thinner-clothed of the mountain slopes of southern Italy.

Among the many wonders of the vegetable world are the flowers that
hang their heads and seem to sleep in the daytime, and that awaken as
the sun goes down, and live their waking life at night. And those that are
most familiar in our gardens have powerful perfumes, except the Evening Primrose (*Œnothera*), which has only a milder sweetness. It is vain
to try and smell the night-given scent in the daytime; it is either withheld
altogether, or some other smell, quite different, and not always pleasant,

[196]

is there instead. I have tried hard in daytime to get a whiff of the night sweetness of *Nicotiana affinis*, but can only get hold of something that smells like a horse! Some of the best of the night-scents are those given by the Stocks and Rockets. They are sweet in the hand in the daytime, but the best of the sweet scent seems to be like a thin film on the surface. It does not do to smell them too vigorously, for, especially in Stocks and Wallflowers, there is a strong, rank, cabbage-like under-smell. But in the sweetness given off so freely in the summer evening there is none of this; then they only give their very best.

But of all the family, the finest fragrance comes from the small annual Night-scented Stock (*Matthiola bicornis*), a plant that in daytime is almost ugly; for the leaves are of a dull-grey colour, and the flowers are small and also dull-coloured, and they are closed and droop and look unhappy. But when the sun has set the modest little plant seems to come to life; the grey foliage is almost beautiful in its harmonious relation to the half-light; the flowers stand up and expand, and in the early twilight show tender colouring of faint pink and lilac, and pour out upon the still night-air a lavish gift of sweetest fragrance; and the modest little plant that in strong sunlight looked unworthy of a place in the garden, now rises to its appointed rank and reigns supreme as its prime delight.

THE SCENTS OF SUMMER I

Best among all good plants for hot sandy soils are the ever-blessed Lavender and Rosemary, two delicious old garden bushes that one can hardly dissociate, so delightfully do they agree in their homely beauty and their beneficence of enduring fragrance, as well as in their love of the sun and their power of resisting drought. I plant Rosemary all over the garden, so pleasant is it to know that at every few steps one may draw the kindly branchlets through one's hand, and have the enjoyment of their incomparable incense; and I grow it against walls, so that the sun may draw out its inexhaustible sweetness to greet me as I pass; and early in March, before any other scented flower of evergreen is out, it gladdens me with the thick setting of pretty lavender-grey bloom crowding all along the leafy spikes.

❀ THE SCENTS OF SUMMER II

What a delicious early summer fragrance is that of a flowering Bean-field, when the sweet scent is offered up as grateful gift to the life-giving sun, and the kindly breeze blows a share of it aside to gladden the heart of the wayfarer. And then the Clover-field, delicious also with sun-released, wind-blown sweetness, less luscious than the breath of the Bean-flower, but with a modest, honeyed homeliness that bears with it an even greater charm.

❀ THE SCENTS OF SUMMER III

The country people say that the roots of Elder must never be allowed to come near a well, still less to grow into it, or the water will be spoilt. The young shoots are full of a very thick pith; we used to dry it in my young days, and make it into little round balls for use in electrical experiments. The scent of the flowers, especially wind-wafted, I think very agreeable, though they smell too strong to bring indoors. If I were not already overdone with home industries, I should distil fragrant Elder-flower water; but I let the berries ripen and make them into Elder-wine, a pleasant, comforting, and wholesome drink for winter evenings.

SPECIAL GARDENS

🌼   BRIER ROSES

I am always dreaming of having delightful gardens for special seasons where one good flower should predominate; but for June with its wealth of flowers there would have to be several special gardens. And, though I have not the means wherewith to do it as fully as I should wish, however strong may be my desire, I can at least show an attempt on a small scale, and also put down what ideas I may have, so that others, more bountifully endowed, may read and profit if they will. For June demands an Iris garden, and a Pæony garden, and an early Rose garden, and a garden for Poppies, besides half wood-like gardens for Azaleas and for Rhododendrons. But in early June the garden-wish that lies nearest to my heart is to have a beautiful planting of Brier Roses.

I have already a sunny bank of Briers some twenty-five yards long and six feet wide, and many will no doubt ask, "Is not that enough?" I can only answer, "No, it is not enough." If one has a picture to paint, whose subject and method of treatment demand a large canvas, one cannot be contented with a small one. I am truly thankful that I have my bank of briers, but satisfied I am not. Because now, seeing how they may be worthily treated, largely, broadly, beautifully, I desire to do it, and to do it carefully on my own ground where I can watch and wait and correct, and at last get it to such a state that it grows into a picture that I am not ashamed to show. And as the blooming time of the Brier Roses is a short one, I should group with them another family of plants whose flowering season would immediately follow. Such a family is at hand in the *Cistineæ*. And I would carpet the whole with the common English Heaths, always allowing the wild *Calluna* to be in chief abundance, with here and there a wide-spreading patch of the white *Menziesia*. Such a garden or half-wild planting would by no means preclude the use of the Briers in other ways, for if I had to deal with a perfectly formal garden, full of architectural detail, the dainty little laughing Briers would be called in to show how well they would also grace the well-ordered refinements of garden-building. For everywhere, and in all sorts of gardens, they are equally at home; looking as well and as rightly placed by the wrought-stone balustrade that bounds the terrace of the palace, as in the narrow spaces given to flowers that border the path from the high-road to the peasant's cottage.

My Brier Rose garden should have grass paths; whether wide or narrow, straight or winding, could only be determined on the spot and in relation to all that was near about it. It is one of the few kinds of gardening that could be easily done on such poor sandy soil as mine, because its hungry dryness suits the companion Cistuses and also the setting of wild Heaths which should be mingled with the fine grasses natural to the heathy soil, while the path and planting should join by a gentle and gradual passing of the one into the other rather than by any hard or abrupt transition. The Briers themselves will want a more careful preparation of the ground; trenching without any manuring will do for the Heath and grass and Cistuses, but though the wild English parent of the garden Briers is at home in sandy heaths, and though it will just exist if planted in the poor ground, it takes so long to grow that it is well moderately to enrich its place with some good leaf mould and spent manure. Then the Briers will grow apace, and though they make but little growth the first year, they are all the time working underground; by the second year they will make good promise, and by the third there should be a fair show.

When I advised the planting of the common Heath (*Calluna*) as a groundwork of the Briers, it was with no thought of its flowering, for that is not till August, but for the sake of its quiet leaf-colouring; grey-green when the Briers bloom, and later of a sober rustiness; its own change of colouring keeping pace with that of the small Rose bushes. In neither case do the companion plants imitate or match each other in colour, but both advance in the progress of the year's transformation by such a sequence of quiet harmonies, that at every season each is the better for the nearness of the other.

❀   THE ROSE GARDEN

It is more helpful to show one simple thing that is easily understood, and that awakens interest and enthusiasm, and to leave those wholesome motive powers to do their own work, than it is to prompt the learner at every step, fussing like an anxious nurse, and doing for him, what, if his enthusiasm is true and deep and not mere idle froth, will give him more pleasure in the doing, and more profit in the learning, than if it were all done for him. For the very essence of good gardening is the taking of thought and trouble. No one can do good decorative work who does it merely from a written recipe.

What a splendid exercise it would be if people would only go round their places and look for all the ugly corners, and just think how they might be made beautiful by the use of free-growing Roses. Often there is some bare yard, and it has come within my own experience to say to the owner, "Why not have rambling Roses on these bare walls and arches?" and to have the answer, "But we cannot, because the yard is paved, or perhaps asphalted." Is not a grand Rose worth the trouble of taking up two squares of flagging or cemented surface?

One of the many ways in which the splendid enthusiasm for good gardening—an enthusiasm which only grows stronger as time goes on—is showing itself, is in the general desire to use beautiful Roses more worthily. We are growing impatient of the usual Rose garden, generally a sort of target of concentric rings of beds placed upon turf, often with no special aim at connected design with the portions of the garden immediately about it, and filled with plants without a thought of their colour effect or any other worthy intention.

Now that there is such good and wonderfully varied material to be had, it is all the more encouraging to make Rose gardens more beautiful, not with beds of Roses alone—many a Rose garden is already too extensive in its display of mere beds—but to consider the many different ways in which Roses not only consent to grow but in which they live most happily and look their best. Beds we have had, and arches and bowers, but very little as yet in the whole range of possible Rose garden beauty.

So the thought comes that the Rose garden ought to be far more beautiful and interesting than it has ever yet been. In the hope of leading others to do more justice to the lovely plants that are only waiting to be well used, I will describe such a Rose garden as I think should be made. In this, as in so much other gardening, it is much to be desired that the formal and free ways should both be used. If the transition is not too abrupt the two are always best when brought into harmonious companionship. The beauty of the grand old gardens of the Italian Renaissance would be shorn of half their impressive dignity and of nearly all their poetry, were they deprived of the encircling forestlike thickets of Arbutus,

SPECIAL GARDENS

Evergreen Oak, and other native growths. The English Rose garden that I delight to dream of is also embowered in native woodland, that shall approach it nearly enough to afford a passing shade in some of the sunny hours, though not so closely as to rob the Roses at the root.

My Rose garden follows the declivities of a tiny, shallow valley, or is formed in such a shape. It is approached through a short piece of near home woodland of dark-foliaged trees, for the most part evergreens; Yew, Holly, and Scotch Fir. The approach may come straight or at a right angle. As it belongs to a house of classic design and of some importance, it will be treated, as to its midmost spaces, with the wrought stone steps and balustraded terraces, and such other accessories as will agree with those of the house itself.

The bottom of the little valley will be a sward of beautifully kept turf, only broken by broad flights of steps and dwarf walls where the natural descent makes a change of level necessary. The turf is some thirty feet wide; then on either side rises a retaining wall crowned by a balustrade. At the foot of this, on the further side, is a terrace whose whole width is about twenty-four feet. Then another and higher retaining wall rises to nearly the level of the wooded land above. This has no parapet or balustrade. The top edge of the wall is protected by bushy and free-growing Roses, and a walk runs parallel with it, bounded by rambling Roses on both sides. On the wooded side many of the Roses run up into the trees, while below Sweet-brier makes scented brakes and tangles.

The lawn level has a narrow border at the foot of the wall where on the sunnier side are Roses that are somewhat tender and not very large in growth. On the terraces there are Roses again, both on the side of the balustrade and on that of the retaining wall. The balustrade is not covered up or smothered with flowery growths, but here and there a Rose from above comes foaming up over its edge and falls over, folding it in a glorious mantle of flower and foliage. It is well where this occurs that the same Rose should be planted below and a little farther along, so that at one point the two join hands and grow together.

So there would be the quiet lawn spaces below, whose cool green prepares the eye by natural laws for the more complete enjoyment of the tinting of the flowers whether strong or tender, and there is the same cool green woodland carried far upward for the outer framing of the picture. In no other way that I can think of would beautiful groupings of Roses be so enjoyably seen, while the whole thing, if thoroughly well designed and proportioned, would be one complete picture of beauty and delight.

In a place that binds the designer to a greater degree of formality the upper terrace might be more rigidly treated, and the woodland, formed of Yew or Cypress, more symmetrically placed. On the other hand there is nothing to prevent the whole scheme being simplified and worked out roughly, with undressed stones for the steps and dry walling for the retaining walls, so as to be in keeping with the other portions of the grounds of any modest dwelling.

If a Rose garden is to be made on a level space where any artificial alteration of the ground is inexpedient, it will be found a great enhancement to the beauty of the Roses and to the whole effect of the garden if it is so planned that dark shrubs and trees bound it on all sides. A simple scheme is where a central space of turf has Rose borders. Outside is a wide grass walk, and beyond that dark shrubs. On the four sides grassy ways pass into the garden; while the whole outer edge of the Rose beds is set with posts connected by chains on which are pillar and free-growing cluster Roses placed alternately.

The background of dark trees is so important that I venture to dwell upon it with some degree of persistence. Any one who has seen an Ayrshire Rose running wild into a Yew will recognise the value of the dark foliage as a ground for the tender blush white of the Rose; and so it is with the Rose garden as a whole.

The wisdom of this treatment is well known in all other kinds of gardening, but with the tender colourings of so many Roses it has a special value. It should be remembered that a Rose garden can never be called gorgeous; the term is quite unfitting. Even in high Rose tide, when fullest of bloom, what is most clearly felt is the lovable charm of Rose beauty, whether of the whole scene, or of some delightful detail or incident or even individual bloom.

The gorgeousness of brilliant bloom, fitly arranged, is for other plants and other portions of the garden; here we do not want the mind disturbed or distracted from the beauty and delightfulness of the Rose. From many of the Rose gardens of the usual unsatisfactory type other kinds of gardening are seen, or perhaps a distant view, or a carriage road, or there is some one or other distracting influence that robs the Roses of the full exercise of their charm. Even in a walled space, unless this is darkly wooded round, it is better not to have Roses on the walls themselves, but rather to have the walls clothed with dark greenery. Any trees of dark or dusky foliage serve well as Rose backgrounds, whether of the greyish tone of the common Juniper or the richer greens of Thuya or Cypress, Yew or Holly.

A GARDEN OF WALL-FLOWERS

I am never tired of watching and observing how plants will manage not only to exist but even to thrive in difficult circumstances. For this sort of observation my very poor sandy soil affords me only too many opportunities. Now, on a rather cold afternoon in April, I go to a sheltered part of the garden, and almost at random place my seat opposite a sloping bank thinly covered with Periwinkles. The bank is the northern flank of a mound of sand, thinly surfaced when it was made with some poor earth from a hedge-bank that was being removed. This place was purposely chosen for the Periwinkles, in order to check their growth and restrain them from running together into a tight mat of runners, as they do so quickly if they are planted in better soil. This poverty of soil and the summer dryness of their place keeps them very much at home, and they make stout, well-flowered tufts, with only a few weak runners. There is something among them on the ground looking like bright crimson flower-buds, about an inch long. I look nearer and see that they are acorns, fallen last autumn from a tree that overhangs this end of the bank. The acorns have thrown off their outer shells, and the inner skin, of a pale greenish-yellow colour when first uncased, has turned, first to pale pink and then to a strong crimson. The first root has been thrown out and has found its way firmly into the ground, though the acorn still lies upon the surface.

Between and among the lesser Periwinkles on the northern bank are spaces where neighbouring Wallflowers have shed their seed, and seed-lings have sprung up. Some of these, evidently on the poorest ground, have branched all round without throwing up a stem, and look like stiff green rosettes pressed close to the earth. Others, a little more well-to-do, have stout stocky stems and dense heads of short, almost horny, dark-green foliage, with promise of compact but abundant bloom. Like the inhabitants of some half-barren place who have never been in touch with abundance or ease of life or any sort of luxury, they are all the more sturdy and thrifty and self-reliant, and I would venture to affirm that their lives will be as long again as those of any sister plants from the same seedpod that have enjoyed more careful nurture and a more abundant dietary. No planted-out Wall-flower can ever compare, in my light soil, with one sown where it is to remain; it always retains the planted-out look to the end of its days, and never has the tree-like sturdiness about the lower portions of its half-woody stem that one notices about the one sown and grown in its place. Moreover, from many years' observation, I notice that such plants only, show the many variations in habit that one comes to recognise as a kind of individual or personal characteristic, so that the plant acquires a much greater and almost human kind of inter-est. I have one such charming seedling that gives me great pleasure. The flower is of a full, clear, orange colour, more deeply tinged to the outer margins of the petals with faint thin lines of rich mahogany, that increase in width of line and depth of colour as they reach the petal's outer edge, till joining together, the whole edge is of this strong, rich colour. The back of the petal is entirely of this deep tint, and though the flower is of some substance, I always think the richness of colouring of the back has something to do with the strong quality of the deep yellow of the face. The calyx, which forms the covering of the unopened bud, is of a full purple-brown. The leaves are of a dark dull green, tinged with brown-bronze, much like the colour of the brown water-cress. The habit of the plant is close and stocky, but does not look dwarfed.

If I had plenty of suitable spaces and could spend more on my garden I would have special regions for many a good plant. As it is, I have to content myself with special gardens for Primroses and for Pæonies and for Michaelmas Daisies. And indeed I am truly thankful to be able to have these; but we garden-lovers are greedy folk, and always want to have more and more and more! I want to have a Rose-garden, and a Tulip-garden, and a Carnation-garden, and a Columbine-garden, and a Fern-garden, and several other kinds of special garden, but if I were able, the first I should make would be a Wall-flower garden.

It should be contrived either in connection with some old walls, or, failing these, with some walls or wall-like structures built on purpose. These walls would shock a builder, but would delight a good gardener, for they would present just those conditions most esteemed by wall-loving plants, of crumbling masonry built of half-formed or half-rotting stone, and of loose joints made to receive rather than to repel every drop of welcome rain. Wall-flowers are lime-loving plants, so the stones would be set in a loose bed of pounded mortar-rubbish, and there would be sloping banks, half wall half bank. I should, of course, take care that the lines of the garden should be in suitable relation to other near portions, a matter that could only be determined on the precise spot that might be available.

But for the planting, or rather the sowing of the main spaces, there would be little difficulty. I should first sow a packet of a good strain of blood-red single Wall-flower, spreading it over a large stretch of the space. Then a packet of a good yellow, either the Belvoir or the Bedfont, then the purple, and then one of the newer pale ones that have flowers of a colour between ivory-white and pale buff-yellow. I would keep the sowings in separate but informal drifts, each kind having its share, though not an equal share, of wall and bank and level. Some spaces nearest the eye should be filled with the small spreading Alpine Wall-flowers and their hybrids, but these are best secured from cuttings. A few other plants would be admitted to the Wall-flower garden, such as yellow Alyssum on sunny banks and Tiarella in cool or half-shady places, and in the wall-joints I would have in fair quantity the beautiful *Corydalis ochroleuca,* most delicate and lovely of the Fumitories. Leading to the Wall-flower garden I should like to have a way between narrow rock borders or dry walls. These should be planted with Aubrietias, varieties of *A. græca,* of full and light purple colour, double Cuckoo-flower in the two shades of colour, and a good quantity of the grey foliage and tender white bloom of *Cerastium tomentosum,* so common in gardens and yet so seldom well used; I would also have, but more sparingly, some groups of double Arabis.

These plants, with the exception of the Cuckoo-flower, are among those most often found in gardens, but it is very rarely that they are used thoughtfully or intelligently, or in such a way as to produce the simple pictorial effect to which they so readily lend themselves. This planting of white and purple colouring I would back with plants or shrubs of dark foliage, and the path should be so directed into the Wall-flower garden, by passing through a turn or a tunnelled arch of Yew or some other dusky growth, that the one is not seen from the other; but so that the eye, attuned to the cold, fresh colouring of the white and purple, should be in the very best state to receive and enjoy the sumptuous splendour of the region beyond. I am not sure that the return journey would not present the more brilliant picture of the two, for I have often observed in passing from warm colouring to cold, that the eye receives a kind of delightful

shock of surprise that colour can be so strong and so pure and so altogether satisfying. And in these ways one gets to know how to use colour
to the best garden effects. It is a kind of optical gastronomy; this preparation and presentation of food for the eye in arrangements that are both
wholesome and agreeable, and in which each course is so designed that it
is the best possible preparation for the next to come.

I think I would also allow some bold patches of tall Tulips in the Wall-
flower garden; orange and yellow and brown and purple, for one distinct
departure from the form and habit of the main occupants of the garden
would give value to both.

❧ THE ROCK GARDEN

A rock-garden may be anything between an upright wall and a nearly
dead level. It is generally an artificial structure of earth and stones, and
alas! only too often it is an aggregation of shapeless mounds and hollows
made anyhow. Such a place is not only ugly but is very likely not suitable
for the plants that are intended to grow in it. If any success in the
cultivation of rock-plants is expected, it is only reasonable to suppose
that one must take the trouble to learn something about the plants, their
kinds and their needs, and it is equally necessary to take the trouble to
learn how their places are to be prepared. Happily for the chances of
success and pleasure in this delightful kind of gardening the right way is
also the most beautiful way. There is no need to surround every little
plant with a kind of enclosure of stones, set on edge and pointing to all
four points of the compass; it is far better to set the stones more or less in
courses or in lines of stratification, just as we see them in nature in a
stone quarry or any mountain side where surface denudation has left
them standing out clear in nearly parallel lines. It matters not the least
whether the courses are far apart or near together; this is naturally set-
tled by the steepness of the ground. In a wall they are necessarily close,

and in very steep ground it is convenient to build them with the courses rather near each other. In such a case as a steep slope with an angle of 45 degrees, the face of the rock-bank could be built in either of two ways. Both will suit the plants. The flatter the angle of the ground the further apart may be the rocky courses, as the danger of the earth washing away is diminished. If the stone is not in large pieces, it will be found a good plan in rather steep banks to begin at the path level with a few courses of dry-walling, and then to make an earthy shelf and then another rise of two or three courses of walling, using the two or three courses to represent one thickness of deeper stone. But in any case the rock-builder should make up his mind how the courses should run and keep to the same rule throughout, whether the stones lie level or dip a little to right or left as they generally do in nature. But whether a stone lies level or not as to the right and left of its front face, it should always be laid so that its back end tips down into the ground, and its front face, when seen in profile, looks a little upward.

This, it will be seen, carries the rain into the ground instead of shooting it off as it would do if it were laid the other way, like the tile or slate on a building.

When the ground is shaped and the rocks placed, the next matter of importance, and that will decide whether the rock-garden is to be a thing of some dignity or only the usual rather fussy mixture, is to have a solid planting of suitable small shrubs crowning all the heights. Most important of these will be the Alpine Rhododendrons; neat in habit, dark of foliage, and on a scale that does not overwhelm the little plant jewels that are to come near them. No shrubs are so suitable for a good part of the main plantings in the higher regions.

By working on such a general plan we shall avoid that rude shock so often experienced when the rock-garden comes into view, from its appearance being so uncompromisingly sudden. Perhaps there is a smooth bit of lawn, with pleasant easy lines of flower or shrub clump; then you pass round some bush, and all at once there is a shockingly *sudden* rock-

garden. I cannot think of any other term that gives the impression I wish
to convey. It often comes of want of space. Only a certain space can be
given to the rock-plants, and it must be made the most of; still, even in
small gardens it might be more or less prepared or led up to. But I am not
just now considering the limitations of the smallest gardens (a tempting
theme, but one that should be taken by itself), but rather the best way to
lay out ground that is not cramped in space or stinted of reasonable
labour. Therefore, where the region of groups of handsome hardy moisture-loving exotics ends, we come to an occasional flattish boulder or
blunt-nosed rock just rising above the ground, as the path rises very
gently. Presently these large plants, of which the furthest back were in
quite moist ground, are left behind, and we are among bushes four to
seven feet high. These give place to lower shrubs, rather more thinly
grouped, while the rocky boulders are more frequent and more conspicuous. Presently, and only by a gentle transition, the rock-mound comes
into view, and we see that there are three paths, each having a slightly
different aspect, while the whole mound, clothed with dark, close-grow-
ing, and for the most part, dwarf shrubs, has a unity of character which
presents no shock to the mind, but only a pleasant invitation to come and
see and enjoy. There is no bewilderment, because there is no jumble or
crowding of irrelevant items. Everything falls into its place, and a quiet
progress through any one of the paths presents a succession of garden-
pictures that look not so much as if they had been designed and made but
as if they had just happened to come so. There is nothing perhaps to
provoke that violent excitement of wonderment so dear to the uneducated, but there will be, alike to the plant lover and to the garden artist, the
satisfaction of a piece of happy gardening, without strain or affectation,
beautiful and delightful in all its parts and growing easily and pleasantly
out of its environment.

It can never be repeated too often that in this, as in all kinds of gardening where some kind of beauty is aimed at, the very best effects are made
by the simplest means, and by the use of a few different kinds of plants

only at a time. A confused and crowded composition is a fault in any picture; in the pictures that we paint with living plants just as much as in those that are drawn and painted on paper or canvas. Moreover, the jumbled crowd of incongruous items, placed without thought of their effect on one another, can only make a piece of chance patchwork; it can never make a design. However interesting the individual plants may be, we want to get good proportion and beautiful combination in order to make the good garden-picture, while the individuals themselves gain in importance by being shown at their best.

❀ SMALL ROCK-GARDENS

An artificial rockery is usually a bit of frankly simple make-believe. Nine times out of ten there is something about it half funny, half pathetic, so innocent, so childish is its absolute failure to look like real rocky ground. And even if for a moment one succeeds in cheating oneself into thinking that it is something like a bit of rocky nature, there is pretty sure to be the zinc label, with its stark figure and ghastly colouring, looking as if it were put there of cruel purpose for the more effectual shattering of the vain illusion. I suppose that of all metallic surfaces there is none so unlovely as that of zinc, and yet we stick upright strips of it among, and even in front of, some of the daintiest of our tiny plants. We spend thought and money, and still more money's-worth in time and labour, on making our little rock terraces, and perhaps succeed in getting them into nice lines and planted with the choicest things, and then we peg it all over with zinc labels! I am quite in sympathy with those who do not know their plants well enough to do without the labels; I have passed through that stage myself, and there are many cases where the label must be there. But I considered that in dressed ground or pure pleasure ground, where the object is some scheme of garden beauty, the label, even if it must be there, should never be seen. I felt this so keenly myself when I first had a piece of rock-garden that I hit upon a plan that can be confidently recommended: that of driving the ugly thing into the earth, leaving only just enough above ground to lay hold of. In this case also the zinc strip can be much shorter; only enough length is wanted to write the name; the writing with metallic ink also remains fresh longer in the damp ground, and shows clear when the peg is pulled up to be looked at. And then one finds out how seldom one really wants the label. In my own later practice, where the number of different plants has been reduced to just those I like best and think most worthy of a place, they are so well known to me that their names are as familiar as those of my best friends; and when I admit a new plant, if I cannot at once learn its name, it is purposely given a big ugly label, as a self-inflicted penance that shall continue until such time as I can expiate by remembrance.

I have two small rock-gardens, differently treated. The upper one leads from lawn to copse, and is made with a few simple parallel ridges of stone, clothed for the most part with small shrubs, such as Gaultheria and Alpine Rhododendron, with hardy Ferns, and groups of two or three plants of conspicuously handsome foliage, such as *Saxifraga peltata* and *Rodgersia podophylla*. The object of this one is to lead unobtrusively from lawn to copse, and at the same time to accommodate certain small shrubs and handsome plants with a place where they would do well, and where I should wish to see them. The other little rock-garden, between the lower end of the lawn and a group of Oaks, has another purpose. It is absolutely artificial, and only pretends to be a suitable home for certain small plants that I love. A rock-garden takes a great deal of skilled labour, and I can only afford it my own, so that its size is limited to little more than I can work with my own hands and see with extremely short-sighted eyes. Four broad and shallow steps lead down to the path-level; there is a long-shaped island in the middle, and sloping banks to right and left, all raised from the path by dry-walling from one to two feet high. The joints of the dry-walling are planted with small Ferns on the cool sides, and with Stonecrops and other dwarf sun-loving plants on the sides facing south. The walling as it rises changes to rocky bank, with again a course or two of walling in the cooler face to suit some plantings of *Ramondia* and the rarer *Haberlea rhodopensis*. The cool, sloping flats between are covered with *Dryas octopetala*, and neat Alpines such as *Hutchinsia* and *Cardamine Trifoliata*, and little meadows of *Linnæa borealis*, *Campanula pulla*, *Veronica prostrata*, and *V. satureioides*, *Linaria pallida* and *L. hepaticæfolia;* while in the joints of the stones and just below them are little Ferns, and in all vacant places tufts and sheets of mossy Saxifrage, coolest and freshest-looking of alpine herbage. These various members of the mossy branch of the great Saxifrage family are some of the most valuable of rock-garden plants, and in a small place like mine can be well employed to give some sort of feeling of unity to what would otherwise be only a piece of floral patchwork, especially if the plants and their mossy setting are placed as much as possible in long drifts rather than in compact patches. I think this principle is of so much importance that I shall not refrain from repeating it, for I have found it to be of value in all kinds of planting, whether of small or large plants in rockery or border, of Daffodils in copse or meadow, or of tree and shrub in larger spaces.

For the effectual destruction of any pictorial effect in a rock-garden, no method of arrangement can be so successful as the one so very frequently seen, of little square or round enclosures of stones placed on end, with the plant inside conspicuously labelled. It always makes me think of cattle-pens in a market, and that the surrounding stones are placed prison-wise, less for the plant's comfort than for its forcible detention. And it leads to the stiffest and least interesting way of planting. If there are three plants they go in a triangle; if four, in a square; if five, in a square with one in the middle, and so on. For even if a little rockery be avowedly artificial, as in many cases it must be, it is better that its details should be all easy and pretty, rather than stiff and awkward and unsightly.

The sunny side of my small rock-garden has long groups of *Othon-*

nopsis, and the woolly-leaved *Hieracium villosum* and Prophet-flower (*Arnebia*), and good stretches of *Achillea umbellata* and of *Iris cristata,* without doubt one of the loveliest among the smaller members of its beautiful family, and of the flowers that bloom in May. This little Iris is only five inches high, and the flowers are two and a half inches across, so that they look large for the whole size of the plant. When placed as it likes best, on a sunny rock-shelf in nearly pure leaf-mould, it shows its appreciation of kind treatment by free growth and abundance of bloom. The leaves, at blooming time only four inches high, though much taller afterwards, are in neat flat little sheaves of from three to five, one leaf always taking a prominent lead. The clear lilac-blue of the flower has a daintily-clean look that is very charming, and taken in the hand I always delight in the delicate beauty of the raised and painted ornament of the lower petals. In the middle of the broadest part is a white pool with a strong purple edging; the white turns to yellow, and runs in a lane an eighth of an inch wide down into the throat, between two little whitish rocky ridges. The yellow stripe is also decorated with a tiny raised serpent wriggling down its middle line, and with a few fine short strokes of reddish-brown.

Another great favourite, equally at home in sun or shade in the rock-walls, is *Corydalis ochroleuca;* masses of feathery daintiness of warm white bloom and fern-like foliage. The flower is of the labiate form, characteristic of the Fumitory group. Its upper member rises from the pouch-like spur in an admirable line of simple strength, and ends above in a narrow turned-back hood, whose outer edge is waved and bluntly toothed in a way that gives an impression of the most delicate decorative finish. The leaves are of the tenderest yellow-green, and the aspect of the whole plant is so refined that it makes all the surrounding growths look coarsely built.

In one corner of the rock-garden are two kinds of Violet, both good and worthy of their place, though both without scent. One is a white Dog-Violet, the white strikingly pure and bright. The leaves are of a very dark green, sometimes with a tinge of blackish-bronze; two rather narrow up-right petals stand up in a way that always reminds me of a frightened rabbit. The other is the splendid North American *Viola cucullata*. Its large round flowers, of a strong pure purple colour, nearly an inch and a half across, are on purplish stems from nine inches to a foot long. Where the lower petal leaves the small white eye there is a sharply-distinct veining of still darker purple. The size of the flower is all the more remarkable because it is a true Violet; there is nothing of the Pansy about it. Pansy and Violet are, of course, closely related, but their characters are quite distinct; and though, as a rough rule, Pansy is large and Violet small, yet there are many small true Pansies, and in this case there is one very large Violet.

No rock-garden should be without *Achillea umbellata* in fair plenty. Even out of flower it is one of the neatest of plants, with its silvery foliage so deeply cut that the leaves are almost like double combs, and its boun-tiful heads of milk-white flowers, whose centres, dusky at first, change to a dull nankeen colour as the bloom becomes perfect. There is no better plant for an informal edging, or for any alpine carpeting, in long pools or straight drifts; it delights in a hot place, and, like many silvery-leaved plants, will bear a good deal of drought.

I am very fond of the double Cuckoo-flower. It has such a clean, fresh look, and the doubling makes such a pretty round rose-shaped flower of each little bloom. The single wild one of the meadows is a pretty plant too, and sometimes grows so thickly that one understands how it came by its old English name of Lady's-smock; for its close masses of whitish bloom might well remind one of linen wear laid out to bleach. Many years ago a dear old friend among our neighbours bought a plant of the double kind. Her meadow was already well stocked with the wild one, and she had the happy idea of planting the double one with it. In course of time it increased and spread over a large space, and was so pretty and pleasant to see that nearly every spring I used to go on purpose to visit it. And one day, to my great delight, I found among it one plant of a much deeper colour, quite a pretty and desirable variety from the type, that has proved a good garden plant. My friend Mr. George Paul, after growing it for a season, thought so well of it that he took it to a meeting of the Royal Horticultural Society, where he received for it a notice of commendation; this, with kindly courtesy, he was good enough to pass on to me, having given my name to the variety. The Cuckoo-flower has a curious way of increasing by dropping its leaflets; they root at the base, and it is easy to make a panful of cuttings in this way, dibbling in the leaflets, and pretty to see the spruce little plants that soon grow from them. It also makes little plants, with roots and all complete, in the axils of the leaves on the lower part of the flower-stems after the bloom is over. These will drop off when mature, but as a good many perish under the natural conditions of my dry garden, I look out for them as soon as the roots are formed and grow them on in boxes till some wet day in July or August, when they can be safely planted out.

There is a good group of this pretty plant at the cooler end of my small rock-garden, where a bit of dwarf dry-walling supports the raised sides. The walling is here only a foot high, and is clothed with the little creeping Sandwort (*Arenaria balearica*). The two plants together make a pretty picture; the Sandwort is rather the later of the two, but is already fairly well in flower before the bloom of the Cuckoo-flower is over. Nothing can be better than this little *Arenaria* for any cool place against stonework. A tuft or two planted at the foot in autumn will creep up and cover a good space of stony face in a short time. One has only to see that it does not cling on to plants as well as stones, for I have had it growing all over the surface of *Ramondia* leaves, only catching it just in time to prevent the *Ramondia* from being smothered. I am watching with some interest a little patch that has found a lodging in the middle of a spreading sheet of *Linaria hepaticæfolia*, another of the small irrepressibles. I want to see which of the two will have the mastery, as it is the habit of both to completely cover any space of ground or stonework they may be on.

ON GARDENING

Any one who wishes to see silvery-green satin of the highest quality should look at the back of the leaves of *Alchemilla alpina*. Indeed the whole plant, though anything but showy, is full of what one may call interesting incident. I remember finding this out one hot afternoon, when after a hard morning's work I sat down, a good bit tired, on the lowest of the steps leading into the little rock-garden. Just under my hand was a tuft of this Lady's-Mantle, and half-lazily, and yet with a faint prick of the moral spur that urges me against complete idleness, I picked a leaf to have a good look at it, and then found how much, besides the well-known beauty of its satin back, there was to admire in it. The satin lining, as is plain to see, comes up and over the front edge of the leaf with a bright-ness that looks like polished silver against the dull green surface. The edge of each of the seven leaflets is plain for two-thirds of its length, and then breaks into saw-teeth, which increase in size, always silver-edged, till they reach the end and nearly meet. And at this point a surprise awaits one, for instead of the endmost jag, in the base of whose body the mid-rib dies away, being as one would expect the stoutest and largest, it is smaller than the two next on each side, so that the tip of the leaflet has a blunt and even depressed shape; indeed the tips of the last five saw-teeth are nearly on a line and at a right angle to the mid-rib, and the middle one is always a little the lowest. Then there is another curious thing to notice, that, though not invariable, is so frequent as to seem to be a law in the plant's structure. The normal number of divisions in a full-sized leaf is seven, and they all join together with the exception of the first and last, at a distance of a quarter of an inch from their common insertion into the stalk. But in most cases either the first or the seventh leaflet has a sub-leaflet of its own, usually smaller, but sometimes nearly as large as itself, joined to it much further up, but with its own mid-rib and distinct system of veining. The heads of small green flowers, set on lesser stalks that leave the main stem by springing out of a frilled collar, half leaf half bract, are not exactly beautiful, but have a curious square-ness of plan, still further accentuated by the four stamens also squarely planted at the inner angles of the petals. Close to the Lady's-Mantle, and also within hand-reach, is a frequent weed, but a weed so lovely that I let it be—the common Speedwell. I remember how delighted I was as a child when I found out for myself how the two lines of fur that run up the stalks between each pair of leaves, changed sides with the next pair of leaves, and ran up the other sides, and how I used to think the little blue flower itself had something the look of a tiny Pansy. I suppose this impression arose from the veins gathering to the middle to a firmer depth of blue, and then giving place to a white eye.

My little rock-garden is never without some stretches of the common Thrift, which I consider quite an indispensable plant. Its usefulness is not confined to the flowering season, for both before and after, the cushion-like growths of sober greenery are helpful in the way of giving an element of repose and quietude to a garden-space whose danger is always an inclination towards unrest and general fussiness. And it should be cautiously placed with regard to the colour of the neighbouring flowers, for its own pink is of so low-toned a quality that pinks brighter and purer spoil it completely. I should say its best companions would be some of the plants of woolly foliage and whitish flower such as Cerastium or the mountain Cud-weeds.

The flowering plants on this small rockery only extend as far as the hand can reach, for convenience of weeding and all requirements of easy access. Beyond this point is a permanent planting of small shrubs, mostly of the Alpine Rhododendrons. These were chosen as the main background for the little flowering plants, because they seemed just to have the desired qualities of a small, neat habit of growth, on a scale not unsuitable to that of the Alpines, a steady moderation of yearly increase, and a richness of deep colouring, highly becoming to the small bright things below them. Beyond them are Gaultherias which will grow a little higher, and then Hollies, so that the whole background of the dainty Alpine jewels will show as a richly-dark and somewhat sombre setting. But besides these dwarf Rhododendrons and the sweet-leaved R. *myrti-*

folium, only a little larger in growth, there is also in the upper part of the rock-work a planting of the smaller Andromedas, with Gaultheria and Skimmia, and groups of *Daphne pontica,* whose abundant yellow-green bloom fills the garden with fragrance in the early days of May. And planted with these, and running down among the flowers, is the white Menziesia, taking an equal place among flower and small shrub, and always delightful with its large white blooms of long ball-shape—just right for fairies' footballs—and its wholesome-looking foliage of deep rich green.

LARGE ROCK-GARDENS

Though I have to be contented with an Alpine garden on a very small scale, I like to plan a large rock-garden in imagination. It is in the lower part of a steep hillside, a little gorge or dell with its own stream and natural rock cropping out. At the desired spot I would build a pond-head across the dell, and following the indication of local stratification, I would arrange large masses of the natural stone so as to form a rocky heading, with deep rifts well packed with soil for Ferns. The water would be led over this rocky head, which should be about twenty feet high, in various ways; in one place by a clear fall into a deep pool, in others by shorter cascades and cunningly-contrived long slides of differing angles. How well I remember such places in the Alps, and how delightful it was to watch the different ways of the water.

In one place there should be a splash on to a rock for the benefit of *Ramondia* and *Soldanella* and *Saxifraga aizoides,* that delight in nearness to water and a bath of spray. Excepting just these plants, I think I should let this region be devoted to Ferns, so as to give a simple picture of one thing at a time, and not even too many different kinds of Ferns, but in some long rocky rifts an abundance of Hart's-tongue, and in some half-dusky region at the foot of the rocky wall, so placed as to be reflected in a quiet backwater of the main pool, a goodly planting of the Lady Fern, and then some handsome tufts of Royal Fern. And in the margin of the pool I would only have, besides the Ferns, one or two native water-plants; and of these the chosen ones would be the Water Plantain (*Alisma*) and the Flowering Rush (*Butomus*), bearing in mind that the Ferns are to have the mastery. I am not even sure that it would not be better to have those spray-loving Alpines in some lower reach of the dell, if just the right place could be contrived for them, and to have Wall-Pennywort in their place in the greater rocky wall, in order to keep the place of rock and pool and Fern as quiet as possible, and to present one simple picture of rock and water, and restful delight of cool and beautiful foliage. And such a picture would also serve to show what could be done with our native plants and these alone. Some stretches of native Heaths, the pink Bell-Heather (*Erica Tetralix*) and the white Irish Menziesia would not be out of place; and in mossy beds such dainty things as *Pyrola, Linnæa,* and *Trientalis* would do well, for while serving as delightful surprises of tender plant-beauty in detail, they would not be so conspicuous as to mar the unity of plan of the main picture as a whole.

The path downward would lead out of this upper place through a planting of some kind of bushy growth hiding the pool, of which the best I can think of would be Sea-Buckthorn, the native Bog-Myrtle, and the broad-leafed American kind—all again carpeted with native Heaths. This rather low-toned mass of bushes of dull colour and dry texture would be a good preparation for arrival at the Fern and water picture, and the sound of the water, more important here than in the trickling of the lower rills, would arouse a feeling of interest, and an anticipation of something pleasant and beautiful hidden beyond the bushy screen.

I should wish that the ground above the glen on both sides should be wooded; not with the largest forest trees, such as Beeches, but mainly with Birch and a good deal of Mountain Ash and Holly, Thorn and Juniper; and some of these would be allowed to seed and spring up in the rocky banks, always watching how they came, and retaining or removing the seedlings so as best to suit the grouping of such a picture as may be intended. As the dell descends it should widen out until it dies away into nearly level ground, and as it flattens, the trees might fall into thinner groups, or be altogether absent if the ground were of Heath or pasture.

But such a little planted valley might also well come down into the rougher part of the garden or shrub plantation or garden-orchard. Given the dell and the stream, an endless variety of simple pictures could be made. By using native plants at the upper end, and then by degrees coming to plantings of foreign things best suited to wild ground, such as the white Wood Lily (*Trillium*) of Canada and the northern States of America, the wilder ground would pleasantly and imperceptibly join hands with the garden, and would be without any of the painful shocks and sudden jolts that so often afflict the soul of the garden-artist on his journey round even well-ordered rockeries of the usual type. I venture to repeat my own firm conviction that this kind of gardening can only be done well and beautifully by a somewhat severe restraint in numbers of kinds. The eye and brain can only take in and enjoy two or three things at a time in any one garden picture. The lessons taught by nature all point to this; indeed one thing at a time is best of all; but as all natural or wild gardening is a compromise, the nature-lessons must be taken mainly as the setting forth of principles. If these principles are well taken in, and digested and assimilated, we shall find no difficulty in rightly using that part of their teaching which bears upon gardening, and we shall see how to treat wild nature, not by slavish imitation, not by driving or forcibly shaping, but by methods that can hardly be described in detail, of coaxing and persuading into pictorial effect.

The upper end of my little dell I suppose to be to the south, so that the rocky wall-head is always in shade, and as one comes downward the right hand slope gets a good deal of sun from noon to the middle of the afternoon. The one on the left is nearly all in shadow, so that for such plants as do best entirely screened from the sun, a suitable place can easily be chosen or arranged. It would be important, in order to preserve a certain unity of effect throughout the whole valley, that there should be a general groundwork of certain plants from end to end. If it were a place of sand and peat, these plants should be the three common wild Heaths, Whortleberry, *Gaultheria Shallon*, and the Bog-Myrtles. Between and under these should be long stretches of common Mosses and Mossy Saxifrages.

I would have everything planted in longish drifts, and above all things it should be planted *geologically;* the length of the drift going with the natural stratification. In all free or half-wild garden planting, good and distinct effect (though apparent and enjoyable to every beholder, even though he may not perceive why it is right and good) is seldom planned or planted except by the garden-artist who understands what is technically known as "drawing." But by planting with the natural lines of stratification we have only to follow the splendid drawing of Nature herself, and the picture cannot fail to come right.

In the planting of my little valley I should be inclined to leave out some of the best-known mountain plants such as Arabis, Aubrietia, Alyssum, and Cerastium. These are so closely associated in our minds with garden use that they have in a way lost their suitability for places where we want to foster the illusion of being among pictures of wild nature.

As the dell becomes shallower, the less sloping sides will want more careful planting. Here I would have on the cool side the bushy Andromedas and Vacciniums, remembering that some of the latter have an autumn leaf-colouring of splendid scarlet, and that therefore other bushes of like colouring would fittingly accompany them; so that here might come the hardy Azaleas, thankful for a place where they have cool peat at the root, and passing shade as of not far distant Birches.

The opposite side in full sun would be a happy home for the Cistuses; the larger pictorial effects being made with bold plantings of *Cistus cyprius* and *C. laurifolius,* and nearer the path *C. florentinus,* and the yellow-flowered *Cistus formosus,* which, though commonly called a

Cistus, is botanically a *Helianthemum*. Then the smaller yellow-flowered and more prostrate *H. halimifolium* and the lesser Rock-Roses. In the most sun-baked spot I would have, on a rocky shelf and hanging over it, a wide planting of Barbary Ragwort (*Othonnopis cheirifolia*), Lavender and Rosemary, and big bushes of Jerusalem Sage (*Phlomis fruticosa*) and yellow Tree-Lupin, and the great Asphodel. It would suit the character of most of these plants to show between them some small stretches of bare sandy soil and bare rock, varied with an undergrowth of the sun-loving Heaths, Lavender-Cotton, and the aromatic Artemisias, in wide plantings and long drifts, always faithfully following the run of the rocks.

These plants and shrubs, among a good many others that might be employed in the same way, came first to mind because of a general likeness or harmony of leaf-colour; for I should think it desirable, had it ever been my happiness to be able to plant such a large wild rock-garden, to avoid too great a mixture of quality of leaf-colour in the main masses. And just so it seemed the better plan in the shaded region of the upper pool to have a preponderance of the cool, fresh yellowish-green of Fern and Moss, so on the sun-baked rocky banks below I should try for a distinct picture of the greyish and low-toned blue-greens so prevalent among those herbs and bushy growths of the Mediterranean region, that are good enough to make themselves at home in more northern latitudes.

Though such a large half-wild rock-garden as I have attempted to sketch may only be possible to a very few among the great number of those who love rock-plants, such a more extensive view of its possibilities does not in the least degree put one out of sympathy with the small rock-gardens now so abundant, and that give their owners so much pleasure. My own covers but a few square yards, but many are even smaller, and perhaps a little worse built and disfigured by labels, and yet I can heartily sympathise with all, for I consider that in dealing with these matters one must never forget, or be afraid to repeat by word or in writing, the plain fact that a pleasure garden is for the purpose of giving pleasure, and that though my own delight in a garden may be worked out in one way, yet other people may take their pleasure quite rightly in ways altogether different.

It has always seemed to me that when there is a very small space to be dealt with, as in the gardens of hundreds of small villas in the suburbs of London and other large towns, that to lay it out as a rock-garden would be the best way of making the most of it. No doubt many clever owners of such houses have done it already, but others may not have thought of it, and though in a restricted area one cannot have large effects, yet there is no reason why one should not have well-designed ones, such as would be in perfect proportion and suitability of scale to the space at command; while such a little garden would admit of a much greater variety of forms of plant beauty than could be appropriately used in any other way.

🌸 THE DRY WALL

One of the best and simplest ways of growing rock-plants is in a loose wall. In many gardens an abrupt change of level makes a retaining wall necessary, and when I see this built in the usual way as a solid structure of brick and mortar—unless there be any special need of the solid wall—I always regret that it is not built as a home for rock-plants. An exposure to north or east and the cool backing of a mass of earth is just what most Alpines delight in. A dry wall, which means a wall without mortar, may be anything between a wall and a very steep rock-work, and may be built of brick or of any kind of local stone. I have built and planted a good many hundred yards of dry walling with my own hands, both at home and in other gardens, and can speak with some confidence both of the pleasure and interest of the actual making and planting, and of the satisfactory results that follow.

The best example I have to show in my own garden is the so-called "Old Wall," before mentioned. It is the bounding and protecting fence of the Pæony ground on its northern side, and consists of a double dry wall with earth between. An old hedge bank that was to come away was not far off, within easy wheeling distance. So the wall was built up on each side, and as it grew, the earth from the hedge was barrowed in to fill up. A dry wall needs very little foundation; two thin courses underground are quite enough. The point of most structural importance is to keep the earth solidly trodden and rammed behind the stones of each course and throughout its bulk, and every two or three courses to lay some stones that are extra long front and back, to tie the wall well into the bank. A local sandstone is the walling material. In the pit it occurs in separate layers, with a few feet of hard sand between each. The lowest layer, sometimes thirty to forty feet down, is the best and thickest, but that is good building stone, and for dry walling we only want "tops" or "seconds," the later and younger formations of stone in the quarry. The very roughness and almost rotten state of much of this stone makes it all the more acceptable as nourishment and root-hold to the tiny plants that are to grow in its chinks, and that in a few months will change much of the rough rock-surface to green growth of delicate vegetation. Moreover, much of the soft sandy stone hardens by exposure to weather; and even if a stone or two crumbles right away in a few years' time, the rest will hold firmly, and the space left will make a little cave where some small fern will live happily.

The wall is planted as it is built with hardy Ferns—*Blechnum,* Polypody, Hartstongue, *Adiantum, Ceterach, Asplenium,* and *A. Ruta muraria.* The last three like lime, so a barrow of old mortar-rubbish is at hand, and the joint where they are to be planted has a layer of their favourite soil. Each course is laid fairly level as to its front top edge, stones of about the same thickness going in course by course. The earth backing is then carefully rammed into the spaces at the uneven backs of the stones, and a thin layer of earth over the whole course, where the mortar would have been in a built wall, gives both a "bed" for the next row of stones and soil for the plants that are to grow in the joints.

SPECIAL GARDENS

The face of the wall slopes backward on both sides, so that its whole thickness of five feet at the bottom draws in to four feet at the top. All the stones are laid at a right angle to the plane of the inclination—that is to say, each stone tips a little down at the back, and its front edge, instead of being upright, faces a little upward. It follows that every drop of gentle rain that falls on either side of the wall is carried into the joints, following the backward and downward pitch of the stones, and then into the earth behind them.

The mass of earth in the middle of the wall gives abundant root-room for bushes, and is planted with bush Roses of three kinds, of which the largest mass is of *Rosa lucida*. Then there is a good stretch of Berberis; then Scotch Briars, and in one or two important places Junipers; then more Berberis, and Ribes, and the common Barberry, and neat bushes of *Olearia Haastii*.

The wall was built seven years ago, and is now completely clothed. It gives me a garden on the top and a garden on each side, and though its own actual height is only 4½ feet, yet the bushes on the top make it a sheltering hedge from seven to ten feet high. One small length of three or four yards of the top has been kept free of larger bushes, and is planted on its northern edge with a very neat and pretty dwarf kind of Lavender, while on the sunny side is a thriving patch of the hardy Cactus (*Opuntia Raffinesquii*). Just here, in the narrow border at the foot of the wall, is a group of the beautiful *Crinum Powelli*, while a white Jasmine clothes the face of the wall right and left, and rambles into the Barberry bushes just beyond. It so happened that these things had been planted close together because the conditions of the place were likely to favour them, and not, as is my usual practice, with any intentional idea of harmonious grouping. I did not even remember that they all flower in July, and at nearly the same time; and one day seeing them all in bloom together, I was delighted to see the success of the chance arrangement, and how pretty it all was, for I should never have thought of grouping together pink and lavender, yellow and white.

[229]

The northern face of the wall, beginning at its eastern end, is planted thus: For a length of ten or twelve paces there are Ferns, Polypody and Hartstongue, and a few *Adiantum nigrum*, with here and there a Welsh Poppy. There is a clump of the wild Stitchwort that came by itself, and is so pretty that I leave it. At the foot of the wall are the same, but more of the Hartstongue; and here it grows best, for not only is the place cooler, but I gave it some loamy soil, which it loves. Farther along the Hartstongue gives place to the wild Iris (*I. fœtidissima*), a good long stretch of it. Nothing, to my mind, looks better than these two plants at the base of a wall on the cool side. In the upper part of the wall are various Ferns, and that interesting plant, Wall Pennywort (*Cotyledon Umbilicus*). It is a native plant, but not found in this neighbourhood; I brought it from Cornwall, where it is so plentiful in the chinks of the granite stone-fences. It sows itself and grows afresh year after year, though I always fear to lose it in one of our dry summers. Next comes the common London Pride, which I think quite the most beautiful of the Saxifrages of this section. If it was a rare thing, what a fuss we should make about it! The place is a little dry for it, but all the same, it makes a handsome spreading tuft hanging over the face of the wall. When its pink cloud of bloom is at its best, I always think it the prettiest thing in the garden. Then there is the Yellow Everlasting (*Gnaphalium orientale*), a fine plant for the upper edge of the wall, and even better on the sunny side, and the white form of *Campanula cæspitosa*, with its crowd of delicate little white bells rising in June, from the neatest foliage of tender but lively green. Then follow deep-hanging curtains of Yellow Alyssum and of hybrid rock Pinks. The older plants of Alyssum are nearly worn out, but there are plenty of promising young seedlings in the lower joints.

Throughout the wall there are patches of Polypody Fern, one of the best of cool wall-plants, its creeping root-stock always feeling its way along the joints, and steadily furnishing the wall with more and more of its neat fronds; it is all the more valuable for being at its best in early winter, when so few ferns are to be seen. Every year, in some bare places,

SPECIAL GARDENS

I sow a little seed of *Erinus alpinus,* always trying for places where it will follow some other kind of plant, such as a place where rock Pink or Alyssum has been. All plants are the better for this sort of change. In the seven years that the wall has stood, the stones have become weathered, and the greater part of the north side, wherever the stone work shows, is hoary with mosses, and looks as if it might have been standing for a hundred years.

The sunny side is nearly clear of moss, and I have planted very few things in its face, because the narrow border at its foot is so precious for shrubs and plants that like a warm, sheltered place. Here are several Choisyas and Sweet Verbenas, also *Escallonia, Stuartia,* and *Styrax,* and a long straggling group of some very fine Pentstemons. In one space that was fairly clear I planted a bit of Hyssop, an old sweet herb whose scent I delight in; it grows into a thick bush-like plant full of purple flower in the late summer, when it attracts quantities of bumble-bees. It is a capital wall-plant, and has sown its own seed, till there is a large patch on the top and some in its face, and a broadly-spreading group in the border below. It is one of the plants that was used in the old Tudor gardens for edgings; the growth is close and woody at the base, and it easily bears clipping into shape.

❁ THE WATER GARDEN

Where there is a stream passing through the outskirts of a garden, there will be a happy prospect of delightful ways of arranging and enjoying the beautiful plants that love wet places. Even where there are no natural advantages of pictorial environment, given a little sinking of the level and the least trickle of water, with a simple and clever arrangement of bold groups of suitable plants, a pretty stream-picture may be made.

But where there is a rather wider and more copious stream, rippling merrily over its shallow bed, there are even wider possibilities. The banks of running water where the lovely Water Forget-me-not grows are often swampy. So we make a path by putting down some rough ballast and ramming it partly into the moist ground, and lay flat stepping stones upon it, and level up to them. In the very wettest places, or if the path has to be taken actually into the water, some small Alder trunks, cut up two feet long and driven into the wet ground, will make a durable and effectual sub-structure. When a water-garden is being prepared by the side of any such stream, the course of the path may well be varied by running first close against the water and then going a yard or two inland; then it might cross on stepping-stones and again run inland and perhaps pass behind a little knoll and then again come back to the stream. Then the stream might divide, and the path be carried between two rills, and so on in a progression of varied incident that would be infinitely more interesting than if the path kept to one bank nearly always at the same distance from the water after the manner of a towing-path.

I am supposing my stream to run along the bottom of a little valley. Close to it the ground is open, except for a few tufts of low wild bushes. As the ground rises it is wooded, first with sparse copse-wood and groups of Birches and Hollies; and after this a rather thick wood of Scotch Fir.

Having pleasantly diversified the path in relation to the stream, we have to think how best it may be planted. Some of the plants suited to the running stream edge will be the same as for the margins of stiller ponds, but some that have a liking for running water will be proper to the stream itself. Such a one is the Water Forget-me-not. If it does not occur in the neighbourhood it is easy to raise quite a large stock from seed; and strong seedlings or divisions of older plants have only to be planted in the muddy soil at the water edge when they will soon grow into healthy spreading sheets and give plenty of the dainty bloom whose blue is the loveliest of any English plant. Next to the Forget-me-not on the water edge, and also a little more inland, I should plant the double Meadow-Sweet, the double garden form of the wild *Spiræa Ulmaria*, and again beyond it, quite out of sight of the Forget-me-not, others of the herbaceous Spiræas, *S. palmata*, *S. venusta*, and *S. Aruncus*—all moisture-loving plants. Drifts of these might spread away inland, the largest of them, which would be of *Spiræa Aruncus*, being placed the furthest from the stream; they are plants of bold aspect, showing well at a little distance.

I should be careful not to crowd too many different plants into my stream-picture. Where the Forget-me-nots are it would be quite enough to see them and the double Meadow-Sweet, and some good hardy moisture-loving Fern, Osmunda or Lady Fern. The way to enjoy these beautiful things is to see one picture at a time; not to confuse the mind with a crowded jumble of too many interesting individuals, such as is usually to be seen in a water-garden.

Close by the stream-side and quite out of view of other flowering plants should be a bold planting of *Iris lævigata*, the handsome Japanese kind, perhaps better known as *Iris Kæmpferi*. It is in varied colourings of white, lilac, and several shades and kinds of purple; but for this stream, where it is desirable to have the simplest effects, the single pure white alone will be best. There are double varieties, but in these the graceful purity of the form is lost and the character of the flower is confused. The best way to grow them in England is in the boggy margin, not in the stream itself; for though seeds will fall and germinate in shallow water, planted roots do better just out of it, but always with their heads in the full sunshine. This is one of the many cases where the natural ways of a plant cannot be followed in our gardens, for in Japan they commonly grow with the roots submerged. Some plants of bright green foliage, such as the handsome branched Bur-reed (*Sparganium ramosum*) will fittingly accompany groups of this noble Water Iris.

The yellow Mimulus (*M. luteus*) is a capital thing for the stream-side; once planted it will take care of itself; indeed it has become naturalised by many streams in England. Another interesting and pretty plant that would do well in its company is the only English representative of the Balsams, *Impatiens Noli-me-tangere*; it is an annual, but will sow itself again.

It should be noted that in such a stream-garden it will usually be the opposite side that is best seen, and this should be borne in mind while composing the pictures and setting out the path.

It is well worth while to consider some pleasant arrangement of colour in the way the varied flower-pictures will present themselves in the course of a walk; thus, after the blue Forget-me-not with the white Spiræas might come the pink and rosy colourings of *Spiræa venusta* and *S. palmata*.

As the stream leads further away we begin to forget the garden, and incline towards a wish for the beautiful things of our own wilds, so that here would be, for the earliest water flowers of the year, the smaller of the wild kinds of Water Buttercup (*Ranunculus aquatilis*). The larger kind, more frequent near London, *R. grandiflorus*, is figured elsewhere. The smaller one is in better proportion to the size of the little stream. Near it, but flowering later, are some strong patches of the native yellow Water Iris (*I. Pseud-acorus*), some of the same being in a swampy patch a yard or two from the bank on the other side of the path, with some of the handsome smooth-leaved rank growth of the Water Dropwort.

A little further the tall yellow Loosestrife (*Lysimachia*) will make some handsome patches; then will come a few yards of rest from bright flowers and a region of Fern-fringed stream bank, where the Lady Fern, one of the most delicately beautiful of waterside plants, should have a good space; some plants almost touching the water and others a little way up the bank.

After this the character of the stream shows a change, for here is a clump of Alders, the advance guard of a greater number that are to be seen beyond. Now it is time to make some important effect with plants of a larger size, that will prepare the eye, as it were, for the larger scale of the water-loving trees. Here, therefore, we have a widespread planting of these large things. By the stream on one bank a long-shaped mass of the rosy Loosestrife (*Lythrum*), and detached patches of the same handsome plant, and grouped near and partly with it the Giant Cow-Parsnip (*Heracleum*). On the other bank is the native Butter-bur (*Petasites*) with its immense leaves, a striking contrast in leaf-form to its neighbours.

Now the stream passes into the swampy region of Willows and Alders, and the path follows it only a little way in; but already we have been among great clumps of Marsh Marigold, some close down to the stream edge in the open, and some in wet hollows a yard or two away. But in the dark pools of mud and water under the Alders the clumps grow larger and more luscious, and in April they are a sight to see, showing sheets of rich yellow bloom, that look all the brighter rising alone from the black pools under the trees. The path that has hitherto accompanied the stream now turns away from it, and on its return journey skirts the streamward side of some boggy pools and oozy places that lie at the foot of the wood's edge.

THE WOOD

It is this quality of singleness or simplicity of aim that I find wanting in gardens in general, where one may see quantities of the best plants grandly grown and yet no garden pictures.

Of course one has to remember that there are many minds to which this need of an artist's treatment of garden and woodland does not appeal, just as there are some who do not care for music or for poetry, or who see no difference between the sculpture of the old Greeks and that of any modern artist who is not of the first rank, or to whom architectural refinement is as an unknown language. And in the case of the more superficial enjoyment of flowers one has sympathy too. For a love of flowers, of any kind, however shallow, is a sentiment that makes for human sympathy and kindness, and is in itself uplifting, as everything must be that is a source of reverence and admiration. Still, the object of this book is to draw attention, however slightly and imperfectly, to the better ways of gardening, and to bring to bear upon the subject some consideration of that combination of common sense, sense of beauty and artistic knowledge that can make plain ground and growing things into a year-long succession of living pictures. Common sense I put first, because it restrains from any sort of folly or sham or affectation. Sense of beauty is the gift of God, for which those who have received it in good measure can never be thankful enough. The nurturing of this gift through long years of study, observation, and close application in any one of the ways in which fine art finds expression is the training of the artist's brain and heart and hand. The better a human mind is trained to the perception of beauty the more opportunities will it find of exercising this precious gift and the more directly will it be brought to bear upon even the very simplest matters of everyday life, and always to their bettering.

Just as wild gardening should never look like garden gardening, or, as it so sadly often does, like garden plants gone astray and quite out of place, so wood paths should never look like garden paths. There must be no hard edges, no conscious boundaries. The wood path is merely an easy way that the eye just perceives and the foot follows. It dies away imperceptibly on either side into the floor of the wood and is of exactly the same nature, only that it is smooth and easy and is not encumbered by projecting tree-roots, Bracken or Bramble, these being all removed when the path is made.

Now we are in the true wood path among Oaks and Birches. Looking round, the view is here and there stopped by prosperous-looking Hollies, but for the most part one can see a fair way into the wood. In April the wood-floor is plentifully furnished with Daffodils. Here, in the region furthest removed from the white Poets' Daffodil of the upper ground, they are all of trumpet kinds, and the greater number of strong yellow colour. For the Daffodils range through the wood in a regular sequence of kinds that is not only the prettiest way to have them, but that I have often found, in the case of people who did not know their Daffodils well, served to make the whole story of their general kinds and relationships clear and plain; the hybrids of each group standing between the parent kinds; these again leading through other hybrids to further clearly

[236]

defined species, ending with the pure trumpets. As the sorts are inter-grouped at their edges, so that at least two removes are in view at one time, the lesson in the general relationship of kinds is easily learnt.

They are planted, not in patches but in long drifts, a way that not only shows the plant in good number to better advantage, but that is singularly happy in its effect in the woodland landscape. This is specially noticeable towards the close of the day, when the sunlight, yellowing as it nears the horizon, lights up the long stretches of yellow bloom with an increase of colour strength, while the wide-stretching shadow-lengths throw the woodland shades into large *phrases* of broadened mass, all subdued and harmonised by the same yellow light that illuminates the long level ranks of golden bloom.

From this same walk in June, looking westward through the Birch stems, the value of the careful colour-scheme of the Rhododendrons is fully felt. They are about a hundred yards away, and their mass is broken by the groups of intervening tree-trunks, but their brightness is all the more apparent seen from under the nearer roofing mass of tree-top, and the yellowing light makes the intended colour-effect still more successful by throwing its warm tone over the whole.

But nearer at hand the Fern walk has its own little pictures. In early summer there are patches of *Trillium*, the white Wood Lily, in cool hollows among the ferns, and, some twenty paces further up, another wider group of the same. Between the two, spreading through a mossy bank, in and out among the ferns and right down to the path, next to a coming patch of Oak Fern, is a charming little white flower. Its rambling roots thread their way under the mossy carpet, and every few inches throw up a neat little stem and leaves crowned with a starry flower of tenderest white. It is *Trientalis*, a native of our most northern hill-woods, the daintiest of all woodland flowers.

To right and left white Foxgloves spire up among the Bracken. When the Foxglove-seed is ripe, we remember places in the wood where tree-stumps were grubbed last winter. A little of the seed is scattered in these places and raked in. Meanwhile one forgets all about it till two years afterwards there are the stately Foxgloves. It is good to see their strong spikes of solid bloom standing six to seven feet high, and then to look down again at the lowly *Trientalis,* and to note how the tender little blossom, poised on its thread-like stem, holds its own in interest and importance.

Further up the Fern walk, near the upper group of *Trillium,* are some patches of a plant with roundish, glittering leaves. It is a North American *Asarum* (*A. virginicum*); the curious wax-like brown and greenish flower, after the usual manner of its kind, is short-stalked and hidden at the base of the leaf-stems. Near it, and growing close to the ground in a tuft of dark-green moss, is an interesting plant—*Goodyera repens,* a terrestrial Orchid. One might easily pass it by, for its curiously white-veined leaves are half hidden in the moss, and its spike of pale greenish white flower is not conspicuous; but, knowing it is there, I never pass without kneeling down, both to admire its beauty and to ensure its well-being by a careful removal of a little of the deep moss here and there where it threatens too close an invasion.

Now there comes a break in the Fern walk, or rather it takes another character. The end of one of the wide green ways that we call the Lily path comes into it on the right, and, immediately beyond this, stands the second of the great Scotch Firs of the older wood. The trunk, at five feet from the ground, has a girth of nine and a half feet. The colour of the rugged bark is a wonder of lovely tones of cool greys and greens, and of a luminous deep brown in the fissures and cavities. Where the outer layers have flaked off it is a warm reddish grey, of a quality that is almost peculiar to itself. This great tree's storm-rent head towers up some seventy feet, far above the surrounding foliage of Oak and Birch. Close to its foot, and showing behind it as one comes up the Fern walk, are a Holly and a Mountain Ash.

This spot is a meeting-place of several ways. On the right the wide green of the Lily path; then, still bearing diagonally to the right, one of the ways into the region of Azalea and Cistus; then, straight past the big tree, a wood walk carpeted with Whortleberry and passing through a whole Whortleberry region under Oaks, Hollies and Beeches, and, lastly, the path which is the continuation of the Fern walk. Looking along it one sees, a little way ahead, a closer shade of trees, for the most part Oak, but before entering this, on the right-hand gently rising bank, is a sheet of bright green leaves, closely set in May with neat spikes of white bloom. It is *Smilacina bifolia*, otherwise known as *Maianthemum bifolium*. The pretty little plant has taken to the place in a way that rejoices the heart of the wild gardener, joining in perfect accord with the natural growth of short Whortleberry and a background of the graceful fronds of Dilated Shield Fern, and looking as if it was of spontaneous growth.

Now the path passes a large Holly, laced through and through with wild Honeysuckle. The Honeysuckle stems that run up into the tree look like great ropes, and a quantity of the small ends come showering out of the tree-top and over the path, like a tangled veil of small cordage.

The path has been steadily rising, and now the ascent is a little steeper. The character of the trees is changing; Oaks are giving way to Scotch Firs. Just where this change begins the bank to right and left is covered with the fresh, strong greenery of *Gaultheria Shallon*. About twenty years ago a few small pieces were planted. Now it is a mass of close green growth two to three feet high and thirty paces long, and extending for several yards into the wood to right and left. In a light, peaty soil such as this, it is the best of undershrubs. It is in full leaf-beauty in the dead of winter, while in early summer it bears clusters of good flowers of the Arbutus type. These are followed by handsome dark berries nearly as large as black currants, covered with a blue-grey bloom.

Now the path crosses another of the broad turfy ways, but here the turf is all of Heath; a fourteen-foot wide road of grey-rosy bloom in August; and now we are in the topmost region of Scotch Fir, with under-growth of Whortleberry.

The wood path next to this goes nearly straight up through the middle of the ground. It begins at another point of the small lawn next the house and passes first by a turf walk through a mounded region of small shrubs and carefully placed pieces of the local sandstone. Andromeda, Skimmia, and Alpenrose have grown into solid masses, so that the rocky ridges peer out only here and there. And when my friends say, "But then, what a chance you had with that shelf of rock coming naturally out of the ground," I feel the glowing warmth of an inward smile and think that perhaps the stones have not been so badly placed.

❈ THE VEGETABLE GARDEN

I have often thought what a beautiful bit of summer gardening one could do, mainly planted with things usually grown in the kitchen garden only, and filling up spaces with quickly-grown flowering plants. For climbers there would be the Gourds and Marrows and Runner Beans; for splendour of port and beauty of foliage, Globe Artichokes and Sea-kale, one of the grandest of blue-leaved plants. Horse-radish also makes handsome tufts of its vigorous deep-green leaves, and Rhubarb is one of the grandest of large-leaved plants. Or if the garden were in shape a double square, the further portion being given to vegetables, why not have a bold planting of these grand things as a division between the two, and behind them a nine-feet-high foliage-screen of Jerusalem Artichoke. This Artichoke, closely allied to our perennial Sunflowers, is also a capital thing for a partition screen; a bed of it two or three feet wide is a complete protection through the summer and to the latest autumn.

❈ THE FRUIT GARDEN

There is a whole range of possible beautiful treatment in fruit-growing that is rarely carried out or even attempted. Hitherto but little has been done to make the fruit garden a place of beauty; we find it almost flaunting its unloveliness, its white painted orchard-houses and vineries, its wires and wire nettings. It is not to be denied that all these are necessary, and that the usual and most obvious way of working them does not make for beauty. But in designing new gardens or remodelling old, on a rather large scale, there need be no difficulty in so arranging that all that is necessarily unbeautiful should be kept in one department, so hedged or walled around as to be out of sight.

In addition to such a fruit garden for strict utility I have in mind a walled enclosure of about an acre and a half, longer than wide. I have seen in large places just such spaces, actually walled but put to no use.

The wall has trained fruit-trees—Peaches spreading their goodly fans, Pears showing long, level lines, and, including hardy Grape Vines, giving all the best exposition of the hardy fruit-grower's art. Next to the wall is a space six feet wide for ample access to the fruit-trees, their pruning, training and root-management; then a fourteen-foot plant border, wholly for beauty, and a path eight feet wide. At a middle point on all four sides the high wall has an arched doorway corresponding to the grassy way between the fruit-trees in the middle space. If the wall has some symmetrical building on the outside of each angle so much the better; the garden can make use of all. One may be a bothy, with lower extension out of sight; one a half-underground fruit-store, with bulb-store above; a third a paint-shop, and a fourth a tea-house.

The middle space is all turf; in the centre a Mulberry, and, both ways across, double lines of fruit-trees, ending with Bays; the Bays are at the ends on the plan. In almost any part of the sea-warmed south of England, below the fifty-first parallel of latitude which passes through the upper part of Sussex, the rows of fruit-trees on the green might be standard Figs; elsewhere they would be bush Pears and Apples. If the soil is calcareous, so much the better for the Figs and Mulberry, the Vines and indeed nearly all the fruits. The angle-clumps in the grass are planted with Magnolias, Yuccas and Hydrangeas.

The border all round is for small shrubs and plants of some solidity or importance; the spaces are too long for an ordinary flower border. It would have a good bush of *Magnolia stellata* at each angle, Yuccas, Tritomas, hardy Fuchsias, Peonies, *Euphorbia Wulfenii*, Hollyhocks, Dahlias, Hydrangeas, Michaelmas Daisies, Flag Iris, the beautiful *Olearia Gunni* and *O. Haastii*, Tree Lupines, Forsythia, Weigela, the smaller Bush Spiræas, Veronicas, Tamarisk, the large-bloomed Clematises, bush kinds of garden Roses, Funkias, and so on.

Surely my fruit garden would be not only a place of beauty, of pleasant sight and pleasant thought, but of leisurely repose, a repose broken only faintly and in welcome fashion by its own interests—in July, August and September a goodly place in which to wander and find luscious fruits in quantity that can be gathered and eaten straight from the tree. There is a pleasure in searching for and eating fruit in this way that is far better than having it picked by the gardener and brought in and set before one on a dish in a tame room. Is this feeling an echo of far-away days of savagery when men hunted for their food and rejoiced to find it, or is it rather the poet's delight of having direct intercourse with the good gift of the growing thing and seeing and feeling through all the senses how good and gracious the thing is? To pass the hand among the leaves of the Fig-tree, noting that they are a little harsh upon the upper surface and yet soft beneath; to be aware of their faint, dusky scent; to see the cracking of the coat of the fruit and the yellowing of the neck where it joins the branch—the two indications of ripeness—sometimes made clearer by the drop of honeyed moisture at the eye; then the handling of the fruit itself, which must needs be gentle because the tender coat is so readily bruised and torn; at the same time observing the slight greyish bloom and the colouring—low-toned transitions of purple and green; and finally to have the enjoyment of the luscious pulp, with the knowledge that it is one of the most wholesome and sustaining of fruit foods—surely all this is worthy garden service! Then how delicious are the sun-warmed Apricots and Peaches, and, later in the year, the Jargonelle Pears, always best eaten straight from the tree; and the ripe Mulberries of September. And how pleasant to stroll about the wide grassy ways, turning from the fruits to the flowers in the clumps and borders, to the splendid Yuccas and the masses of Hydrangea bloom, and then to the gorgeous Tritomas and other delights; and to see the dignity of the stately Bay-trees and the incomparable beauty of their every twig and leaf.

The beautiful fruit garden would naturally lead to the orchard, a place that is not so often included in the pleasure-ground as it deserves. For what is more lovely than the bloom of orchard-trees in April and May, with the grass below in its strong, young growth; in itself a garden of Cowslips and Daffodils. In an old orchard how pictorial are the lines of the low-leaning old Apple-trunks and the swing and poise of their upper branches, best seen in winter when their graceful movement of line and wonderful sense of balance can be fully appreciated. But the younger orchard has its beauty too, of fresh, young life and wealth of bloom and bounteous bearing.

Then if the place of the orchard suggests a return to nearer pleasure-ground with yet some space between, how good to make this into a free garden orchard for the fruits of wilder character; for wide-spreading Medlars, for Quinces, again some of the most graceful of small British trees; for Service, Damson, Bullace, Crabs and their many allies, not fruit-bearing trees except from the birds' and botanists' points of view, but beautiful both in bloom and berry, such as the Mountain Ash, Wild Cherry, Blackthorn, and the large-berried White-thorns, Bird-cherry, White Beam, Holly and Amelanchier. Then all these might be inter-grouped with great brakes of the free-growing Roses and the wilder kinds of Clematis and Honeysuckle. And right through it should be a shady path of Filberts or Cobnuts arching overhead and yielding a bountiful autumn harvest.

❋ THE HERB GARDEN

One other department of the garden is a source of pleasure, namely, a border or little garden for the sweet-herbs. Where house and garden are newly made I like to arrange places for these herbs, not in the kitchen

[243]

garden only, but so that there should be also close to the house, and somewhere near the door that gives access to the kitchen, a little herb-garden for the cook, so that any herb can be had at once. Here should be two or three plants each of the Thymes, Basils, and Savories, Tarragon and Chervil, a bush of Sage, some clumps of Balm, Marjoram, and Fennel, Soup-celery and Parsley for flavouring, Borage and a little Mint, and within reach a Bay-tree.

It is much better for the cook to go out and compose the little *bouquet* for the special flavouring of some delicate soup or sauce, picking the right quantity and proportion straight from the fragrant growing things. Moreover, having them all before her, she has a better chance of getting a knowledge of their natures and separate identities, and the little plants and their ways and uses must necessarily acquire in her eyes a more distinctly living interest.

FLOWERS
IN THE HOUSE

❋   CUT FLOWERS

As in all matters of decoration, so also it should be borne in mind in the use of flowers indoors that one of the first and wholesomest laws is that of restraint and moderation. So great is the love of flowers nowadays, and so mischievous is the teaching of that hackneyed saying which holds that "you cannot have too much of a good thing," that people often fall into the error of having much too much of flowers and foliage in their rooms. There comes a point where the room becomes overloaded with flowers and greenery. During the last few years I have seen many a draw-ing-room where it appeared to be less a room than a thicket. Where a good mass of greenery is wanted in a house, it is best kept in the hall or some place near the entrance, and even in quite a large room, one very large arrangement of foliage and flower will probably be enough, though of pot-plants in suitable receptacles and of smaller things of carefully arranged and disposed cut flowers it may take a large number. But it must be borne in mind that it can be easily overdone.

The elaborate system of flower arrangement practised by the Japanese shows firstly, and throughout, a recognition of beauty of line as the supreme law. It may be of one main line only, or of a grouping of several, but it is always there. It has become a fashion to attempt to imitate this system; and among some successes at the hands of those who cannot be content with anything short of "good drawing" there are the many absurd failures of those to whom it is nothing but sticking flowers and branches upright in shallow vessels, and whose only reason for doing it is because it is the fashion. Delightful and desirable as are the results of this kind of arrangement in the best hands, I cannot think that it will ever supersede, or even seriously compete with, the loose and free ways of using our familiar garden flowers. For one thing, to do it well, ample leisure and a quiet mind are needed, as well as mechanical dexterity and highly-trained eye, for it is like seriously composing a picture; and in our case one whole group of motives that is absorbingly present to the mind of the Japanese decorator is absent, namely, those that have to do with traditional law and symbolism. For, happily, we can pick a bunch of Primroses in the wood and put it in water without having to consider whether we have done it in such a way as to suggest a ship coming home or a matrimonial engagement in contemplation. I do not say this in any spirit of derision, for I gladly acknowledge how much we may learn from the Japanese in the way they insist on beauty of line; but, at the same time, I cannot but rejoice that we are not hampered by other considerations than those that lead us to combine and place our flowers so as to be beautiful in themselves and fitting for our rooms.

The room itself must be considered; and though in most forms of decoration, both indoors and out, my own liking and what knowledge I may have gained lead me to prefer using colour in harmonies rather than in contrasts, in the case of cut flowers I find in practice that I use as many of the one as of the other.

If I may suggest a general rule, I should say, use warm colours (reds and yellows) in harmonies, and cold ones (blues and their allies) in contrasts. But one must be content to be able to suggest in the vaguest way only when writing about colour, except in the case of a flower or substance whose colour is constant, for except by such reference no tint can be accurately described. It is very easy to say pink, but pink covers a wide range, from warm ash-colour to pale salmon-red, and from the tint of a new-born mushroom to that of an ancient brick. One might prepare a range of at least thirty tints—and this number could easily be multiplied—all of which might be called pink; yet with regard to some room, or object, or flower of any one kind of red, only a few of these will be in friendly accordance, a good number will be in deadly discord, and the remainder more or less out of relation.

To give a few illustrations: if the walls and main furnishings of a room are blue, all pale yellow and warm-white and creamy-coloured flowers will do well, such as sulphur Hollyhocks and Iris flavescens, Evening Primrose and shrubby Spiræas such as *S. ariæfolia, S. lindleyana* and double Meadowsweet, and all pale yellowish-green foliage, as that of Maize and *Funkia*. If the room has walls of pale yellow or ivory-white, the colour of the flowers would be reversed, and one would use Delphiniums, pale and dark, avoiding those of purplish colour; *Clematis Flammula*, and bowls of Forget-me-not. In a room with warm-white walls any colour of flowers does well, so long as they are kept to one range of colouring at a time. I do not say that colours may not be mixed, but it is best and easiest to begin with restriction in their number. In a white or neutral-coloured room, if a mixture is desired, the colours would be best in the simple mixtures as proposed in the case of flower and room colour, as blue and pale yellow flowers, or blue and warm-white with pale green foliage.

In a red room, other than a rosy red, scarlet and yellow flowers have a fine effect—*Gladiolus, Tritoma,* perennial Sunflowers, scarlet and yellow Dahlias; these are also fine in a white-walled room. My house has the

[249]

walls of all rooms plainly lime-whited, giving a white of delicately warm colour, and though at first I thought I should feel quite free to use all kinds of coloured flower-schemes in it, yet I find that the different rooms have their distinct preferences. For instance, the sitting-room, whose window curtains are of madder-dyed cloth, and whose other furniture is mostly covered with stuff of a dull orange colour, likes to have the furniture colour repeated in its flowers, and is never so happily beflowered as with double orange Day-Lily or orange Herring-lilies (*Lilium croceum*), and with this it often insists on some bowls of purple flowers. This is where they show on the warm-white wall, away from the madder-dyed curtains, in combination with the cool grey-brown of the large oak beams and braces.

The aspect of a room will also have much to do with the colours of the flowers that look well in it; the same flower even, seen in a sun-lighted room of south aspect and in a northern one, the quality of whose lighting is largely affected by a blue sky, will appear to be of quite a different tone.

It should also be remembered how the colour of flowers is affected by artificial light. There are some forms of electric light of the colder qualities that show colours almost as in daylight, but under all other forms of artificial light it is safest to use white, red, and yellow flowers mainly. Flowers of full blues and violets become dull and colourless; in pale blues the purity is lost, while some reddish-purples show as a dull red. In all colourings of mauve and lilac the warm quality is increased, so that though purple flowers are best avoided for evening decoration, many kinds, such as the lighter and warmer-coloured of the Michaelmas Daisies, are very pretty and useful. Bright fresh greenery, such as the leaves of *Funkia grandiflora* and of forced Lily-of-the-Valley, are all the brighter under the yellow light, and all reds and yellows are much intensified.

In the earlier part of the year, unless there is an old-established shrubbery to cut from, it is sometimes difficult to find good greenery to go with flowers. In March I make a good deal of use of the leaves of the wild Arum, so abundant in hedges, pulling up the whole sheaf of leaves and preparing it by standing it deep in water. It goes capitally with Trumpet Daffodils. The later Daffodils look well with leafy twigs of Birch, which comes just in time to accompany them; and later still, in the end of April and beginning of May, Poet's Narcissus and Sweet-brier branches go happily together.

Many of the flowers of May and June—Lilac, Guelder-Rose, Rhododendron, and Pæony—are well furnished with their own greenery, and from then onwards there is plenty to choose from. Still for autumn I find it useful to have a line or patch of one of the maize-like Sorghums or Millets; the one I use is the *Sorgho à balais* of the French. If when half grown the main stem is cut out, it branches into a number of side shoots, good to group with Gladiolus, or to wreathe about with the white clusters of the late-blooming *Clematis Flammula* of September and the still finer *C. paniculata* of October.

And with late autumn what a wealth of beautifully-coloured foliage there is to choose from, both in the garden and in the wood; of Vine and Virginia Creeper and Scarlet Oak; of yellowing Beech and ruddy Bramble and Guelder-Rose; the single Guelder-Rose grand with berry also. *Rosa lucida*, always one of the best of Roses for clumps and bushes in any shrubbery spaces, is brilliant in late autumn with the red and yellow of its foliage and the abundant clusters of its ripe scarlet fruit.

Even in middle winter one can make green foliage groups without flowers that are worthy room-ornaments, for there are always sprays of green Ivy to be found and fronds of Hart's-tongue and Polypody Ferns, and in woodland places where scrub Oak was cut down last winter the yearling shoots bear their large green leaves far into the next, giving us a handsome type of deciduous leafage otherwise not to be had. Sprays of Oak are of value also early in the year, for some bear small strongly waved leaves of a golden green in May and June, while for bowls of Tea-Roses in late summer no leaf-accompaniment that I can think of is better than the young summer shoots of Oak, richly beautiful in their "subdued splendour" of crimson and red and russet-bronze.

✳︎ OUTDOOR FLOWERS AND FOLIAGE NOVEMBER TO FEBRUARY

Even in the depth of winter, when flowers are least plentiful, good room decoration may be done with but very few, or indeed with foliage only.

In an average garden that is not quite new, there is always something to be found. A country house is hardly ever without its masses of shrubbery. More than once it has happened that the mistress of such a house bewailed herself to the writer, that there was nothing pickable in the garden; whereas the old shrubberies were simply unworked mines of endless wealth.

In the latest case, in a comparatively small place, it was easy to show her how much there was only waiting to be used. First there was an old, overgrown Aucuba in a shady place among tall shrubs. Its rather pale green leaves were large and wide, and its branches were flung abroad in a way that would evidently suit a large jar of Italian majolica, that my hostess wished to fill with something worthy.

The most vigorous in growth of the garden varieties of Aucuba is the one with yellow-spotted leaves. A branch or two of this in any large jar, preferably one of the blue and white Oriental porcelain, is a fine winter ornament.

All this was pointed out to my hostess, and it was pleasant to see her growing interest as she became aware of the value of the material that could be brought into use. "We will have some side boughs of the Aucuba," I said, "and I see some straight shoots of a Laurel beyond it, that will do to go with those Arum flowers we saw in the greenhouse." It was the broad-leaved Laurel; the one known as "round-leaved" in nurseries. The pieces chosen were some with unusually large leaves of a bright pale-green colour. They looked as if they had grown quickly under some unusual stimulus, such as a sudden spell of heat and moisture during the past summer, and they had escaped damage from winter cold from their sheltered place near the middle of the bush, so that in general effect they were Laurel branches with leaves unusually large, and yet refined by being of softer texture; branches that made one think rather of a Greek mountain side than of a neglected English shrubbery.

A little further was a batch of Berberis; some of it finely coloured. It was easy to choose some straggling pieces nearly three feet long, with good tops of different outward inclination; some nearly upright, and others bending to right and left; and a good branching piece for the middle. Then, greatest prize of all, against a garden shed, was an old bush of the yellow-bloomed winter Jasmine (*Jasminum nudiflorum*) in full flower. Some large and long branches with their pendulous front sprays were soon cut, to be arranged with the Berberis.

By now we were fully loaded, but we had to stop again to examine an old tree of golden Holly. A search among the lower branches produced what was hoped for—some small twigs whose leaves were pale yellow all over:—"These will be charming in one of your silver bowls with just a few white flowers, Christmas Roses or small white Hyacinths."

It may safely be said that a raid in any old shrubbery will produce—not necessarily exactly this—but enough material of like utility, such as, eked out with a very few flowers, will suffice for satisfactory room decoration.

The yellow Jasmine (*Jasminum nudiflorum*) is well known. Bloom can be cut from it throughout the winter in all open weather, but frost spoils the expanded flowers. It is therefore advisable to have covers of some material like Willesden scrim, and some arrangement whereby these can be easily hooked up or removed, according to the weather. It is usual to grow it against a wall or fence, so that this should not be a difficult matter.

For ordinary garden decoration it should be remembered that there is also another use for this capital winter-blooming shrub. Its habit may be described as straggling-pendulous; fitting it for use among stiffer bushes, or for tumbling about in rocky places. In many pleasure-grounds, where the land is steeply graded, or especially in half-wild places, where rising banks occur or ascending broken ground, such a planting as common white Thorn, kept in bush form, with the yellow Jasmine trained through and over, will show the rambling plant to great advantage; and the partial protection will save much of the bloom from frost.

Arbutus furnishes many a delightful branch and twig of flower and even fruit in the winter months, but it is happiest in the south.

Of all the lovely forms of branch and leaf, the one that may be said to be of supremest beauty—that of the Sweet Bay—may be enjoyed in winter. For then the whole bush, or tree as it is in the south, is at its best and glossiest. To any one who has a keen delight in the beauty of form, that of a twig of Bay is little less than amazing. The stem is slender but strong, the leaves are beautifully set on; the leaf itself, with its richly waved edge telling of strength, its tough and yet refined texture, its firm pale green midrib—again for strength; its form, broadly lance-shaped, narrowing to a finely-pointed tip that inclines downward—the whole structure showing the most admirable design for strength and beauty, grace and refinement—is truly a thing to marvel at, and to have and hold with the utmost reverence and thankfulness.

The foliage of Ilex or Evergreen Oak is singularly becoming to many winter flowers. It should be remembered that the Ilex leaves are at their best in winter. By April they become spotted and discoloured, and a few weeks later the young growths will be sprouting.

There are several shrubs with variegated foliage that are of great use in winter decorations. One of the best of these is the gold-variegated Privet, holding its leaves till well after Christmas; a worthy companion to the winter yellow Jasmine and any white flowers. The variegated Elæagnus is also a capital thing; the branches and twigs are extremely stiff-wooded, and when they are arranged they form a strong scaffolding for the introduction and support of any flowers that are to go with them. They are also long-enduring in water, and for this reason are admirable companions for long-lived flowers, such as free-sprayed stove Orchids. The gold-variegated Euonymus, both narrow and broad-leaved, is also of much value for winter cutting.

❧   WINTER ARRANGEMENT

Throughout January, and indeed from the middle of December, is the time when outdoor flowers for cutting and house decoration are most scarce; and yet there are Christmas Roses and yellow Jasmine and Laurustinus, and in all open weather *Iris stylosa* and Czar Violets. A very few flowers can be made to look well if cleverly arranged with plenty of good foliage; and even when a hard and long frost spoils the few blooms that would otherwise be available, leafy branches alone are beautiful in rooms. But, as in all matters that have to do with decoration, everything depends on a right choice of material and the exercise of taste in disposing it. Red-tinted Berberis always looks well alone, if three or four branches are boldly cut from two to three feet long. Branches of the spotted Aucuba do very well by themselves, and are specially beautiful in blue china; the larger the leaves and the bolder the markings, the better. Where there is an old Exmouth Magnolia that can spare some small branches, nothing makes a nobler room-ornament. The long arching sprays of Alexandrian Laurel do well with green or variegated Box, and will live in a room for several weeks. Among useful winter leaves of smaller growth, those of *Epimedium pinnatum* have a fine red colour and delicate veining, and I find them very useful for grouping with greenhouse flowers of delicate texture. *Gaultheria Shallon* is at its best in winter, and gives valuable branches and twigs for cutting; and much to be prized are sprays of the Japan Privet, with its tough, highly-polished leaves, so much like those of the orange. There is a variegated Eurya,

[255]

small branches of which are excellent; and always useful are the gold and silver Hollies.

There is a little plant, *Ophiopogon spicatum*, that I grow in rather large quantity for winter cutting, the leaves being at their best in the winter months. They are sword-shaped and of a lively green colour, and are arranged in flat sheaves after the manner of a flag-Iris. I pull up a whole plant at a time—a two-year-old plant is a spreading tuft of the little sheaves—and wash it and cut away the groups of leaves just at the root, so that they are held together by the root-stock. They last long in winter, and are beautiful with Roman Hyacinths or Freesias or *Iris stylosa* and many other flowers. The leaves of Megaseas, especially those of the *cordifolia* section, colour grandly in winter, and look fine in a large bowl with the largest blooms of Christmas Roses, or with forced Hyacinths. Much useful material can be found among Ivies, both of the wild and garden kinds. When they are well established they generally throw out rather woody front shoots; these are the ones to look out for, as they stand out with a certain degree of stiffness that makes them easier to arrange than weaker trailing pieces.

I do not much care for dried flowers—the bulrush and pampas-grass decoration has been so much overdone, that it has become wearisome— but I make an exception in favour of the flower of *Eulalia zebrina*, and always give it a place. It does not come to its full beauty out of doors; it only finishes its growth late in October, and therefore does not have time to dry and expand. I grew it for many years before finding out that the closed and rather draggled-looking heads would open perfectly in a warm room. The uppermost leaf often confines the flower, and should be taken off to release it; the flower does not seem to mature quite enough to come free of itself. Bold masses of Helichrysum certainly give some brightness to a room during the darkest weeks of winter, though the brightest yellow is the only one I much care to have; there is a look of faded tinsel about the other colourings. I much prize large bunches of the native Iris berries, and grow it largely for winter room-ornament.

FLOWERS IN THE HOUSE

❧ JASMINE NUDIFLORUM

What a precious winter flower is the yellow Jasmine (*Jasminum nudiflorum*). Though hard frost spoils the flowers then expanded, as soon as milder days come the hosts of buds that are awaiting them burst into bloom. Its growth is so free and rapid that one has no scruple about cutting it freely; and great branching sprays, cut a yard or more long, arranged with branches of Alexandrian Laurel or other suitable foliage— such as Andromeda or Gaultheria—are beautiful as room decoration.

❧ SPRING HOUSE FLOWERS

In March and April Daffodils are the great flowers for house decoration, coming directly after the Lent Hellebores. Many people think these beautiful late-flowering Hellebores useless for cutting because they live badly in water. But if properly prepared they live quite well, and will remain ten days in beauty. Directly they are cut, and immediately before putting in water, the stalks should be slit up three or four inches, or according to their length, and then put in deep, so that the water comes nearly up to the flowers; and so they should remain, in a cool place, for some hours, or for a whole night, after which they can be arranged for the room. Most of them are inclined to droop; it is the habit of the plant in growth; this may be corrected by arranging them with something stiff like Box or Berberis.

Anemone fulgens is a grand cutting flower, and looks well with its own leaves only or with flowering twigs of Laurustinus. Then there are Pansies, delightful things in a room, but they should be cut in whole branches of leafy stem and flower and bud. At first the growths are short and only suit shallow dishes, but as the season goes on they grow longer

[257]

and bolder, and graduate first into bowls and then into upright glasses. I think Pansies are always best without mixture of other flowers, and in separate colours, or only in such varied tints as make harmonies of one class of colour at a time.

The big yellow and white bunch Primroses are delightful room flowers, beautiful, and of sweetest scent. When full-grown the flower-stalks are ten inches long and more. Among the seedlings there are always a certain number that are worthless. These are pounced upon as soon as they show their bloom, and cut up for greenery to go with the cut flowers, leaving the root-stock with all its middle foliage, and cutting away the roots and any rough outside leaves.

?❧ DAFFODILS

When the first Daffodils are out and suitable greenery is not abundant in the garden (for it does not do to cut their own blades), I bring home handfuls of the wild Arum leaves, so common in roadside hedges, grasping the whole plant close to the ground; then a steady pull breaks it away from the tuber, and you have a fine long-stalked sheaf of leafage held together by its own underground stem. This should be prepared like the Lent Hellebores, by putting it deep in water for a time. I always think the trumpet Daffodils look better with this than with any other kind of foliage. When the wild Arum is full-grown the leaves are so large and handsome that they do quite well to accompany the white Arum flowers from the greenhouse.

✳ APRIL AND MAY

These months hang together in the garden and therefore in its products for house decoration.

FLOWERS IN THE HOUSE

Fresh-picked Wallflowers are delightfully sweet in rooms. Hardly any flower is more richly brilliant under artificial light than the so-called blood-red colourings. The purples are beautiful arranged with white Tulips. The purples and browns mingle very pleasantly in the sunlight of the spring garden, though this combination indoors is rather too heavy.

Care should be taken to strip off most of the leaves of cut Wallflowers that will be under water, as they quickly decay, and the water should be often changed, for it soon becomes offensive. This is the case with Stocks also and with flowers of the *Cruciferæ* in general. They belong to the same tribe as cabbages, and most people know only too well the bad smell of decaying cabbage leaves.

The most beautiful flowering shrub of April is the neat and pretty *Magnolia stellata*. A well-established plant is about six feet high and through, and bears its milk-white bloom in the greatest profusion. It grows so freely that whole branches can be cut, each branch having many flowers. These alone, or with some sprays of Pyrus Japonica, are charming in rooms, and look especially well in silver bowls.

It should be remembered that to do a spring garden justice it ought to be a garden of spring flowers and no others. The usual way of growing the early blooming parts where they are to be followed by those of summer, not only restricts the choice but makes it impossible to grow some of the best of the early plants which are perennials, such as *Dielytra, Dicentra, Doronicum,* Solomon's Seal, Anemones, *Dentaria, Uvularia, Mertensia, Tiarella,* and others. This is a fact that is very commonly overlooked, and, though it does not exactly bear on the subject of flowers for cutting (as cutting does not go on in gardens that are for the display of flower-beauty) yet it is well to mention it at any opportunity. Flowers for cutting should be grown in the reserve garden in narrow beds set apart for the purpose. Four feet is a convenient width for the beds. Here the April flowers will comprise some of the Daffodils, beginning with the yellow trumpet Tenby and the early *Incomparabilis* Stella. Then will follow the beautiful Leedsi group, the large Sir Watkin and good store of

[259]

the bright-cupped Barri conspicuus, also the large trumpets Horsfieldi, Emperor and Empress, with the later Grandee and the useful Campernelle Jonquil. Many other kinds of the good Daffodils may well find a place in the cutting garden, but these will be essential and may be taken as a useful restricted selection, but it must include the Poet's Narcissus and its double variety for May.

Anemones are excellent house flowers, lasting long in water and opening well in a sunny window. *Myosotis dissitiflora* should not be forgotten. Like all the Forget-me-nots, it lasts well when cut, and is always prettier than the deeper-coloured forms of *M. sylvatica*. By the end of April, with the last of the Daffodils whose bloom runs on into May with the Poet's Narcissus, the true Jonquil, the Tazetta group and, latest of all, N. gracilis, we get to the time of Tulips. But before leaving the Daffodils, it should not be forgotten that a charming mixture in a room is the Poet's Narcissus, either single or double, with Sweetbrier, now in sweetest, tenderest leaf; a charming association both for scent and sight.

There is one of the Star of Bethlehem family, *Ornithogalum nutans*, that is remarkably beautiful in water, arranged with some dark, polished foliage such as that of Portugal Laurel or Japan Privet. It has a rare satin-like quality. The bloom is white and yet scarcely white, but is like white satin in half shade. It lasts long in water and becomes more starry and pretty as the days of its indoor life go by. I only hesitate to recommend it because it becomes one of the worst weeds that can be introduced into a garden; and, according to my own experience in more than one place, it cannot be eradicated.

Meanwhile great sheets of a good garden form of *Myosotis dissitiflora* have been coming into bloom. It is an early Forget-me-not of charming quality, better than the garden forms of *M. sylvestris*, which are so much used in spring gardening. With this we grow in long drifts some of the paler of the best forms of Bunch Primroses. This capital Forget-me-not also arranges charmingly, both indoors and out, with another contemporary, the double Arabis; also with Primroses of pale canary colour and yellow Alyssum; the Alyssum arranged cloudily among the other flowers and standing a little above them—all in a rather flat, wide bowl.

I always think that this, the time of Tulips, is the season of all the year when the actual arranging of flowers affords the greatest pleasure. The rush and heat of summer have not yet come; the days are still fairly restful, and one is so glad to greet and handle these early blossoms. There are not as yet too many flowers. The abundance of June, with its many floral distractions, is not yet upon one. Moreover, the early flowers that come on slowly last long in water. The flowers of middle and late summer, pushing quickly into life, much sooner fade; they come and go in a hurry—one feels that the time spent in setting them up is somewhat wasted. But the steadfast Tulips will last for nearly a week, thus giving a better return for the time devoted to them.

The Darwin Tulips, in their many varieties of tall-stemmed one-coloured bloom, are among the most decorative of the round-petalled forms. Among the splashed and striped mixed Bybloemen, the discarded blooms from among which the more regularly-marked show flowers are chosen, there are examples of the highest decorative quality. It matters but little for room ornament that the "flames" or "feathers" should be symmetrical; it concerns us more that the flowers should be bold and handsome. They are beautiful in jars of blue and white china, or pewter, of rather upright form.

Among Tulips the most refined of form (not considering show standards) is the clear pale yellow *T. retroflexa;* with its sharp-pointed turned-back petals. This remarkable Tulip is one of the most graceful of its kind; its freedom of form, and one might almost say freedom of action, making it quite unlike any other. Parrot Tulips have something of the same habit as to wayward contortion of stem. This makes them a little difficult to arrange, but, when cleverly placed so that the weight of the heavy head is adequately carried, and the flower poised in accordance with the action of the stalk, the effect is excellent. Silver-crown and Sulphur-crown have somewhat the same form as *retroflexa,* but less accentuated. Among the showiest colourings the tall scarlet *Gesneriana major,* and, later, the sweet-scented *T. macrospeila,* are capital room flowers; and where the colouring is suitable, the tall and large Bleu Celeste is a grand object. It is absurdly named, for no tulip is anything like blue. It is a double Tulip of massive form of a rather subdued and yet effective purple colour, and is among the latest.

The third week of May is the week of Lily of the Valley. It is intensely sweet in rooms, and needs no description or extolling. It is best in glasses quite by itself.

Dielytra and Solomon's Seal will be in every garden where good cutting plants are grown, and Pansies in quantity. Pansies are not so often grown for indoor use as they deserve; perhaps because people do not think of the best way of using them. This is to cut, not the bloom only, but the whole shoot. When fair-sized sorts are grown, they can be cut nine inches long. They are delightful in wide bowls with the colours properly assorted, as white and yellow, white and blue, or white and purple together, and the rich and pale purples mixed; and the rich browns of the wallflower colours, either with or without the deeper yellows.

Then let anyone try a bowl of Woodruff and Forget-me-not, with a few pure white Pansies; and enjoy, not their pleasant fresh colouring only, but their faint perfumes, so evenly balanced and so kindly blending.

❦ ROSES

There is scarcely any Rose that we can wish to have in our gardens that is not also delightful in the cut state. A china bowl filled with wellgrown Hybrid Perpetuals, grand of colour and sweetly scented, is a room decoration that can hardly be beaten both for beauty and for the pleasure it gives, whether in a sitting-room or on the breakfast table. The only weak point about cut Roses is that their life is short. The day they are cut they are at their best, the next day they will do, but the third day they lose colour, scent, and texture. Still it is so delightful to any one who lives a fairly simple life in the country to go out and cut a bunch of Roses, that the need for their often renewal is only an impulse towards the fulfillment of a household duty of that pleasant class that is all delight and no drudgery.

＊ ROOM AND CONSERVATORY DECORATION

Anyone who is accustomed to arrange flowers in certain rooms year after year must have observed how, after a time, the room "finds itself." How, first of all, there are certain places where flowers always look well, so that one always puts a vase of flowers there; and how one gets into the way of putting other vases into other special places. Some day one thinks, perhaps, the putting of the same glass or bowl in the same place is only a habit or a piece of mental indolence. The thing is taken away—put somewhere else. It does not do so well in the new place and the old place calls out for it. It looks empty—unfurnished. One moves about the room, studying it from every point. Yes, it must go back to the old place. Then conscience is at rest. The thing has "found itself."

Then one finds out that certain rooms demand certain colours, and that different aspects must be differently treated. By degrees one gets to know the wants of every room, so that in the end the raid round the garden in search of flowers is governed by certain limitations, and the quest is thereby simplified.

As to colour one can only suggest very broadly that a room whose colouring is blue will be thankful for white and pale yellow flowers with bright green leaves: but if the walls are pale blue it will also be well suited with very tender pink and grey foliage. A green-walled room will also be well-dressed in the very tenderest pink, but will admit flowers of almost any colour except strong scarlet and crimson. A buff or yellow room will take strong reds; a white room all colours, but, of course, not all at one time.

✳ DINNER-TABLES

As in so many matters that concern social life, the treatment of the dinner-table has always been subject to moods and vagaries of fashion. For a year or two one way of doing a table is "the thing," when something else comes in; what was right two years ago is hopelessly out of fashion, and some new crank reigns.

So it was that when we began to think of decorating our dinner-table with flowers—the time is well within my recollection—we passed successively under the tyranny of the three-tier glass tazza, the pools of looking-glass, the fountains, the blocks of ice; the elaborate patterns of leaves and flowers on the tablecloth, and the centres of bright-coloured damasks and brocades. We have been of late somewhat under the dominion of the shallow pool of water, and are now hesitating between the desirability of inventing something new and the better alternative of being guided by more rational motives.

With all these past and passing fashions, *as fashions,* I have nothing whatever to do. Good decorations, in good hands, have been done with all of them; and with every one of them good things may be done to this day if done just rightly. But surely it is better to keep the mind quite free, and to do the best one can with what one has at hand, whether the particular form of decoration happens to be in fashion or not. After all, the best components and accessories of table decoration can never be out of fashion. Silver, glass and china of fine design do not stale in one's estimation. A china bowl of lovely Roses is for all time an acceptable thing on a table.

The flowers to avoid are those of blue and purple colourings. Pale blues lose all their purity, dark blues tell as black, and purples, unless they have a good deal of red in them, become colourless and heavy. Pale yellow is pretty with some combinations of yellow-green foliage, but tells as a warm white. Deep orange, and colours inclining to a bright mahogany tint, such as African or French Marigolds, Wallflowers, and the red-brown Pansies, are of splendid richness.

Pink, and light and dark rose-colours are always charming. The pink tulips of the earlier year, and the pale and rosy Peonies of the more refined kinds of middle summer, are noble table flowers. Sweet peas are charming on the dinner-table, especially in their pink, rose, and red colourings. One need not even fear at night some of the rose-colours that incline to amaranth or magenta, such colours as in daylight we should reject, for the yellow light of lamp or candle neutralises the harshness, just as on a summer evening out of doors the yellowing rays of the setting sun improve the rank colour-quality of the Crimson Rambler Rose. But Sweet Peas alone, on a large table, want the addition of more solid flowers, such as Roses.

The blue and purple flowers that cannot be used at night are in place on the luncheon table, and, especially at breakfast, it is cheering to see the lovely blue of Water Forget-me-not, with perhaps a few pale pink China Roses and white Pansies on long stalks, or a bowl of any freshly-gathered Roses with the morning dew still upon them.

Fruit and flowers are so nearly allied on our tables that I should like to remind my readers of a simple and desirable way of arranging fruit for lunch or home dinner. In small gardens there may not be fruit enough of any one or more kinds to fill separate dishes. But, if arranged all together, a few fruits of each kind make quite a good show. There is something essentially decorative about Melons and Grapes, but if there is no Melon, a small ornamental gourd will serve, or one of the cheap Spanish Melons that can be bought for sixpence in the fruit shops. In the case of a moderate household where fruit has to be bought, a modest expenditure will secure a handsome dish. Some important foliage, such as a branch of Vine or Fig or Hop greatly helps, and a flowing spray of Autumn Clema-

[265]

tis not only adds to the effect, but may help to bring the dish of fruit into harmonious relation with any bowls of flowers that may also be upon the table in which the same Clematis also appears.

The setting up of such dishes of fruit is one of the many decorative hints that I have learnt in Italy, where fruit so arranged goes by the name of a *Trionfo*. Indeed when Grapes, Melons and smaller fruits of bright colour and tempting scent are handsomely piled and wreathed with suitable foliage, the group adds to the table, if not a triumphant, at least an exhilarating, aspect. Any large dish, preferably of some metal—silver, brass or pewter, does for the base of the trophy.

A COUNTRY
MISCELLANY

❀ SOME NAMES OF PLANTS

It is interesting to try and trace some of the ways by which familiar garden plants come by their popular names.

Many of our oldest favourites have names only slightly altered from the Latin; in this way we get Rose, Lily, Tulip, Pæony, Lavender, Rosemary, Violet, and numbers of others. Some of the most familiar names of the sweet-herbs of the kitchen garden come to us in the same way; hence we have Mint, Borage, Fennel, Coriander, Thyme, and Chervil, and the vegetables, Carrot, Cauliflower, and Beet, and some trees, as Elm, Poplar, Juniper, Tamarisk, and Cypress. And all these names are so familiar and have become such good English that we forget how we came by them, and that they are only the Latin names with the corners rounded off. And of the older names these seem to be the most permanent, for though we may retain many of what one may call old English names, such as Canterbury Bell and Snowdrop, Hollyhock, Honeysuckle, and Sweet-William, yet a great number, though still known, have gone out of use.

Nobody now says Gilliflower, though it is a much better name than the vague Carnation; and the pretty Eglantine, though the sound of it is still known, is put away in the lumber-room of things not used or wanted; and most people have even forgotten that it was the older name for Sweetbrier. And as for all the rollicking company of Bobbing Joan and Blooming Sally and Bouncing Bet, they have long been lost, reappearing only in the more dull and decorous guise of Wild Arum and French Willow and Soapwort.

But let us treasure the best of our old plant-names, Sweet Sultan and Bachelors' Buttons, Eyebright, Foxglove, Nightshade, and London Pride, and especially those that have about them a flavour of poetical feeling or old country romance, such as Travellers' Joy, Meadowsweet, Speedwell, Forget-me-not, Lads'-love, Sweet Cicely, Love-in-a-mist.

Some of our popular names, as indeed are most of the botanical ones, are descriptive of the appearance of the flower or whole plant, or of some prominent form of the seed-vessel. A few examples are Monkshood, Snapdragon, Pennywort, Shepherd's Purse, Grape Hyacinth, Cockscomb, Marestail, Dutchman's Pipe, Hose-in-hose, Gardeners' Garters, Cottongrass, Hartstongue, Snowdrop, Woodbine.

Some derive names from their economic uses—as Broom, Spindle-tree, and Butcher's Broom—while others are among the oldest words of our language; pure Anglo-Saxon, many of them coming down to us almost unaltered in sound. Among this roll of honour are the bread-grains, Wheat, Barley, Oats, and Rye, also Flax and Hemp, Hazel, Heath, Bracken and Bramble, Oak, Ash, Yew, Beech and Holly, Daisy, Daffodil, Ivy, Mullein and Teazel, Nettle, Dock, Thistle, Rush, Sedge, Yarrow, Hemlock, and Groundsel. Some plants take their name from the time of year when they are in bloom, as May, Lent Lily, Christmas Rose, and Michaelmas Daisy.

I am afraid we must allow that our ancestors were happier than we are in inventing names for garden varieties of flowers; for when I look in nurserymen's plant-lists and find such a name as "Glare of the Garden" for a beautiful and desirable plant, I cannot help feeling how painfully such a name contrasts with the more pleasantly descriptive and often pretty one, such as Parkinson quotes in his chapter on Carnations: Faire Maid of Kent, the Daintie, the Lustie Gallant, the Pale Pageant, the Dainty Lady. The last-named Carnation (then Gilliflower) we still grow, but have corrupted the name into the Painted Lady. It is a pretty kind that should be more grown, with fringed petals that are rosy-scarlet on the face and white at the back. It is not perhaps easy to get, and probably not much in favour in nurseries because "the grass has no neck"; that is to say, the shoots, instead of spreading outwards with long joints at the base that are easy to layer, have the joints so short that the shoots are crowded together into one close tuft.

Sometimes when the botanical name is descriptive, it is simply translated into the English equivalent, as *Helianthus* into Sunflower and *Chrysocoma* into Goldilocks.

Some flowers have names referring to Bible stories or incidents, such as Aaron's Rod, Jacob's Ladder, Solomon's Seal, and Star of Bethlehem, all still in use, though others that might be classed with them, such as Grace-of-God (*Hypericum*), Gethsemane (*Orchis*), and Hallelujah (*Oxalis*) have been lost.

Though it is undoubtedly desirable to have a popular name for every flower that has become familiar, the numbers of fine plants that have been introduced of late years have been many more than have as yet found fitting names in our own tongue. And in spite of vigorous effort on the part of those who have earned the best right to give English names to plants comparatively new to cultivation, but now well established in English gardens, the fact remains that the names which are used or proposed have to follow that strange but undoubted law in the progress of language, that all words belonging to it must grow and cannot be made. Sometimes a new name will be adopted at once; the good white and yellow varieties of *Chrysanthemum frutescens* that came to us from France were very soon called "Paris Daisies" by the market people, and Paris Daisies they remain. In this case no doubt the general want of a popular name was only a part of the reason for one being quickly found, for to many people "Chrysanthemum" means only the garden varieties of *C. sinense*, and an easy English name became necessary in order to avoid confusion.

But language is like the horse in the proverb, you may lead it to the water but you cannot make it drink. A word that is really wanted may be invented; it may be graceful and suitable and placed temptingly before the public eye; it may be taken up or it may be left—there is no saying.

The strangest thing of all is the way some perfectly good, strong, much-wanted words drop out of use, such as the old English "Sperage" for Asparagus. Here is a fine old plant-name with its honourable pedigree written on its face, recalling on the way the ancient use of the feather-brush-like sprays of the wild plant in the old Roman churches of Southern Europe for "asperging" the congregation. And for some unknown reason this good old word goes out of use, in order to revert to the much more cumbersome Latin.

In our common speech many an example may be found of the same capricious waywardness, that shows itself in neglecting the good word or in perverting it from its true meaning, and putting in its place some other word which is weaker and in all ways worse. In some cases a whole swarm of poor substitutes only show the more clearly how much the good old word is wanted, and yet it is left unused till at last it dies. These fine old words die first in common speech, though they may linger long in literature. Why are we shy of the good word "trustworthy," or why for once that it is used do we hear fifty times the weak and ill-construed "reliable" or the still worse "dependable"?

Why do we hover all round the fine old verb to "thrust" with feebler words like "push" or "poke" or vulgarities like "shove"?

What has become of the name of the old virtue "fortitude," seldom heard in speech and only living in the best literature? What other word can express the magnificent combination of courage and endurance that we only hear spoken of in terms of schoolboy cant as "pluck," or in those of racing slang as "staying-power."

In many cases the botanical names of plants have been so long in popular use that they have actually become a part of our language. When this is so, and the Latin or Greek name has become perfectly familiar, there is no need to cast about for an English one, especially in the case of those plants whose names are pretty and pleasant and neither long nor cumbersome. So we have Iris and Ixia, Azalea, Kalmia, Daphne, Anemone, Clematis, Verbena, and Cistus and many others. They have passed into the language by general adoption and approval, and there can be no need of other names in their places. A few long awkward names such as Rhododendron have passed in with them, but as they are generally known they must also remain.

But among well-known plant-names there are some curious vagaries, for we commonly call the fine flowering shrub *Philadelphus* "Syringa," which is the botanical name of the Lilac, and it is much more generally known as Syringa than by the English name Mock-Orange. Another example of the botanical name of one plant being used as the popular name of another is that of the family *Tropæolum*. Who can say why we call it "Nasturtium," which is the botanical name of the Water-cress?

Sometimes a plant is popularly known by its own specific botanical name as in the cases of Oleander, Auricula, and Hepatica. These are botanically *Nerium Oleander, Primula Auricula,* and *Anemone Hepatica.* But there is a reasonable excuse for this practice, because they were classed by the older botanists under these names as generic which are now retained as specific only; and according to botanical usage, which by no means disregards the concerns of etymology, this fact in the plant's history is recorded by the capital letter being retained in the specific name.

I can only think of one English plant-name that is made from a true specific name. This is the Tuberose (*Polianthes tuberosa*). It reminds me of a dear old garden friend and true lover of plants, whose apprehension of botanical names was somewhat vague, but whose use of them was entirely without restraint, who asked me if I had got any of that beautiful "speciosum." Putting my mind into a suitable attitude I answered, "Oh yes, and any amount of the still more glorious 'spectabile' "!

Considering how much of our language and civilisation came many centuries ago from France, it seems strange how few names of French origin remain among our flowers. There are no doubt others, but I can only think of Dandelion (*Dent de Lion*), aptly named after the toothed edge of the leaf. The much more modern "Mignonette" has a French sound but at any rate now is purely an English name, for the French for Mignonette is always the botanical name Réséda. I often ask cottage folk what they call the familiar garden flowers. The answers are not always satisfactory, as except in the case of those that cannot be mistaken, such as Rose, Lily, Pansy, and Violet, they are apt to apply well-known names rather indiscriminately.

Indeed I have known several cases in which all garden flowers were called "Lilies," and all weeds "Docks." An old woman that we had some years ago to weed the lawn was one of those who held to this broad and simple distinction in botanical nomenclature, for though there was not a Dock in the grass, and her work was to fork up Daisies and Dandelions, Plantains and Hawk-weeds; yet whenever one asked how she was getting on, and of what kinds of weeds she found the greater number, her broad brown face would beam her appreciation of the interest shown in her work, and her stout figure would make a sudden subsidence in the good old country bob-curtsey, as she gave the invariable answer "Docks, m'm."

Sometimes the country folk will make a name of their own. I think this must have been the case in a village in the south of Sussex in whose neighbourhood I was often on a visit to a dear friend, now, alas, no longer living. There was a grand growth of *Bignonia rudicans* along the front of some cottages, whose occupiers called it by the capitally descriptive name of Flowering Ash. And from the same friend I learnt the most remarkable country plant-name I ever heard; for she told me that one day, asking the mistress of a cottage home what she called the well-known Stonecrop with spreading heads of bright-yellow flowers on six-inch-high stalks that grew on the low old wall in front of the cottage garden, the woman said: "Well, m'm, *we* call it Welcome-home-husband-be-he-ever-so-drunk"!

THE DONKEY

All my life I can remember my old friend with the donkey-cart, in intimate association with the lanes near my home. He worked under the road-surveyor, trimming overgrowing hedges and road edges, and removing incidental obstructions, as of the many Hazels pulled down and left hanging into the road by nut-hunting boys in September, and boughs blown down by winter storms, and drifts of dead leaves in November. The white donkey, who carried tools and worker, waited all day on some handy wayside patch of grass where he found food and rest. Man and beast grew old together in many a long year's companionship of toil, until at length neither could work any longer. A farmer who was a kind neighbour to the old man told me a pathetic story of how he had come to ask him to shoot the old donkey, who could no longer feed and was evidently very near his end. "The old man he sobbed and cried something turrible," said my friend the farmer. Afterwards, when I asked how old the donkey was, and how long the two had worked together, the old road-man said: "I know his age exactly; he is the same age as my youngest son, and that's twenty-seven." When he had made an end of the poor old beast, the farmer observing what a thick long coat the donkey had, took off the skin and had it cured at the tannery. Some months later, seeing what a

ON GARDENING

handsome pelt it made, I bought it of him, and now my friends take it for the skin of a polar bear, for it is almost white, and the mass of soft hair is nearly three inches deep.

🙞 MR. WEBB

I shall never forget a visit to that nursery [Calcot, near Reading] some six-and-twenty years ago. It was walled all round, and a deep-sounding bell had to be rung many times before any one came to open the gate; but at last it was opened by a fine, strongly-built, sunburnt woman of the type of the good working farmer's wife, that I remember as a child. She was the forewoman, who worked the nursery with surprisingly few hands—only three men, if I remember rightly—but she looked as if she could do the work of "all two men" herself. One of the specialties of the place was a fine breed of mastiffs; another was an old Black Hamburg vine, that rambled and clambered in and out of some very old greenhouses, and was wonderfully productive. There were alleys of nuts in all directions, and large spreading patches of palest yellow Daffodils— the double *Narcissus cernuus,* now so scarce and difficult to grow. Had I then known how precious a thing was there in fair abundance, I should not have been contented with the modest dozen that I asked for. It was a most pleasant garden to wander in, especially with the old Mr. Webb who presently appeared. He was dressed in black clothes of an old-looking cut—a Quaker, I believe. Never shall I forget an apple-tart he invited me to try as a proof of the merit of the "Wellington" apple. It was not only good, but beautiful; the cooked apple looking rosy and transparent, and most inviting. He told me he was an ardent preacher of total abstinence, and took me to a grassy, shady place among the nuts, where there was an upright stone slab, like a tombstone, with the inscription:

TO ALCOHOL.

He had dug a grave, and poured into it a quantity of wine and beer and spirits, and placed the stone as a memorial of his abhorrence of drink. The whole thing remains in my mind like a picture—the shady groves of old nuts, in tenderest early leaf, the pale Daffodils, the mighty chained mastiffs with bloodshot eyes and murderous fangs, the brawny, wholesome forewoman, and the trim old gentleman in black. It was the only nursery I ever saw where one would expect to see fairies on a summer's night.

THE MAKING OF POT-POURRI

"Do tell me how you make your Pot-pourri?" is a question that comes often during the year; and it is so difficult to give a concise answer or a short written recipe, that I will just put down all I can think of about the material and method that go to its making, in the hope that it may help others who wish to prepare the fragrant compound on their own account. And though any one can make Pot-pourri after a fashion, yet to make it well and on rather a large scale, a good deal of care and a good deal of time are needed, besides suitable space and appliances, and a proper choice of material.

The greater part of the bulk is of Rose petals and Sweet Geranium leaves, then, in lesser quantity, Lavender, leaves of Sweet Verbena, Bay, and Rosemary, prepared Orange peel, and finally Orris-root powder, and various sweet gums and spices.

There are of course the two kinds of Pot-pourri, the dry and the moist. The dry is much the easier and quicker to make, but is neither so sweet nor so enduring, so now the moist is the only kind I care to have. One of the chief reasons why it cannot be done by a fixed recipe is that the materials have first to be got to a certain state—limp and leathery—neither too wet nor too dry; and this state can only be secured by trying, and feeling one's way, and getting to know. When the ingredients are dried to the right degree, they are packed tightly into jars with a certain mixture of salt, which seems to combine with the remaining moisture, and serves both to retain the mass at the right degree of dampness, and also to preserve it from any kind of decay or mouldiness. In my own case, as a considerable quantity is made, I find it best to prepare a jar of each ingredient by itself, and then to mix all together; but when the whole making is small, there is no reason why it should not all go into one receptacle until the time comes for adding the spices. In the whole arrangement the matter that wants most care is the proper preparation of the Rose petals. And the Roses must be in good order. They may be full blown, but must not be faded or in any way injured, and above all they must be quite dry. A Rose is a great hand at holding water. If it has been rained into when first opened, it will still hold the wet in its inner depths two days afterwards. Dew does not seem to go so far in, and is generally dried by noon; but in any case it is safest to gather the Roses on a warm sunny afternoon.

So every two or three days, when Roses are in plenty, we bring them in, perhaps a bushel-basket full at a time. If they cannot be picked over at once, they are laid out, not more than three inches thick, on a rough hempen wrapper about three yards long by two yards wide; if they were left in the basket they would soon begin to "heat" and spoil. The shady, paved garden-court on the north side of the house is the chosen place, and the Rose-cloth is spread where the broad passage upstairs overhangs, so that we can sit below in shelter even in rain. Then at the earliest opportunity the Rose petals are pulled off their hard bases, and carefully sifted through the fingers so as to separate them as much as possible. Sometimes visitors are pressed into the service, sometimes the little nieces come down from their home close by, and often I go and pick them over after dark in the pleasant summer evening. It is just as easy to do without any light, and then one enjoys all the more the wonderful

fragrance and the pleasant cool texture; and plunging hands or face into the mass, delicious alike to scent and touch, one calls to mind how such generous measures of plucked Roses played their part in the feasts of ancient Rome.

The separated petals lie on the cloth for two days, or for a longer or shorter time, as the air may be more or less drying, in order that they may lose a part of their moisture; how much I cannot say, but perhaps half, as they seem to be shrivelled to about half their size; and now they are ready to go into their preparation jars. After making shift for some years with various odds and ends of jars, the best of them being a big blue and grey German one and some South Italian oil jars, I had some made on purpose at Doulton's pottery. The material has to be firmly and evenly pressed, as it lies in the jar layer on layer, and as this is difficult to arrange in any vessel of bulging form, my jars were made quite cylindrical, and they answer admirably. They stand twenty-two inches high and have a diameter over all of ten inches, and have flat flanged lids with loop handles. They are of the strong buff stoneware, like salt-jars, glazed inside and out. In order to keep the material well pressed down, I had some leaden discs cast, of such a diameter as to go easily inside; these are five-eighths of an inch thick, and weigh fourteen pounds each, and have also handles to lift by.

The Rose petals are thrown in, about two good handfuls at a time, and are made to lie close together by gentle ramming, and have a thick sprinkling (not quite a covering) of the salt mixture. This is of equal parts bay salt and kitchen salt; the bay salt, which comes in hard lumps, being roughly pounded, so that the greater part of it is in pieces the size of peas or smaller. The Rose leaves are put in as before, two handfuls or so, rammed, salted, and so on till all are in, then the leaden weight goes in, and the jar is covered till the next supply is ready.

The process is the same with the leaves of Sweet Geranium, only that they are taken off their stalks before they are dried, and all but the smallest are pulled into three or four pieces. They take about as long to dry as the Rose petals, and are laid out in the same way on the Rose-cloths. Sweet Verbena is of such a quick-drying nature that it only has to be stripped from the stalk and can be put in the jars at once; also Bay leaves, Rosemary leaves, and Lavender; but all are treated alike in that they are put into the jars in moderate layers, lightly rammed, salted and pressed.

Lavender, whether for Pot-pourri or for drying, should be cut as soon as a good proportion of the lower flowers in the spike are out. My friends often tell me that my Lavender smells better than theirs; but it is only because I watch for the right moment for cutting, and am careful about the drying. If it is picked for drying, and is laid too thickly, it soon goes mouldy; it must be laid thinly and turned once or twice till it is dry enough to be safe.

An important ingredient in good Pot-pourri is strips of Seville Orange peel stuck with Cloves. The peel is taken off and cut in pieces from end to end of the Orange, so that each is about half an inch wide in the middle and two inches long; holes are pricked in it, and the shaft of the Clove pressed in so that the heads nearly touch each other. The pieces are then packed into a jar firmly with the hand—they would not bear ramming—with sprinklings of salt in between and over the top. This is the first ingredient to be made ready, as the Oranges are in season from the end of February to the middle of March; the last batches of preparation being made towards the middle of September, of the later pickings of Sweet Geranium.

The materials seem to be mellower and better for being left for some time in the preparation jars, so I put off the final amalgamation till near the end of October. The jars now hold the produce of some seven or eight bushels of Rose petals, about four bushels of Sweet Geranium, and an-other bushel of various sweet leaves, all of course much reduced in bulk by drying and ramming; with this is about fifty pounds of the mixed salt.

Now we have to get together the spices, sweet gums, and Orris-root. As

an improvement on plain Orris-root it is advisable to use Atkinson's Violet Powder; we therefore have—

> 5 large packets Violet Powder,
> 1 pound ground Allspice,
> 1 pound ground Cloves,
> 1 pound ground Mixed Spice,
> ½ pound ground Mace,
> 1 pound whole Mace,
> 1 pound whole Cloves,
> 1 pound pounded Gum Benzoin,
> 1 pound pounded Gum Storax or Styrax.

All the powders are mixed together in a large bowl, and the whole Mace and Cloves are in another bowl, and now we are ready for the grand mixing. A space is swept on the brick floor of the studio just in front of the raised hearth of the broad ingle; the full jars are brought into a wide half-circle; the home children and their elders, and perhaps one or two neighbours, are convened to the Pot-pourri party, with tea to follow; one mixer is posted at each jar or bowl, and the materials are thrown handful by handful on to the floor in the middle space.

When first I made Pot-pourri it could be mixed in a large red-ware pan; as I grew more ambitious the mixing was done in a hip-bath, in later years in a roomy wooden tub; but now the bulk is so considerable that it can only be dealt with on a clear floor space.

The heap rises, and from time to time has to be flattened as the jolly party all round throw on their handfuls. The post of honour seems to be the distribution of the Orange peel stuck with Cloves, but the claim for the supreme dignity of this office is clearly though tacitly contested by the holder of the large basin of "sauce" of sweet powders. The pressed stuff in the jars is so tightly compacted that it has to be loosened by vigorous stabs and forkings with an iron prong, by one whose duty it is to go round and fork it up so that it can be handled; this official can hardly get round in time to satisfy the many calls of "Please give me a stir up." The heap grows like one of the big ant-hills in the wood, until at last all the jars are empty, and every one's hands are either sticky with salt or powdery with sweet spices. Now the head Pot-pourri maker takes a shovel, and turns the heap over from left to right and then from right to left, and backwards and forwards several times till all is duly mixed. Then the store cask is brought forward: a strong iron-hooped oak cask with a capacity of fifteen gallons. It looks as if the fragrant heap could never be got into it, but in it goes shovelful by shovelful, and again it is rammed, until all is in, leaving only a bare two inches of space on the top. The cask has been made on purpose, and has no uppper head, but a lid with a wood-hooped rim that fits over the edge, and a knob-handle set out of the centre, the easier to lift the cover by jerking it to one side.

The full cask is now so heavy that it is a job to get it back to its place against a farther wall; it must weigh a hundredweight and three-quarters, possibly more. If the mixture stays some weeks or even months in the cask before any is taken out, by remaining untouched for awhile it seems to acquire a richer and more mellow scent.

The studio floor is left in a shocking state of mess. A wide space in front of the ingle shows a dark patch of briny moisture; footmarks of the same are thick in the neighbourhood of the site of the heap, and some small tracks further afield show where little feet have made more distant excursions; but it is growing dark, and we must leave it and wipe our shoes and go in to tea, and there will be a half-day's work for the charwoman to-morrow.

The foregoing description answers my friends' questions as to how *I* make Pot-pourri; but it does not follow that they may not make it in different and better ways, according to the degree of personal intelligence and ingenuity that they may bring to bear on the material they have at disposal.

In making Pot-pourri by the lazier and less effective dry process, it is the drying of the Rose petals that requires the most care. The Roses must be picked quite dry, the petals pulled apart and laid thinly on